ESSENTIAL
AS PSYCHOLOGY
FOR AQA(A)

Richard Gross & Geoff Rolls

Hodder & Stoughton
A MEMBER OF THE HODDER HEADLINE GROUP

To Eve, Billy and Ella. xxx G.R.

To Jan, Tanya and Jo. With my love. R.G.

Orders: please contact Bookpoint Ltd, 130 Milton Park, Abingdon, Oxon OX14 4SB. Telephone: (44) 01235 827720. Fax: (44) 01235 400454. Lines are open from 9.00 – 6.00, Monday to Saturday, with a 24 hour message answering service. You can also order through our website www.hodderheadline.co.uk.

British Library Cataloguing in Publication Data
A catalogue record for this title is available from the British Library

ISBN 0 340 846402

First Published 2003
Impression number   10 9 8 7 6 5 4 3 2 1
Year   2007 2006 2005 2004 2003

Typeset by Fakenham Photosetting Ltd, Fakenham, Norfolk.
Printed in Dubai for Hodder & Stoughton Educational, a division of Hodder Headline Plc, 338 Euston Road, London NW1 3BH.

Contents

26830

Introduction

Essential AS Psychology is written for the AQA (A) Specification, although it could also prove useful for students following other Specifications. As the title suggests, we've included only the information you really need to be able to achieve a top grade in the AS exam – no more and no less!

Key features include:

- **Essential Study boxes**, in which the study is examined under the five headings which can be used in exam questions. These are **A**ims, **P**rocedures, **F**indings, **C**onclusions, and **C**riticisms (**APFCC**). The criticisms can be both positive (indicated by ✓) and negative (indicated by ✗). Positive and negative criticisms are of equal importance. The same format is used outside Essential Study boxes under the heading 'Evaluation of . . . '

- **Concise chapter summaries**, with key points listed under the three headings that the chapter is divided into.

- **Essential Study summary boxes** at the end of each chapter. A useful summary, which can be used as a revision aid.

- **Self-assessment questions (SAQs)** at the end of each chapter. These are examples of Part a and Part b questions (worth 40% of your exam). They relate to AO1, that is, **knowledge and understanding**.

- **Exam tips boxes**, which recur throughout each chapter. These are designed to provide you with pointers for answering specific Part c questions (worth 60% of your exam). These relate to both AO1 and AO2 (**analysis and evaluation**). We must stress that *there's no single correct way of answering any question*, and these boxes offer you guidelines and advice only. We also invite you to have a go at the question yourself, using our suggestions. Please note that we've included *most* of the Part c questions you could be asked in the exam, but we *haven't* tried to cover every possibility.

- **Sample answers (SAs)** at the end of the book. These correspond to the Exam tips Boxes. It's because there are several ways of gaining the same marks that we haven't called these 'model answers' (which implies 'this is how this question *should* be answered'). Instead, we offer you an idea of how a particular question *could be answered*.

- **Essential Glossary**. These are the terms and concepts which examiners can ask you to define or explain in Part a questions. If they don't appear in the Glossary, then they *cannot* be asked about in the exam.

- We also include a short chapter on **Preparing for the AS exam**. This:

a) defines exactly what's meant by AO1 and AO2, as well as AO3 (which is assessed only in the Research Methods section)

b) gives examples of Part a, b, and c questions and how these relate to AO1/AO2/AO3

c) explains mark allocations for AO1 and AO2

d) provides hints for writing evaluation (AO2)

e) gives some examples of how to write your commentaries for AO2

f) offers some tips on how to make the most effective use of your time both before and during the exam.

Much of the text is broken down into **bullet points**. These bite-sized chunks of information are easier to take in, whether you're working through the material for the first time, or using it for revision. We've done a lot of the selection for you. This means that instead of reading through the text and deciding what's crucial and what's not, you can safely assume that *all* the material is important. Although it's still important to make your own notes and organise these in a way that suits you, we've tried to be very economical in the way we've used language. Why use several words when a few will do? You too should aim for conciseness in your exam answers.

Sometimes the Specification refers to particular theories or areas of research, such as 'The multi-store model of memory (Atkinson & Shiffrin)', or 'Bowlby's maternal deprivation hypothesis'. The examiner can ask you specifically about these, using the same wording as used in the Specification. Everything that appears in the Specification in this way is covered in this book.

In other parts of the Specification, areas of research or research studies are given as 'e.g.s' in brackets. For example, 'Research into sources of stress, including life events (e.g. Holmes and Rahe)', and 'Research studies into conformity (e.g. Sherif, Asch, Zimbardo)'. It's up to you which study you choose. Mostly, the examples given in the Specification are the ones we've included in the book. Although we've limited the number of *additional* studies, we've provided enough material to allow you to answer all types of exam question.

Just as examiners use 'positive marking', so we are very much on your side. We hope you find this book easy and enjoyable to read, and that it helps you both to learn and to revise the essentials.

ACKNOWLEDGMENTS

I'd like to thank Richard Gross and Tim Gregson-Williams for asking me to help with this book. Richard, you're the original and still, without doubt, the best. I've found working with you an absolute pleasure. Thank you.

I'd also like to thank my brilliant fellow Psychology staff at Peter Symonds' including James Larcombe, Alex Banks, Andy Pond and Chrissie Rycroft. Thanks for your helpful suggestions (most of which were physically impossible). Much of the material has been tried out on the hundreds of students that now take Psychology at Symonds. You make the teaching worthwhile. Thanks also to Neil Hopkins for supporting the writing of the book.

GR

RG would like to thank Geoff Rolls for his guidance and efficiency in this joint venture, and for his support through a difficult few months. Your kindness has meant a lot to me.

Emma Woolf at Hodder has been an absolute star, driving forward the project at all stages. Many thanks Emma. Thanks also to Jasmine Brown for the skilful editing of the book. Stewart Larking deserves credit for the cover and Ian West for his fantastic cartoons.

What's covered in this chapter?

SHORT-TERM AND LONG-TERM MEMORY

- Research into the nature and structure of memory including encoding, capacity and duration of short-term memory (STM) and long-term memory (LTM)
- The multi-store model (MSM) of memory (Atkinson and Shiffrin)
- At least ONE alternative to the MSM model
  - Working memory (Baddeley and Hitch)
  - Levels of processing (Craik and Lockhart)

FORGETTING

- Explanations of forgetting in STM (e.g. decay and displacement)
- Explanations of forgetting in LTM (e.g. retrieval failure and interference)
- Research into the role of emotional factors in forgetting (flashbulb memories and repression)

CRITICAL ISSUE: MEMORY RESEARCH INTO EYEWITNESS TESTIMONY (EWT) INCLUDING:

- Reconstructive memory (Bartlett)
- Loftus' research (e.g. the role of leading questions)

SHORT-TERM MEMORY (STM) AND LONG-TERM MEMORY (LTM)

The term 'memory' can mean the system of retaining information, the actual storage system or the material that has been retained. There are three memory stores: sensory memory, STM and LTM. Sensory memory is the store that contains the information received through the senses. It's the 'gate-keeper' of information, and passes material on to STM and LTM for more permanent storage.

There are three basic processes in memory (see Figure 1.1):

● **Encoding**: transforming a sensory input (e.g. sound or visual image) for it to be registered in memory

● **Storage**: retaining or holding information in memory until it's required

● **Retrieval**: locating information which has been stored and extracting it from memory.

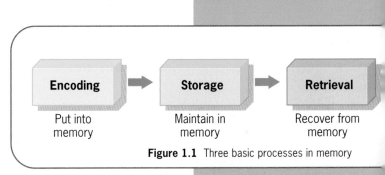

| **Encoding** | **Storage** | **Retrieval** |
| Put into memory | Maintain in memory | Recover from memory |

Figure 1.1 Three basic processes in memory

STM

STM is a temporary place for storing information received through the senses where it receives little processing.

ENCODING

Information arrives in sensory memory in its original form (e.g. sound, vision and so on). This information needs to be encoded in a form that STM can deal with. For example, if the input into sensory memory is the word 'banana', you could encode this visually by thinking of an image of a banana. Alternatively, you could encode it acoustically by repeating 'banana' over and over again (probably best done quietly!). Or you could encode it semantically (through meaning) by applying your pre-existing knowledge of bananas. This might involve thinking about what desserts you can make with bananas, or the time you slipped on one!

Since memory processes are often unconscious, people cannot accurately report what type of encoding they use. Substitution error studies help to examine coding in both STM and LTM. These involve participants confusing one item in a memory list with another.

Conrad (1964) presented participants with a visual list of six consonants (e.g. HBRTFS) that they then had to write down. Recall errors were mainly related to a letter's sound, not its visual appearance. For example, B was often mistaken for V, but F was hardly ever mistaken for E. These acoustic confusion errors suggest that:

- the visually presented information must have been encoded acoustically

- STM is primarily encoded on the basis of sound.

ESSENTIAL STUDY 1.1

Encoding in STM •••••• **Baddeley** (1966): **Acoustic/Semantic** (AS) **study**

Aim (AO1)

To investigate whether encoding in STM is acoustic (sound) or semantic (meaning).

Procedures (AO1)

Participants were presented with four word lists which were either:

List A: acoustically similar (such as 'cat', 'mad', 'sat', 'sad')

List B: acoustically dissimilar (such as 'pen', 'day', 'cow')

List C: semantically similar (such as 'big', 'huge', 'great')

List D: semantically dissimilar (such as 'old', 'late', 'thin')

75 participants heard one list repeated four times. Immediately after this (to test STM), they were given a list that contained all the original words but in the wrong order. Their task was to rearrange the words in the correct order.

Findings (AO1)

Those participants given List A (acoustically similar) performed the worst (recall of 10%). Recall for the other lists was comparatively good (60–80%) (see Figure 1.2).

Conclusion (AO1)

Since List A was recalled the worst, it would appear that there's acoustic confusion in STM. Therefore, STM tends to be encoded on an acoustic basis.

Criticisms (AO1/AO2)

✓ **Results make 'cognitive sense'.** For example, if you were asked to remember a shopping list for a short time you'd probably repeat it aloud (acoustic rehearsal) as you walked to the supermarket.

✗ **STM is not restricted to acoustic coding.** Some semantic coding has been demonstrated in STM. However, the small difference in recall between semantically similar (64%) and semantically dissimilar (71%) lists suggests that, at best, there's *minimal* semantic coding in STM.

✗ **Visual images?** We can also remember visual images (e.g. faces) in STM that would be very difficult to encode on the basis of sound. For example, how would your face be encoded acoustically? (Friends say my face would be encoded as the sound of fingernails being scraped down a blackboard!)

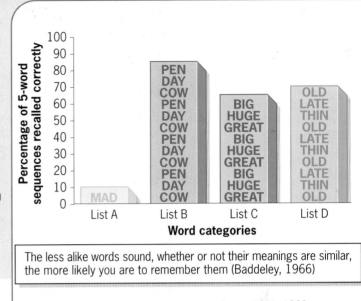

> The less alike words sound, whether or not their meanings are similar, the more likely you are to remember them (Baddeley, 1966)

Figure 1.2 Baddeley's 1966 Acoustic/Semantic (AS) study findings

CAPACITY

STM has a limited capacity, that is, we can only hold a small amount of information in it before it's forgotten. **Serial digit span studies** demonstrate this. Participants are presented with an increasingly long sequence of digits that they have to report back in order (e.g. 26478, 968423, 2975841 and so on). When they fail on 50% of the trials, they've reached their digit span capacity.

Capacity in STM • • • • • • **Jacobs (1887) Study of Immediate Digit Span** (SIDS)

Aim (AO1)

To investigate the capacity of STM.

Procedures (AO1)

Jacobs read aloud lists of either letters or numbers. He gradually increased the length of these lists until participants could only successfully recall them 50% of the time. Jacobs used a wide age range in his sample.

Findings (AO1)

• STM capacity for numbers was 9, whereas for letters it was 7

• STM increased with age – 8-year-olds recalled 7 numbers, whereas 19-year-olds recalled 9 numbers.

Conclusion (AO1)

• STM has a limited capacity of between 5 and 9 digits

• Age does affect STM capacity, since people may improve their recall strategies with age and/or through practice.

The longest place name in Wales – digit span this!

Criticisms (AO1/AO2)

✓ **Other support:** Jacobs' findings have been replicated. Miller (1956) coined the phrase *'the magic number seven plus or minus two'* $7+/-2$ to describe the capacity of STM.

✗ **Other factors influence STM capacity:** For example, performance is improved if items are read aloud rather than sub-vocally. Also, LTM can affect STM capacity (see chunking below).

✗ **Mnemonics:** The capacity of STM can be affected by *mnemonic* (memory improvement) *techniques* such as chunking, or by presenting items in a rhythm. This is why we tend to group telephone numbers into chunks of three digits.

✗ **Digit span findings are culturally specific:** Welsh speakers have a shorter digit span than English speakers. Because there are more syllables in Welsh, Welsh speakers take longer to repeat the Welsh items in their STM (Ellis & Hennelly, 1980).

The capacity of STM can be increased if separate 'bits' of information are grouped together into larger 'chunks'. For example, the number 19391945 can be 'chunked' as the start and end dates of the Second World War. Reading involves chunking letters into words and words into sentences. For Miller (1956), the capacity of STM is seven plus or minus two *chunks* rather than individual pieces of information.

Simon (1974) tested his own immediate digit span. He found the length of 'chunk' affected capacity. The larger chunks were more difficult to rehearse. He consistently found his digit span to be 5 chunks.

DURATION

You'll not be surprised that the duration of STM is short, that is, less than 30 seconds (see Essential Study 1.3).

Duration in STM •••••• Peterson and Peterson (1959) **Trigram Retention Experiment** (TRE)

Aim (AO1)

To investigate the duration of STM when no rehearsal is allowed.

Procedures (AO1)

Participants were read a nonsense **trigram** (three consonants which have no meaning e.g. LTB). Immediately after this, participants had to count backwards in threes starting from a very large 3-digit number (e.g. 576) for a specified time period. This time period was called the **retention interval** and varied from 3 to 18 seconds. The counting backwards task was called the **distractor task**. It was designed to prevent rehearsal of the trigrams. At the sound of a tone, participants had to recall the trigram.

Findings (AO1)

Approximately 90% of the trigrams were recalled after a 3-second retention interval. Only about 10% were recalled after 18 seconds. Letters had to be in exactly the same place in the recalled trigram as in the original.

ESSENTIAL STUDY 1.3

Conclusion (AO1)

Without rehearsal, the duration of STM is very short indeed (less than 18 seconds).

Criticisms (AO1/AO2)

✓ **The findings have been replicated.**

✓ **The study was highly controlled:** The use of trigrams ensured that participants couldn't impose any meaning on the material to be recalled. They all started from the same 'base level' and thus recall scores could be compared.

✗ **Low ecological validity:** The laboratory situation and the use of trigrams meant that the study was not really representative of learning in real life. When was the last time you were asked to remember complete nonsense (not including your last psychology lesson!)?

✗ **Additional cognitive task:** The counting distractor task did prevent rehearsal. But it also meant that participants had to perform an additional cognitive processing task. This may have affected their recall scores.

✗ **Interference confusion:** It was also shown that participants confused later trigrams with earlier ones. This suggests that they still had some memory of the earlier trigrams for *longer* than 18 seconds.

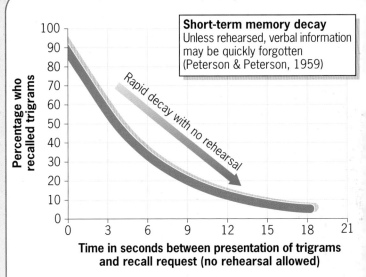

Short-term memory decay
Unless rehearsed, verbal information may be quickly forgotten (Peterson & Peterson, 1959)

Rapid decay with no rehearsal

Percentage who recalled trigrams

Time in seconds between presentation of trigrams and recall request (no rehearsal allowed)

Figure 1.3 Peterson & Peterson (1959) Trigram Retention Experiment findings

Despite methodological problems, researchers agree that:

- STM has a limited duration (less than 30 seconds)
- information is rapidly lost from STM if it's not rehearsed.

LTM

LTM involves the permanent storage of information.

ENCODING

With verbal material, coding in LTM appears to be mainly semantic (see Essential Study 1.4).

Encoding in LTM •••••• **use Baddeley** (1966): **Acoustic/Semantic** (AS) **study** (see Essential Study 1.1)

Aim (AO1)

To investigate whether LTM encoding is acoustic (sound) or semantic (meaning).

Procedures (AO1)

This was the same as the STM study in Essential Study 1.1 except that recall of the lists wasn't immediate. There was a 20-minute retention interval, during which the 72 participants conducted another task. This ensured that recall would involve LTM.

Findings (AO1)

Those participants given List C (semantically similar) performed the worst. Recall for the other lists was comparatively good (70%–85%).

Conclusion (AO1)

Since List C was recalled the worst, it appears there's semantic confusion in LTM. Therefore, LTM tends to be encoded on a semantic basis.

ESSENTIAL STUDY 1.4

Criticisms (AO1/AO2)

✓ **Replication**: The study is easily replicated and the findings are consistent.

✓ **The findings make 'cognitive sense'** in everyday life. For example, try to remember a TV programme you watched a while ago. You'll remember the overall content (meaning), not the actual words (acoustic).

✗ **There are many different types of LTM**: 'Knowing how' to perform various tasks (e.g. riding a bike) is called 'procedural' memory. Autobiographical or personal memories of events or places are called 'episodic' memories. These types of LTM are rarely examined in laboratory memory studies. 'Flashbulb' memory is another LTM not covered within this study (see page 20).

✗ **LTM doesn't only use semantic coding**: Songs must be encoded acoustically, and it's hard to see how smells and tastes can be encoded on the basis of meaning. LTM coding must involve a very large, long-lasting and flexible system.

✗ **There are other factors that influence encoding in LTM**: These include participant's age and the nature of the material. For example, 'concrete' words such as 'beach' are more likely to be visually processed, whereas abstract words such as 'hate' lend themselves to semantic coding.

CAPACITY

The potential capacity of LTM is unlimited. Anokhin (1973) estimated that the number of possible neuronal connections in the human brain is 1 followed by 10.5 million kilometres of noughts! He concluded that *'no human yet exists who can use all the potential of his/her brain. This is why we don't accept any estimates of the limits of the human brain'*. There are no studies that you need to learn on LTM capacity.

DURATION

A memory can last a lifetime, so the duration of LTM just depends on how long you live. Many older people love to tell (interesting?) stories from their childhood. Material in STM that's not rehearsed is quickly forgotten. This is *not* true of LTM. We couldn't keep repeating information over and over again in order to store it in our LTM. For example, you may not have ridden a bike for many years, but it's unlikely that you'll have forgotten how. The duration of LTM was demonstrated by Bahrick *et al* (1975) – see Essential Study 1.5.

ESSENTIAL STUDY 1.5

Duration in LTM •••••• **Bahrick *et al* (1975) High School Yearbook Photo (HSYP) study**

Aim (AO1)

To investigate the existence of very long-term memories (VLTM) using real-life memories.

Procedures (AO1)

400 participants ranging in age from 17 to 74 were asked to remember the names of classmates from their high school (**a free recall task**). They were also shown a set of photos and a list of names, some of which were of their ex-school friends. They had to identify their ex-school friends (**a recognition task**).

Findings (AO1)

Those who'd left high school within the previous 15 years recalled 90% of the faces and

ESSENTIAL STUDY

names in the recognition task. Those who'd left 48 years previously recalled 80% of the names and 70% of the faces.

Free recall of the names was comparatively poor.

Conclusion (AO1)

- Recognition is easier than free recall. This suggests that we possess a lot of information in our LTM, but we need clues or cues in order to access it (see retrieval-cue forgetting page 16).
- People do possess VLTM (very long-term memories), although these decline a little over time.

Criticisms (AO1/AO2)

✓ **Experimental support:** These findings support those of Shepard (1967), who demonstrated people's long-term memories for adverts.

✓ **High ecological validity:** The study involved people's real-life memories rather than nonsense trigrams in the laboratory.

✗ **The study lacked some important controls.** For example, participants may have been in contact with friends or looked at the yearbook since they left high school.

✗ **Recognition, not recall:** The study only found the existence of VLTM with recognition, not recall. In addition, they were only testing one form of LTM (visual LTM).

Summary table of STM/LTM differences

	STM		LTM	
Encoding	Mainly acoustic (sound)	Baddeley (1966): (AS) study	Mainly semantic (meaning)	Baddeley (1966): (AS) study
Capacity	Small (7+/−2 chunks of information)	Jacobs (1887) (SIDS)	Unlimited	Not applicable
Duration	Short (<30 seconds)	Peterson and Peterson (1959) (TRE) study	30 seconds to a lifetime	Bahrick et al (1975) (HSYP) study

Multi-store model (MSM) of memory (Atkinson & Shiffrin, 1968)

DESCRIPTION

The MSM explains how information flows from one storage system to another. The model proposes that sensory memory, STM and LTM are permanent structures of memory. We've already described some of the key characteristics of these stores. Information received through the senses (sound, sight, touch, smell) enters the sensory store. If attention is paid to it, the information is transferred and processed further by STM. If it's not attended to, the sensory information is immediately forgotten, or not even processed in the first place. If the information now in STM has been rehearsed sufficiently, it can be transferred to LTM. The greater the amount of STM rehearsal, the greater the likelihood it will transfer to LTM for more permanent storage.

Figure 1.4 below shows why it's called the multi-store model. The key processes involved are attention, rehearsal and forgetting.

EVALUATION OF THE MSM

✔ **Influential, useful:** The MSM was an influential, early model which psychologists still find useful.

✔ **STM/LTM differences:** There's considerable evidence that there are two distinct types of memory store, namely STM/LTM (see above).

✔ **Serial position effect:** Murdock (1962) presented participants with a list of words that they had to recall in any order (a free recall task). Murdock found that those words at the beginning and the end of the lists were recalled better than those in the middle. This is known as the serial position effect. Those words at the beginning of the list (the primacy effect) are recalled because they've been rehearsed over and over again and have been transferred to LTM. Those words from the end of the list (the recency effect) are recalled because they're still in STM. Thus, the primacy and recency effect provides support for the existence of the two separate memory stores (STM and LTM, see Figure 1.5).

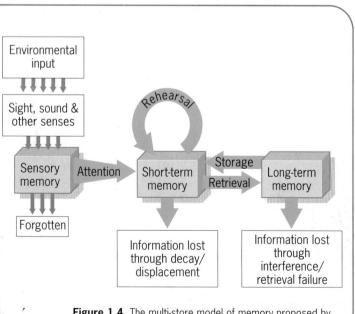

Figure 1.4 The multi-store model of memory proposed by Atkinson and Shiffrin (1968, 1971)

✗ • ✓ **Clinical case studies:** Shallice & Warrington (1970) reported the case of KF. As a result of a motorbike accident, he had an extremely poor STM (only one or two digits). Yet his LTM for events after the accident was normal. This supports MSM. However, KF's deficit in STM was only for verbal information. His STM for visual and acoustic material was normal. This suggests the existence of more than one type of STM, not incorporated in the MSM.

✗ **Mere rehearsal doesn't ensure transfer from STM to LTM:** Bekerian & Baddeley (1980) found that people didn't know of the changes to BBC radio wavelengths despite hearing the information, on average, well over a thousand times.

✗ **The MSM is over-simplified:** It assumes a single STM and a single LTM. It's been demonstrated that there are different types of STM (see Baddeley and Hitch working memory below) and different types of LTM (procedural, episodic and semantic memories, see page 6).

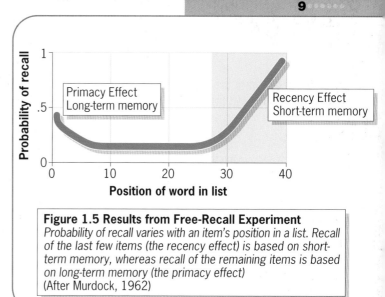

Figure 1.5 Results from Free-Recall Experiment
Probability of recall varies with an item's position in a list. Recall of the last few items (the recency effect) is based on short-term memory, whereas recall of the remaining items is based on long-term memory (the primacy effect)
(After Murdock, 1962)

✗ **The 'one-way' (linear) direction of the MSM appears to be incorrect:** There is a *two-way* flow of information between STM and LTM. Morris *et al* (1985) demonstrated how previous knowledge and interest in football could help in the recall of fictitious football scores. Participants listened to 'made-up' football results, and then had to recall them immediately (a STM task). Participants who were interested in football recalled the most. This suggests that they'd used their greater knowledge of football (LTM) to impose meaning on the results (STM). Information thus flows from LTM to STM. This isn't possible according to the MSM.

EXAM tips BOX

Outline and evaluate the multi-store model of memory. (18 marks)

- You could structure your answer in terms of three paragraphs each about 100–130 words long. The first paragraph could involve a *description* of the MSM. You could include a diagram and describe each of the stores (AO1 worth 6 marks).

- In the second paragraph you could *analyse and evaluate* from a positive viewpoint and provide evidence that supports the model (e.g. Murdock, 1962; K.F. case study).

- In the final paragraph you could *analyse and evaluate* from a negative viewpoint and provide evidence that contradicts the model (Berkerian & Baddeley, 1980, Morris *et al*, 1985; different types of STM/LTM) (AO2 worth 12 marks).

- You can choose to write an answer that concentrates entirely on the positive points or the negative points of the model – it's up to you.

Try to write out a suitable answer using about 300–350 words. There is an SA (sample answer) at the end of the book, but try not to look at it until you've tried to answer the question yourself.

Alternatives to the MSM Working Memory (WM) (Baddeley & Hitch, 1974)

Description

Baddeley and Hitch questioned the existence of a single STM store (they weren't concerned with LTM). They argued that STM was far more complex than a mere 'stopping off' point for transferring information to LTM. They saw STM as an 'active' store that holds several pieces of information whilst it's being worked on (hence 'working' memory). Working memory holds the information you are consciously thinking about now.

Working memory has been compared to a computer screen, where several operations are performed on current data. To replace the single STM, Baddeley and Hitch proposed a multi-component WM (see Figure 1.6):

- The **central executive** is involved in higher mental processes such as decision-making. It allocates resources to the other slave systems depending on the task in hand. For example, sometimes it's difficult to concentrate on driving and talking at the same time. For a difficult manoeuvre, the central executive would direct your attention to the driving task, and you'd probably have to stop talking. The central executive has a limited capacity, but it's very flexible and can process information from any of the senses.

- The **articulatory loop** is a verbal rehearsal loop that holds words we're preparing to speak. Information is represented as it would be spoken (so it's called the '**inner voice**'). The capacity of the loop is about 2 seconds. There's also the phonological store or '**inner ear**', which receives auditory information (the things you hear), and stores it in an acoustic code. This is important for language acquisition.

- The **visuo-spatial scratch** (or sketch) pad helps to rehearse visual or spatial information (what things look like). It uses a visual code, analysing features in terms of size, colour and shape (and so is called the '**inner eye**'). It can process movements and actions, as well as static visual patterns.

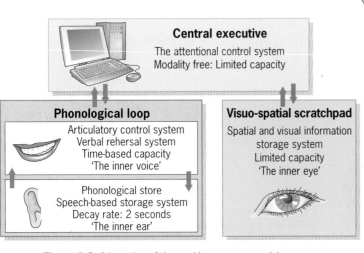

Figure 1.6 Adaptation of the working memory model

Research to support the WM model has involved doing two tasks at once (**the dual task method**). According to WM, it should be easier to do two tasks that use a different processing system (verbal and visual) rather than two tasks that use the same 'slave' system. Baddeley (1973) got participants to follow a moving spot of light with a pointer (**a tracker task**). At the same time, half the participants had to describe the angles on a 'hollow' letter F. This group found the two tasks extremely difficult, because they were using the visuo-spatial sketchpad for both tasks. The other participants performed the tracking task along with a verbal task and had little difficulty performing both tasks simultaneously. They were using different 'slave' systems (verbal and visual).

EVALUATION OF WM

✔ **Research support:** from dual task studies (Baddeley 1973), although such laboratory studies are rather artificial. K.F. could remember visual, but not verbal stimuli in STM, so there must be at least two systems in STM.

✔ **Importance of rehearsal?** The WM model doesn't over-emphasise the importance of rehearsal for STM retention, in contrast to the MSM.

✔ **Physiological evidence:** WM is supported by studies involving brain scans. PET (Positron Emission Tomography) scans have shown that different areas of the brain are used whilst undertaking verbal and visual tasks. These areas may correspond to the components of WM (Paulescu *et al*, 1993).

✘ **Only STM:** WM only concerns itself with STM and so it isn't a comprehensive model of memory.

✘ **Function of central executive?** Least is known about the most important component, namely the central executive. It isn't clear how it works or what it does. This vagueness means that it can be used to explain almost any experimental results. For example, if two tasks *cannot* be done together, then it can be argued that two processing components in the model conflict or that the tasks exceed the central executive's capacity. If the two tasks *can* be done simultaneously, then it can be argued that they don't exceed the available resources. It's a circular argument ('heads I win, tails you lose'). Eysenck (1986) claimed that a single central executive might be as inaccurate as a single STM store.

✘ **The capacity of the central executive** has never been measured.

✘ **Practice or time:** The WM model doesn't explain changes in processing ability that occur as the result of practice or time.

✘ **Another store?** Recently an episodic buffer store was added to combine information from LTM with other slave systems (Baddeley, 2001). The model is getting more complicated with each new finding it cannot explain!

It's better to see STM as a number of independent components rather than a unitary STM store as the MSM suggests. However, there remain a number of problems with WM and even Baddeley stated: '*We've a long way to go before we can be sure of the details of the model*'.

Levels of processing (LOP) (Craik & Lockhart, 1972)

DESCRIPTION

(Note: you only need to know *one* alternative model to the MSM: WM *or* LOP will do.)

Craik and Lockhart's LOP approach emphasises the processes involved in memory, rather than the storage systems. They believed that memories occur as a by-product of the processing of information. The processing of information is on a continuous dimension but can be tested at three levels:

- A superficial level analysing the basic features of a word, such as its shape ('**visual**' processing).

- An intermediate level analysing, say, the sound of a word ('**acoustic**' processing).

- A deeper level analysing the meaning of the word ('**semantic**' processing).

Craik and Lockhart argued that the deeper information is processed, the better it will be remembered. The level of the processing depends on:

- the nature of the stimulus

- the tasks to be completed

- the time available.

Studies on interference have used the **paired associate technique**. Participants have to learn two word lists, with the first word the same in each case e.g.

List A   List B
Desk – boy   Desk – tree
Flower – car   Flower – chair

When given the first word of the pairs (e.g. desk) and asked to recall List A (e.g. boy), participants often report the words from List B (e.g. tree). This is evidence for retroactive interference .

EVALUATION OF INTERFERENCE THEORY

✗·✓ **Experimental studies support interference** (e.g. Keppel & Underwood 1962). But many of these studies lack ecological validity.

✓ **Makes 'cognitive sense':** Most people would agree that it's more difficult to remember similar material than dissimilar material. For example, if someone was trying to remember a telephone number, you'd shout out random numbers in order to put them off.

✗ **Only one type of forgetting:** Interference is demonstrated best using the paired associate word technique, and so only explains one aspect of forgetting.

✗ **Use of meaningless word lists:** Interference is less easy to demonstrate with meaningful (semantic) material (Solso, 1995).

✗ **Not easy to demonstrate with experts:** Experts in a particular field should find it difficult to learn new information, since it should interfere with their large amount of pre-existing knowledge. This is clearly not the case, probably due to their well-organised memory.

✗ **Learning is artificially compressed in time:** Typically, participants have little time in the laboratory to learn and recall material. This artificial compression of time is more likely to cause interference. Learning in real life is more 'spread out' in time and is less affected by interference effects.

✗ **Not a popular theory:** Psychologists don't believe it's a convincing theory. Retrieval failure has recently become a more popular explanation.

Retrieval failure

DESCRIPTION

The retrieval failure explanation of forgetting suggests that you can't remember because there aren't enough cues or clues to help recall. Memories are there in your memory (available) but cannot be accessed at that time. It's demonstrated by the 'tip of the tongue' phenomenon (TOT). People are asked questions and are certain they *know* the answer but cannot actually answer it at the time. Giving them a clue or cue, such as the first letter of the word, often helps them to retrieve it (Brown & McNeill, 1966). According to the 'encoding specificity principle', the closer the cue is to the information you're trying to remember, the more it will aid recall.

Research concentrates on two types of cues:

● **External cues: context-dependent forgetting (or remembering).** This suggests that the context or place where material is learnt can affect recall. Godden & Baddeley (1975) got underwater divers to learn word lists either on dry land or underwater. They then had to recall the words in each of these places. Results showed that words learnt and recalled in the same context were remembered better. However, Fernandez & Glenberg (1985) tried to replicate such studies and never found consistent support for context-dependent effects.

● **Internal cues: state-dependent forgetting (or remembering).** This suggests that the physiological state a person is in can affect recall. Goodwin *et al* (1969) examined this effect with alcohol. Participants who hid money whilst drunk were more likely to remember the hiding place when they were back in their original drunken state. Darley *et al* (1973) found similar effects for marijuana. Studies have also investigated the effect of mood on recall but results have been inconclusive. Ucros (1989) with a meta-analysis (review) of all the research concluded that there was a small state-dependent effect of mood.

Darley and Goodwin always had plenty of volunteers ... but were the samples representative?

E V A L U A T I O N   O F   R E T R I E V A L   F A I L U R E   T H E O R Y

✓ **Psychological research** supports retrieval failure forgetting (see above).

✓ **Retrieval failure theory makes 'cognitive sense':** Often sounds, smells, particular songs 'spark off' long lost memories and provide cues for remembering. Returning to your old school may have the same effect.

✗ **Impossible to disprove:** We cannot disprove the idea that all memories are stored but that we lack sufficient cues to access them.

✗ **Procedural memories** ('knowing how') aren't explained by retrieval failure. Most procedural memories (e.g. riding a bike) aren't forgotten or affected by retrieval cues.

✗ **Contextual effects not large:** Contexts have to be *very* different in order to reliably demonstrate contextual effects.

EXAM tips BOX

Consider psychological research into explanations of forgetting in long-term memory. (18 marks)

● Again, it may be best to think of answering this question in three paragraphs each about 100–130 words long.

● In the first paragraph, you could *describe* both proactive and retroactive interference and *very briefly* mention context- and state-dependent forgetting as supporting retrieval failure (AO1 worth 6 marks).

● In the second paragraph, you could *analyse and evaluate* studies that support or reject interference theory (e.g. Keppel & Underwood 1962.

● In the final paragraph you could *analyse and evaluate* studies that support or reject retrieval failure (e.g. Godden & Baddeley 1975, Goodwin *et al* 1969) (AO2 worth 12 marks).

Try to write out a suitable answer using about 300–350 words. Remember, there is no single way of answering such questions. The material outlined above is designed to guide you. There's a 'sample answer' at the end of the book but don't be tempted to look at it until you have tried to answer the question yourself.

Weighing up the competing explanations for forgetting, Eysenck (1998) concluded that *'it seems probable that this [retrieval failure] is the main reason for forgetting in LTM'.*

EXAM tips BOX

To what extent is there psychological evidence to support the idea of repression in forgetting? (18 marks)

● You could structure your answer in three paragraphs, each about 100–130 words long.

● The first paragraph could involve a brief description of repression (AO1 – 6 marks). With this question, it might be best to mix material that supports and rejects repression throughout the remaining two paragraphs.

● In the second paragraph you could *analyse and evaluate* Freud's evidence and that provided by cases of psychogenic amnesia. In the final paragraph you could include studies by Levinger & Clark (1961) and Kline (1972) as well as more general criticisms (AO2 – 12 marks). Remember that mere *description* of studies will not gain any AO2 marks. You must use this material as an aid to analysis and evaluation.

Try to write out a suitable answer using about 300–350 words. There's a 'sample answer' at the end of the book but don't be tempted to look at it until you have tried to answer the question yourself.

A hijacked plane flies into one of the World Trade Centre's Twin Towers in New York on September 11th 2001. Both towers collapsed shortly after. An example of flashbulb memory?

Flashbulb (FB) memories

DESCRIPTION

FB memories refer to a special kind of 'episodic' memory, which we can vividly recall in great detail (e.g. September 11th 2001 terrorist attacks in the US or Princess Diana's death). It's called a FB memory because the memory is recalled in almost photographic detail. FB memories can also be about more personal events, such as the birth of a brother or sister. For FB memories to occur, the event must be surprising, unexpected and emotionally and personally significant.

People with FB memories tend to recall the same six pieces of information surrounding the event, namely:

● Where they were

● What they were doing

● Who told them

● What they felt about it

● What others felt about it

● What happened immediately afterwards.

EVALUATION OF FB MEMORY RESEARCH

✓ **Accurate FBs:** Conway *et al* (1994) showed that UK participants had very accurate FB memories of Margaret Thatcher's resignation. Inaccurate FB memories involve events that weren't surprising, unexpected or of great personal significance.

✗ **The same as other memories:** FB memories are recalled in detail simply because they're repeated over and over again. This rehearsal leads to enhanced recall like any other memory.

✗ **FB memories are inaccurate:** McCloskey *et al* (1988) found inaccurate memories of the Space Shuttle Challenger disaster. Wright (1993) found similar results for the Hillsborough tragedy involving Liverpool FC. This was despite people believing their memories to be accurate.

Flashbulb Memory of Sept 11th 2001 (FM 9/11): **Conway, Skitka, Hemmerich & Kershaw** (2003)

Aims (AO1)

To investigate whether salient events, which are accompanied by strong affect and emotion, are recalled with accuracy over a long time period or whether memory of these events is susceptible to distortion. The event in question was the World Trade Centre attacks on Sept 11th 2001.

Procedures (AO1)

- A random national sample of 678 participants were tested for their memory recall immediately after the attacks on the World Trade Centre and then one year later.

- The data was collected by a marketing company via Web-TV, which is an internet connection via television.

Findings (AO1)

- Nearly half of all Americans (+/− 3%) had a perfect flashbulb memory of 9/11.

- 75% of Americans (+/− 3%) had a near perfect recall of 9/11.

Conclusion (AO1)

- Flashbulb memories are more detailed, vivid and accurate than ordinary memories.

- Flashbulb memories do appear to exist for particularly salient, surprising or consequential events.

Criticisms (AO1/AO2)

✓ **Sample:** A national representative sample was obtained. The Web-TV method of data collection allows a more representative sample than internet via computer, which is skewed toward more wealthy and educated folks.

✓ **Sept 11th:** This is the first piece of research investigating flashbulb memories for 9/11 – arguably, the world event which will be most cited in the future as an example of FM.

✓ **Other research support for relevance of event:** This study tested Americans' memories for a disaster that occurred in America. Results are supported by the 'racial relevance' study where it was found that 75% of black people had a FM for the assassination of Martin Luther King (a black civil rights leader) compared to only 33% of white participants (Brown & Kulik, 1977). It seems that *personal relevance* of the event is a vital factor in FM.

✗ **Only one year follow-up:** Flashbulb memories have only been tested up to one year later. Work in progress will test whether flashbulb memories of 9/11 endure.

ESSENTIAL STUDY 1.7

EXAM tips BOX

Briefly describe and evaluate research into the way emotional factors influence forgetting. (18 marks)

● You could structure your answer in terms of three paragraphs each about 100–130 words long.

● In the first paragraph, you could *briefly* describe the effects of mood, repression and/or flashbulb memories on forgetting (AO1 – 6 marks). In the final two paragraphs, you might choose to concentrate solely on repression and/or flashbulb memories.

● In the second paragraph, you could *analyse and evaluate* research that supports or questions repression (e.g. Freud, 1901; Levinger & Clark 1961; Eysenck & Wilson, 1973).

● In the final paragraph you could *analyse and evaluate* research on flashbulb memories (e.g. Conway et al, 2003, 1977; Wright, 1993) (AO2 – 12 marks).

● This is a difficult question since there's so much material that could be included. There might be a 'trade-off' in your answer between breadth and depth. That is, the fewer studies you mention the more detail required and vice versa. It's normally better to cover three or four studies in reasonable detail than list lots of studies and have no time to expand on them.

● You could choose to write an answer that only presents one side of the argument, that emotional factors do/don't influence forgetting.

Note: The examiners could ask you a question about FB memories alone since they're explicitly mentioned in the specification. However, we've not prepared a 'sample answer' for several reasons. FB memories are more concerned with remembering than forgetting (the actual sub-section) and it's more likely that they'd ask about FB memories as part of an 'emotional factors influencing forgetting' question. However, if the Chief Examiner reads this s/he may change his/her mind! You have been warned!

CRITICAL ISSUE: EYEWITNESS TESTIMONY

Reconstructive memory (Bartlett)

DESCRIPTION

Bartlett (1932) stated that memory doesn't work accurately like a camera, rather it's prone to inaccuracies and interpretations based on prior experiences i.e. memories are reconstructed (see Essential Study 1.8).

Schemas are our ready-made expectations that help us to understand our world. We use schemas to:

● interpret the world. They help us 'fill in the gaps' in our knowledge.

● simplify the processing of information.

However, schemas can lead to memory distortions when information doesn't readily fit into existing schemas. Cultural expectations or stereotypes also influence memory.

Allport & Postman (1947) illustrated the powerful effect of schemas on memory. They asked participants to view a cartoon and then describe what they'd seen. Typically, white participants reported that the black man had been holding the cut-throat razor. This is a shocking finding, since white participants must have held a schema or stereotype suggesting black men were more prone to violence. It's hoped that results would be very different today.

Reconstructive memory •••••••• **Bartlett** (1932) **'War of the Ghosts'** (WAROG) **study**

Aims (AO1)

To investigate the reconstructive nature of memory by examining the effect that prior expectations and experiences have on memory recall.

Procedures (AO1)

A short story or drawing was shown to participants. The best known story was called 'The War of the Ghosts'. Participants had to reproduce it after different time periods (15 minutes to years later). This is called a **repeated reproduction technique**.

Findings (AO1)

Over time, the reproductions became shorter, more coherent, more conventional and more clichéd. The reproductions were adapted to fit the participant's own cultural expectations. Typical errors that participants made in their recall included: *Omissions*: important details were left out (e.g. 'something black came from his mouth'); *Normalisation*: the story was made more 'normal' (e.g. 'boats' instead of 'canoes'; 'fishing' instead of 'hunting' seals); *Intrusions*: extra details were added to the story in order to make more sense; *Gist recall*: participants recalled only the 'gist' or basic storyline.

Conclusion (AO1)

Interpretation plays a major role in remembering. Remembering is an active process of reconstruction. Bartlett called this **'effort after meaning'**, that is, making the past more coherent to fit into existing knowledge or **schemas**.

Criticisms (AO1/AO2)

✓ **Status of research:** This study is regarded as a 'classic' in psychology and Bartlett's work on reconstructive memory remains influential.

✓ **Other research support:** The reproductive nature of memory has been demonstrated by others (Allport & Postman, 1947) and with other formats (e.g. drawings).

✗ **Poorly controlled study:** Analysis of the reproductions was too subjective and Bartlett may have been inadvertently biased in his interpretation of the stories.

✗ **Low ecological validity:** The stories used were rather artificial and unusual. Wynn & Logie (1998) repeatedly asked undergraduates about their first week at university and memory distortions weren't evident over time. This is because they examined real-life, everyday memories.

HOW DO YOU MAKE YOUR GIRLFRIEND CRY WHEN YOU'RE HAVING SEX?

I DON'T KNOW

RING HER UP...

Jokes often work by using schema theory to provide a surprising punchline

EVALUATION OF RECONSTRUCTIVE MEMORY

✓ **Schemas do play a major part in memory recall** and help to explain the reconstructive nature of memory.

✗ **Schemas are themselves influenced by memory:** Schemas can be updated and changed. It's not a one-way process whereby existing schemas lead to reconstructed memories. Experience and memories also affect our schemas.

✗ **The idea of schemas is rather vague.** What exactly are they? How are they acquired?

✗ **Accuracy of memory:** Schema theory over-emphasises memory inaccuracies. For example, it cannot easily explain FB memories.

The role of leading questions (Loftus)

DESCRIPTION

Loftus' EWT research also illustrated the reconstructive nature of memory. Loftus showed that eyewitness memories can be affected by the wording of questions (see Essential Study 1.9). This has serious implications for the judicial system, since jurors seem to be particularly convinced by EWT.

There are two types of misleading questions which appear to affect EWT:

● *Leading questions*: a question which makes it likely that a participant's schema will influence them to give a desired answer (see Essential Study 1.9).

● *'After-the-fact information' questions*: here new misleading information is added in the question after the incident has occurred (see Loftus, 1974 study below).

Estimated speed of a car crash can be affected by the type of verb used (Loftus & Palmer, 1974)

EXAM tips BOX

'There are so many factors that influence memory that we cannot be sure that any memories are not merely biased reconstructions.' To what extent does psychological research support this view of reconstructive memory? (18 marks)

● Again, you could structure your answer in three paragraphs, each 100–130 words long.

● In the first paragraph, you could *describe* what reconstructive memory refers to, introduce Bartlett's views and refer to schemas and stereotypes (AO1 – 6 marks).

● In the second paragraph, you could *analyse and evaluate* studies that support the reconstructive nature of memory (e.g. Bartlett, 1932; Allport & Postman, 1947).

● In the third paragraph, you could also use eyewitness testimony research as support (see Loftus below), although criticisms of the methods employed should be mentioned. Finally, you could cite research that analyses and evaluates the reconstructive (inaccurate) nature of memory (Yuille & Cutshall, 1986). This could also include Wynn & Logie (1998) and research into flashbulb memories (AO2 – 12 marks).

Try to write out a suitable answer using about 300–350 words. There is a 'sample answer' at the end of the book, but try not to look at it until you've tried to answer the question yourself.

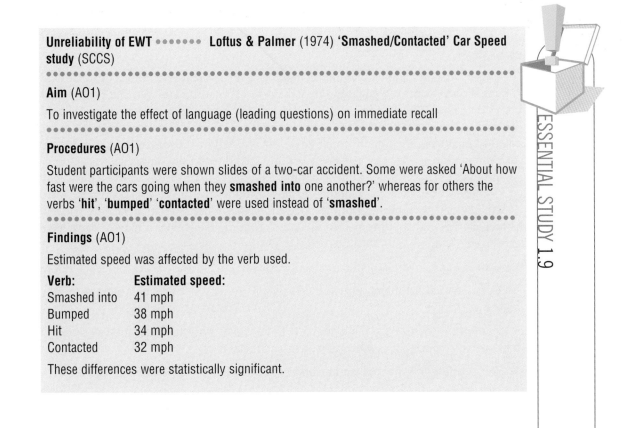

Unreliability of EWT •••••••• **Loftus & Palmer** (1974) **'Smashed/Contacted' Car Speed study** (SCCS)

Aim (AO1)

To investigate the effect of language (leading questions) on immediate recall

Procedures (AO1)

Student participants were shown slides of a two-car accident. Some were asked 'About how fast were the cars going when they **smashed into** one another?' whereas for others the verbs '**hit**', '**bumped**' '**contacted**' were used instead of '**smashed**'.

Findings (AO1)

Estimated speed was affected by the verb used.

Verb:	Estimated speed:
Smashed into	41 mph
Bumped	38 mph
Hit	34 mph
Contacted	32 mph

These differences were statistically significant.

ESSENTIAL STUDY 1.9

Conclusion (AO1)

- Memory recall can be distorted by the language used.
- Participants have different interpretations of the speed and force from the use of different verbs. Leading questions do affect memory recall.

Criticisms (AO1/AO2)

✓ **Well controlled experiments:** The independent variable (use of verbs) is manipulated and all other variables are controlled.

✓ **Other experimental support:** There have been many studies which support Loftus.

✗ **Lacks ecological validity:** Witnessing a video clip lacks the emotional effects of watching a real-life event (see Yuille & Cutshall, 1986 below).

✗ **Sample:** Students are not representative of the wider population, so the results cannot be generalised.

✗ **Change of verb:** Did participants merely change their speed estimates due to verb change (demand characteristics) or did it actually alter their memory of the accident?

Other EWT research studies

Two groups of participants watched a film of a car being driven through the countryside (Loftus, 1975). Group A were asked '*How fast was the white car going when it passed the 'Stop' sign while travelling along the country road?*' (there was a 'Stop' sign in the film). Group B were asked '*How fast was the white car going when it passed the barn while travelling along the country road?* (there was no barn but the question presupposes there was one). A week later 17% of Group B reported seeing a barn compared to just 2% of Group A. The 'after the event' question had falsely suggested to them that there had actually been a barn. The explanation for this is source **misattribution**, where witnesses confuse the *actual* event itself with **post-event information**.

Yuille & Cutshall (1986) conducted research into a **real-life** crime. A thief had attempted to steal from a gun shop in Vancouver, Canada. However, the shop owner shot and killed the thief in front of 21 witnesses. 13 of the witnesses were interviewed four months later and they were asked misleading questions. However, witness accounts remained highly accurate and weren't adversely affected by the misleading information. Misleading information may not affect real-life memories to the same extent as laboratory-produced memories due to the emotions experienced at the time. This incident may have been encoded like a flashbulb memory, and so wasn't easily distorted. Also, participants had previously been interviewed by the police. Researchers only tried to deliberately mislead them four months later. Thus their memories may already have been 'fixed'.

There are a number of factors, apart from misleading questions, which influence EWT:

- **Race:** errors are more likely to occur when the suspect and witness are racially different.

- **Clothing:** witnesses pay more attention to transient characteristics (such as clothing) than stable characteristics (such as height and facial shape).

- **Social influence:** People are influenced by other people's memories of events.

EVALUATION OF EWT RESEARCH

✓ **Strong experimental support:** EWT can be affected by misleading post-event information.

✗ **Demand characteristics:** Participants in EWT studies respond to the experimental situation and provide answers they're expected to give.

✗ **Participant expectations and consequences:** Participants don't expect to be deliberately misled by university researchers, and therefore the reconstructive findings should be expected since they believe the researchers to be telling the truth. The consequences of inaccurate memories are minimal in a research setting compared to real-life crimes. Foster *et al* (1994) showed that eyewitness identification was more accurate for a real-life crime as opposed to a simulation.

✗ **Deliberately misleading information:** Memory for important events isn't easily distorted when the information is obviously misleading.

✗ **Minor aspects of memory:** Misleading information only affects minor, relatively unimportant, aspects of the memory (e.g. 'barn' details above).

EXAM tips BOX

To what extent has psychological research shown eyewitness testimony to be unreliable? (18 marks)

● Again, you could structure your answer in three paragraphs, each 100–130 words long.

● In the first paragraph, you could describe some studies that show EWT to be unreliable (e.g. Loftus & Palmer, 1974, Loftus, 1975) (AO1 – 6 marks).

● In the second paragraph, you could *analyse and evaluate* such studies.

● In the final paragraph, you could *analyse and evaluate* evidence that shows EWT to be reliable (e.g. Yuille & Cutshall, 1986; Foster *et al*, 1994) (AO2 – 12 marks).

Try to write out a suitable answer using about 300–350 words. There is a 'sample answer' at the end of the book, but try not to look at it until you've attempted the question yourself.

Does misleading information alter and replace the original memory (Loftus' view) or is the original memory merely obscured while remaining intact (McCloskey & Zaragoza, 1985)? Baddeley claimed that EWT research doesn't prove destruction of the memory trace, but merely interference with its retrieval. However, even when participants are explicitly told about misleading information, they find it hard to ignore.

Dr Elizabeth Loftus, the world's leading expert in EWT research

ESSENTIAL STUDY SUMMARY

Topic	Research study	Researcher date	Page
Encoding in STM	Acoustic/Semantic (AS) study	Baddeley (1966)	2
Capacity in STM	Study of Immediate Digit Span (SIDS)	Jacobs (1887)	3
Duration in STM	Trigram Retention Experiment (TRE)	Peterson & Peterson (1959)	4
STM	*Use any study on STM (above)*	–	–
Encoding in LTM	Acoustic/Semantic (AS) study	Baddeley (1966)	4
Duration in LTM	High School Yearbook Photo (HSYP) study	Bahrick *et al* (1975)	6
LTM	*Use any study on LTM (above)*		
Repression	Emotionally Charged Words (ECW) study	Levinger & Clark (1961)	19
Flashbulb memory	FM 9/11 study	Conway *et al* (2003)	21
Emotional factors in forgetting	*Use either study on Repression or Flashbulb memory*		
Reconstructive memory	'War of the Ghosts' (WAROG) study	Bartlett (1932)	23
Eyewitness testimony	'Smashed/Contacted' Car Speed (SCCS) study	Loftus & Palmer (1974)	25

AS Module 1:
Developmental Psychology

What's covered in this chapter?

ATTACHMENTS IN DEVELOPMENT

a. **The development and variety of attachments**

- The development of attachments (e.g. Schaffer). Research into individual differences, including secure and insecure attachments (e.g. Ainsworth) and cross-cultural variations.
- Explanations of attachment (e.g. learning theory, Bowlby's theory).

b. **Deprivation and privation**

- Bowlby's maternal deprivation hypothesis. Research into the effects of deprivation/separation (e.g. Robertson & Robertson, Bowlby).
- Research into the effects of privation (Hodges & Tizard's study of institutionalisation).

CRITICAL ISSUE: DAY CARE

- The effects of day care on children's cognitive and social development.

THE DEVELOPMENT AND VARIETY OF ATTACHMENTS

What are attachments?

According to Kagan *et al* (1978), an attachment is:

- an intense emotional relationship specific to two people
- which endures over time, and
- in which prolonged separation from the attachment figure is accompanied by stress and sorrow.

This definition applies to attachments at any point in a person's life. But our earliest attachment serves as a *prototype* (or model) for all later attachments. The crucial first attachment is usually taken to be with our mother.

Phases in the development of attachments

The attachment process can be divided into several phases (Schaffer, 1996):

- The **pre-attachment phase** (birth–3 months). From about six weeks, babies develop an attraction to other human beings. They prefer other people to physical objects and events. One way in which they show this preference is through smiling in response to people's faces. They direct this **social smile** to just about anyone.

● The **indiscriminate attachment phase** (3–7/8 months). Babies begin to discriminate between familiar and unfamiliar people. They smile much more at people they know, and the social smile has disappeared. But they'll still let strangers handle and look after them. They don't become visibly distressed, provided they're treated properly.

● The **discriminate attachment phase** (7/8 months onwards). Babies begin to develop specific attachments. They show this through (a) actively trying to stay close to particular people (especially the mother), and (b) becoming distressed when separated from them (*separation anxiety*). The baby can now consistently tell the difference between its mother and other people. It also understands that the mother continues to exist even when she's out of sight (*object permanence*).

Also at this time, babies avoid close contact with unfamiliar people. Some display the *fear-of-strangers* response. This includes crying and trying to move away. It usually only occurs if the stranger tries to make contact with them.

● The **multiple attachment phase** (9 months onwards). The baby forms strong emotional ties with (a) other major caregivers (such as the father, grandparents, and siblings), and (b) non-caregivers (such as other children). The fear-of-strangers response weakens. But the attachment to the mother remains the strongest.

Individual differences in attachment

ESSENTIAL STUDY 2.1

Ainsworth *et al's* (1971, 1978) **Strange Situation study of Attachments** (SSoA)
● ●

Aims (AO1)

In 1971 and 1978, Ainsworth and her colleagues reported their findings from the Baltimore study of attachment. This was a replication (in Baltimore, US) of an earlier study Ainsworth had conducted in Uganda, Africa (called the Ganda project, 1967). In that earlier study, she observed babies aged 15 weeks to two years over a nine-month period. She also interviewed their mothers. Ainsworth's main interest was in *individual differences* between mother–child pairs in the quality of their attachments.
● ●

Procedures (AO1)

Like the Ganda project, the Baltimore study was longitudinal. Ainsworth *et al* visited 26 mother–child pairs at home every 3–4 weeks for the baby's first year of life. Each visit lasted 3–4 hours. Also like the earlier study, both interviews and naturalistic observation were used. But observation now played a much greater role.

To make sense of the vast amount of data collected for each pair, Ainsworth *et al* needed some standard against which to compare their observations. The standard they chose was the *Strange Situation*. This comprises eight episodes (each lasting about three minutes, except for episode 1, which lasts 30 seconds), as shown in Table 2.1.

Table 2.1 The eight episodes of the Strange Situation

Episode	Persons present	Brief description
1	Mother, baby, observer	Observer introduces mother and baby to experimental room, then leaves
2	Mother, baby	Mother is passive while the baby explores
3	Stranger, mother, baby	Stranger enters. First minute: stranger silent. Second minute: stranger converses with mother. Third minute: stranger approaches baby. After three minutes, mother leaves unobtrusively
4	Stranger, baby	*First separation episode.* Stranger's behaviour is geared to the baby's
5	Mother, baby	*First reunion episode.* Stranger leaves. Mother greets and/or comforts baby, then tries to settle baby again in play. Mother then leaves, saying 'bye-bye'
6	Baby	*Second separation episode*
7	Stranger, baby	*Continuation of second separation.* Stranger enters and gears her behaviour to the baby's
8	Mother, baby	*Second reunion episode.* Mother enters, greets baby, then picks up baby. Meanwhile, stranger leaves unobtrusively

Every aspect of the participants' reactions is observed and videotaped. But most attention is given to the baby's response to the mother's return (*reunion behaviours*). In the Baltimore study, the Strange Situation was used when the babies were 12 months old. This is the age-group it's designed for.

Findings (AO1)

As a group, babies explored the playroom and toys more enthusiastically when the mother was present than *either* (a) after the stranger entered *or* (b) when the mother was absent. But Ainsworth *et al* were fascinated by the unexpected variety of reunion behaviours.

Ainsworth *et al* classified the babies in terms of three types of attachment.

• 15 per cent of the sample were classified as ***anxious-avoidant (Type A)***. They typically ignored the mother, showing *indifference* towards her. Their play was hardly affected by whether she was present or absent. They showed few signs of stress when she left the room, and actively ignored or avoided her when she returned. They responded to the mother and stranger in very similar ways. They were most distressed when left on their own.

• 70 per cent were classified as ***securely attached (Type B)***. They played happily while the mother was present (whether or not the stranger was there). But they became very upset when the mother left, and their play was seriously disrupted. When she returned, they wanted immediate comfort from her. They quickly calmed down and started playing again. Overall, they treated the mother and stranger very differently.

• 15 per cent were classified as ***anxious-resistant (Type C)***. These babies were fussy and wary even when the mother was present. They cried a lot more than Types A and B. When the mother left, they became very distressed. When she returned, they wanted contact with her, but *at the same time* showed anger and resisted contact. For example, they put their arms out to be picked up, but then immediately struggled to get down again. This showed their *ambivalence* towards her.

Conclusions (AO1)

The Baltimore study's findings largely confirmed those of the Ganda project. The mother's *sensitivity* is the crucial factor that determines the quality of children's attachment. Sensitive mothers see things from their baby's perspective, correctly interpret their signals, and respond to its needs. They're also accepting, co-operative, and accessible. Sensitive mothers tend to have babies who are *securely attached*, whereas insensitive mothers tend to have *insecurely attached* (either *anxious-avoidant* or *anxious-resistant*) babies.

Criticisms (AO1/AO2)

✓ **Status of the research:** The Baltimore study is the most important study in the history of attachment research (van Ijzendoorn & Schuengel, 1999).

✓ **Research support:** Several more recent studies, using larger samples, have tested and supported the original claim that parental sensitivity actually *causes* attachment security (van Ijzendoorn & Schuengel, 1999).

✗ • ✓ Most debate has focused on the Strange Situation itself (see below).

✗ **Small samples:** Both the Ganda and Baltimore studies used rather small samples.

EVALUATION OF THE STRANGE SITUATION

✓ **Established methodology:** The Strange Situation is the most widely used method for assessing infant attachment to a caregiver.

✗ **A stable characteristic?** Attachment type (based on the Strange Situation) is often taken to measure a *fixed characteristic* of the child. But if the family's circumstances change (such as the mother's stress levels), how the child is classified can change. This couldn't happen if attachment style were a permanent characteristic.

✗ **Different parental relationships:** Attachment to mothers and fathers are *independent*. So, the same child might be securely attached to its mother, but insecurely attached to its father. This shows that attachment patterns reflect *qualities of distinct relationships*, rather than characteristics of the child.

✗ **Low ecological validity:** Some regard it as highly artificial (i.e. it lacks *ecological validity*).

✗ **Ethics:** It's designed to see how young children react to an increasingly stressful situation. Mothers *do* leave their children for brief periods, often with strangers (such as unfamiliar babysitters or childminders). But we must question the ethics of any method used in psychological research which *deliberately* exposes children to stress.

EXAM tips BOX

Consider psychological research into individual differences in attachments. (18 marks)

- You could structure your answer in terms of three paragraphs, all about 100–130 words long.

- The first paragraph could include a *description* of research into individual differences in attachments, either the findings from studies using the Strange Situation, or the Strange Situation itself, or a combination of the two (AO1, worth 6 marks).

Note that studies of 'cultural variations' (i.e. cross-cultural studies) may count as 'individual differences'.
Note also that 'research' includes both 'studies' and 'theories'.

- In the second and third paragraphs, you could *analyse and evaluate* the findings, and/or the Strange Situation method. You might do this by considering whether Ainsworth *et al's* findings have been replicated (including cross-cultural studies), how attachment types have been interpreted, and the ethical acceptability of the Strange Situation (AO2, worth 12 marks).

Try to write a suitable answer in about 300–350 words. As with all questions, there's no single correct way of answering it. The above are just pointers. There's a sample answer at the end of the book. Try not to look at it until you've had a go at doing it yourself.

Note that you could be asked a very similar question that refers to 'cultural variations' instead of 'individual differences' (see Essential Study 2.2 below).

Cultural variations in attachment

The pioneering cross-cultural study was Ainsworth's (1967) Ganda project (see Essential Study 1.1 above). Cross-cultural studies using the Strange Situation have shown important differences, both within and between cultures.

Van Ijzendoorn & Kroonenberg's (1988) **Review of Patterns of Attachment** (RPA)

Aim (AO1)

Van Ijzendoorn and Kroonenberg wanted to compare the findings of studies using the Strange Situation conducted in different cultures. They were interested in *patterns* of attachment type (secure, avoidant, resistant) both between and within cultures.

Procedures (AO1)

They reviewed 32 world-wide studies involving eight countries and over 2,000 children (see Table 2.2 below). These studies had been conducted by *other* researchers. Van Ijzendoorn and Kroonenberg were comparing the studies in order to find any general trends.

ESSENTIAL STUDY 2.2

Findings (AO1)

Table 2.2 Percentage of children displaying attachment types in eight countries

Country	No. of studies	Percentage of each type of attachment		
		Type B (Securely attached)	Type A (Anxious-avoidant)	Type C (Anxious-resistant)
West Germany	3	57	35	8
Great Britain	1	75	22	3
Netherlands	4	67	26	7
Sweden	1	74	22	4
Israel	2	64	7	29
Japan	2	68	5	27
China	1	50	25	25
US	18	65	21	14

Conclusions (AO1)

• There are marked differences *within* cultures. For example, in one of the two Japanese studies, there were *no* Type A children at all, but a high proportion of Type C. In the other, the pattern was more like Ainsworth *et al*'s findings.

• The overall world-wide pattern was similar to Ainsworth *et al*'s 'standard' pattern. This was also true of the 18 American studies overall. But there was also considerable variation *within* the US studies.

• Overall, Type B is the most common of the three. But Type A is relatively more common in Western European countries, and Type C in Israel and Japan.

Criticisms (AO2)

✗ • ✓ **Cultural diversity:** The countries included in the study are both Western and non-Western (China and Japan). But only three of the 32 studies were carried out in China and Japan.

✗ • ✓ **Sub-cultures:** There are several *sub-cultures* within highly populated countries. The variation *within* cultures shows that there isn't a *single* British or American form of child-rearing. This makes it difficult to compare different cultures.

✗ **The meaning of the Strange Situation:** The Strange Situation affects children from different cultures in different ways (it has a *different meaning*). Japanese children are rarely separated from their mothers. So, the separation episodes in the Strange Situation are the most upsetting for these children. For children raised on Israeli kibbutzim (small, close-knit groups), it's the arrival of the stranger that's most distressing. We need to know about child-rearing practices in different cultures if we're to validly interpret the findings.

EXPLANATIONS OF ATTACHMENT

Learning theory

• This refers to **behaviourist** attempts to explain all behaviour in terms of **conditioning** (see Chapter 4, pages 90–1).

• Through classical conditioning, babies learn to associate their caregivers with food. Food is an **unconditioned** or **primary reinforcer**. The caregiver is a **conditioned** or

secondary reinforcer. The baby feels secure when the caregiver is present, that is, she's rewarding in her own right.

● This theory is a '**cupboard love**' theory. According to learning theory, babies become attached to people who satisfy their physiological needs.

EVALUATION OF LEARNING THEORY

✖ It's based largely on research involving non-human animals. We cannot be sure that these findings apply to attachment in children.

✖ Harlow (1959) studied learning using rhesus monkeys. He separated newborns from their mothers, and raised them in cages on their own. Each cage contained a 'baby blanket'. The babies became extremely distressed whenever the blanket was removed for any reason. This behaviour was similar to how baby monkeys react when they're separated from their mothers. This suggested to Harlow that attachment *isn't* based on association with food.

✖ To test this hypothesis, Harlow placed baby rhesus monkeys in cages with two 'surrogate' (substitute) mothers. One was made from wire and had a baby bottle fitted to 'her'. The other surrogate was made from soft, cuddly terry cloth (but didn't have a bottle fitted: see Figure 2.1). The babies spent most of their time clinging to the cloth mother, even though she provided no milk. Harlow concluded that monkeys have an unlearned need for *contact comfort*. This is as basic as the need for food, at least in baby rhesus monkeys.

✖ The ethics of Harlow's research is dubious.

✖ Schaffer & Emerson (1964) studied 60 babies, every four weeks, throughout their first year. They were studied again at 18 months. Mothers were asked about the baby's protests in various separation situations. These included being left alone in a room, being left with a babysitter, and being put to bed. The babies were clearly attached to people who weren't involved in their physical care (notably the father). Also, in 39% of cases, the mother (usually the main carer) *wasn't* the baby's main attachment figure. Clearly, there's more to attachment than 'cupboard love'.

✖ For Schaffer (1971), 'cupboard love' theories of attachment put things the wrong way round. Babies don't 'live to eat', but 'eat to live'. They're *active seekers of stimulation*, not passive recipients of nutrition.

Bowlby's theory

● This is the most comprehensive theory of human attachment.

Why do babies form attachments to their parents?

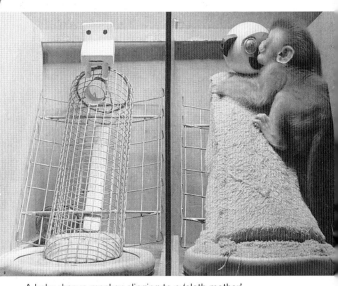

A baby rhesus monkey clinging to a 'cloth mother'

Lorenz being followed by goslings which had imprinted on him after hatching

● Bowlby drew on several sources. These included Harlow's rhesus monkey research, and Lorenz's (1935) study of *imprinting* in goslings and other bird species (as in the photo).

● Bowlby was also a trained psychoanalyst. So, his theory was partly based on Freud's theories, as well as on his own work with children and adults.

● Newborn human babies are completely helpless. Consequently, they're *genetically programmed* to behave towards their mothers in ways that ensure their survival (Bowlby, 1969, 1973).

● These *species-specific* behaviours include cuddling, looking, smiling, and crying. Babies use them to shape and control their caregivers' behaviour.

● The mother also inherits a genetic blueprint. This programmes her to respond to the baby's attachment behaviours. But the baby doesn't have to be her biological child. Babies need adequate *mothering* (a mother-figure), rather than their biological mother.

● There's a **critical period** for the formation of attachments (Bowlby, 1951). That is, mothering must take place within a certain time period for a child to form an attachment. Mothering is useless for *most* children if delayed until after 12 months. It's useless for *all* children if delayed until after two-and-a-half to three years.

● The child's attachment to the mother helps regulate how far away from her s/he will move. Also, it determines how much fear of strangers the child will show (see page 32). Generally, attachment behaviours are more evident when the child is distressed, unwell, afraid, or in unfamiliar surroundings.

● Babies display **monotropy,** a strong innate (inborn) tendency to become attached to one particular adult female (usually the biological mother). This attachment is *unique*. It's the first to develop and it's the strongest of all.

● For Bowlby (1951): *'Mother love in infancy is as important for mental health as vitamins and proteins for physical health'*.

EVALUATION OF BOWLBY'S THEORY

✘ Babies and young children display a whole range of attachment behaviours towards various attachment figures *other than their mothers.* In other words, the mother *isn't* special in the way Bowlby claimed (Rutter, 1981).

✘ Bowlby didn't deny that children form *multiple attachments*. But Schaffer & Emerson (1964: see above) showed that multiple attachments seem to be the rule (rather than the exception).

✘ For Bowlby, fathers aren't of any *direct* emotional importance for the baby. Their main role is to provide emotional and financial support to the mother. But Schaffer and Emerson's findings suggest that fathers are attachment figures *in their own right*.

Bowlby's maternal deprivation hypothesis

● We saw earlier that Bowlby claimed there's a *critical period* for attachment formation.

- He combined this with his theory of *monotropy* to form his *maternal deprivation hypothesis* (MDH).

- This claimed that if the mother–infant attachment were broken in the first years of life, the child's emotional and intellectual development would be seriously and permanently harmed.

- For Bowlby (1951):

  'An infant and young child should experience a warm, intimate and continuous relationship with his mother (or permanent mother figure) in which both find satisfaction and enjoyment'.

- Bowlby's MDH was based largely on studies (conducted in the 1930s and 1940s) of children brought up in residential nurseries and orphanages.

- Goldfarb (1943) studied 15 children raised in institutions (group 1) from about six months until three-and-a-half years. They were matched with 15 children who'd gone straight from their natural mothers to foster homes (group 2). The group 1 children lived in almost complete social isolation during their first year.

- At age three, group 1 lagged behind group 2 on measures of abstract thinking, social maturity, rule-following, and sociability. Between ages 10 and 14, group 1 continued to perform more poorly, and their average IQs (intelligence quotients) were 72 and 95 respectively.

- Spitz (1945, 1946) studied children raised in some very poor South American orphanages. Staff were overworked and untrained, and rarely talked to the babies. They hardly ever picked them up, even for feeding. They showed them no affection, and didn't provide any toys.

- The orphans showed *anaclitic depression* (a reaction to the loss of a love object). This includes fear, sadness, weepiness, withdrawal, loss of appetite, loss of weight, inability to sleep, and developmental retardation.

- Spitz & Wolf (1946) studied 91 orphanage infants in the US and Canada. Over one-third died before their first birthdays – despite good nutrition and medical care.

EXAM tips BOX

Give a brief account of *one* explanation of attachment and consider its strengths *and* limitations. (18 marks)

- You could structure your answer in terms of three paragraphs, all about 100–130 words long.

- The first paragraph could include a *description* of one explanation of attachment. *Note that the questions only asks you for* **one** *explanation so don't do more than you have to.* The two most likely choices are learning theory, and Bowlby's theory. (AO1, worth 6 marks).

- In the second paragraph, you could consider the *strengths* of the explanation of attachment. You might do this by considering the evidence the theory was originally based on, looking at subsequent evidence that supports the theory, and/or by comparing and contrasting it with another explanation.

- In the third paragraph, you could repeat the exercise, this time focusing on the *limitations* of your chosen explanation. *But try not to simply repeat points you made in the second paragraph.* Alternatively, you could examine strengths and limitations in *both* paragraphs. (AO2, worth 12 marks).

Try to write a suitable answer in about 300–350 words.
As with all questions, there's no single correct way of answering it. The above are just pointers. There's a sample answer at the end of the book. Try not to look at it until you've had a go at doing it yourself.

EVALUATION OF BOWLBY'S MATERNAL DEPRIVATION HYPOTHESIS

According to Bowlby, Goldfarb, Spitz, and Wolf, all these institutions had one factor in common, namely, lack of maternal care. This was the crucial harmful influence on the children growing up in them (which Bowlby later called maternal deprivation). But this interpretation fails to:

✗ recognise some of the methodological weaknesses of these studies. For example, in Goldfarb's study the children weren't assigned randomly to the two 'conditions' (groups 1 and 2) as would happen in a true experiment. It's possible that group 2 children were brighter, more easy-going, sociable and healthy from a very early age, and that this is *why* they were fostered (rather than sent to an institution). The poorer development of these children may have been due as much to these early differences as to the time they spent in institutions.

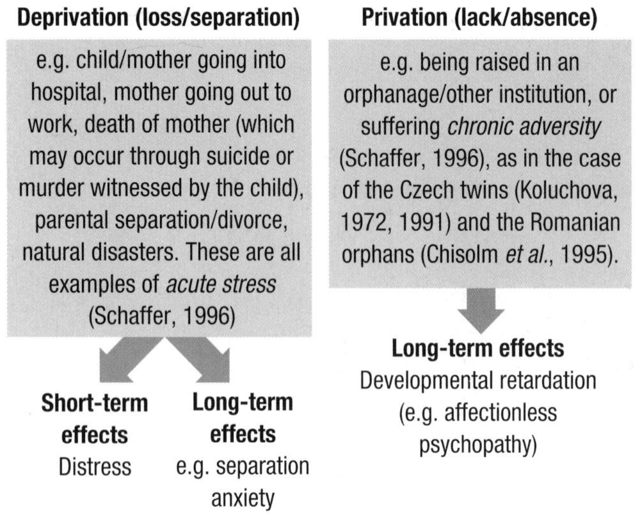

Deprivation (loss/separation)	Privation (lack/absence)
e.g. child/mother going into hospital, mother going out to work, death of mother (which may occur through suicide or murder witnessed by the child), parental separation/divorce, natural disasters. These are all examples of *acute stress* (Schaffer, 1996)	e.g. being raised in an orphanage/other institution, or suffering *chronic adversity* (Schaffer, 1996), as in the case of the Czech twins (Koluchova, 1972, 1991) and the Romanian orphans (Chisolm *et al.*, 1995).

Short-term effects
Distress

Long-term effects
e.g. separation anxiety

Long-term effects
Developmental retardation (e.g. affectionless psychopathy)

Figure 2.1 Examples of the difference between deprivation and privation, including their effects

✖ recognise that the institutions were extremely unstimulating environments for young children. This lack of stimulation could have been responsible for their poor development, in addition to (or instead of) the absence of maternal care. In other words, a crucial variable in intellectual development is the amount of *intellectual stimulation* a child receives, *not* the amount of mothering.

✖ distinguish between the effects of deprivation and privation (Rutter, 1981). *Deprivation* ('de-privation') refers to the *loss through separation*, of the (maternal) attachment figure. This assumes that an attachment has already developed. *Privation* refers to the *absence* of an attachment figure. There's been no opportunity to form an attachment with anyone in the first place.

✖ The studies of Goldfarb etc. are most accurately seen as demonstrating the effects of *privation*. Yet Bowlby's theory, and his own research, were mainly concerned with *deprivation*. Figure 2.1 opposite shows that deprivation and privation refer to two very different types of early experience. Each has very different types of effect, both short- and long-term.

EXAM tips BOX

Give a brief account of and evaluate Bowlby's maternal deprivation hypothesis. (18 marks)

● You could structure your answer in terms of three paragraphs, all about 100–30 words long.

● The first paragraph could include a *description* of Bowlby's maternal deprivation hypothesis. The two central components of this are the idea of a critical period for developing attachments, and monotropy. (AO1, worth 6 marks).

● In the second paragraph, you could consider the studies on which Bowlby based his MDH. Since you're meant to be *analysing and evaluating* the MDH, you should only give the briefest outline of these studies. What you should be concentrating on are (a) the methodological weaknesses of these studies, and/or (b) the validity of the conclusions that Bowlby, and other researchers, drew from them.

● In the third paragraph, you could consider the concept of 'maternal deprivation' itself. For example, Rutter's distinction between deprivation and privation suggests that Bowlby should have used two separate terms, instead of just one. Also, did Bowlby overestimate the importance of mothers as attachment figures? Here, you could draw on points made when evaluating Bowlby's theory of attachment (pages 37–8). (AO2, worth 12 marks).

Try to write a suitable answer in about 300–350 words. As with all questions, there's no single correct way of answering it. The above are just pointers. There's a sample answer at the end of the book. Try not to look at it until you've had a go at doing it yourself.

DEPRIVATION AND PRIVATION

The effects of deprivation/separation

One example of short-term deprivation (days/weeks, rather than months/years) is a child going into a nursery while its mother goes into hospital. Alternatively, the child might stay with foster parents. Again, children sometimes have to go into hospital themselves.

ESSENTIAL STUDY 2.3

Robertson & Robertson's (1969) study of John

Aim (AO1)

This was one of a series of films (*Film Series: Young Children in Brief Separation*) made by James and Joyce Robertson (who were colleagues of Bowlby) between 1967 and 1971. The Robertsons wanted to document how young children's brief separation from their mothers affected their mental state and psychological development. The film series had actually begun (in 1953) with Laura, a two-year-old who went into hospital for eight days for a minor operation.

Procedures (AO1)

James Robertson used a 16mm camera to record John's experience during a nine-day stay in a residential nursery. The study involved *naturalistic observation*. It's also a case study, an in-depth study of a single individual.

John's mother went into hospital to have another baby. Joyce Robertson provided a verbal commentary. She also appears in the film. She sits in the corner of the room, taking notes, trying to stay as 'invisible' as possible.

John was 17 months old at the time.

Findings (AO1)

The nursery was approved for the training of nursery nurses, and was highly thought of. But at that time, nurses were assigned to *duties* rather than to individual children. As a result, no *one* nurse had responsibility for John's care. He was taken there by his parents in the middle of the night, when his mother's labour began.

He suddenly found himself one among several children. Most of the other children had been there since birth, and they were 'noisy, aggressive, self-assertive and demanding'.

By contrast, John was a rather sensitive child who'd enjoyed a very close and stable relationship with his mother. In fact, he'd had very little contact with other children before (he was the first-born).

Day 1: He was friendly with the nurses, especially Mary who dressed him, then put him to bed that night. But she didn't stay with him, and he shouted in protest.

Day 2: This began fairly well. John tried to get a nurse to mother him, but he was pushed aside by other children. He was quiet and uncomplaining most of the day. But as his father (who visited after work) left to go home, John cried and struggled to go with him. Nurse Mary was able to comfort him. But when she left, John became tearful again.

Days 3–5: From day 3 onwards, John became increasingly distressed. Sometimes, he stood sadly at one end of the room; at other times he cried sadly for long periods. He still tried to get close to one or other of the nurses. But he was more likely to play quietly in a corner, or crawl under a table to cry alone. Gradually, his approaches to the nurses became fewer. Even when one tried to comfort him, he was likely to be unresponsive. He sought comfort from a giant teddy bear, which he hugged. He still cried a great deal, 'in quiet despair, sometimes rolling about and wringing his hands'.

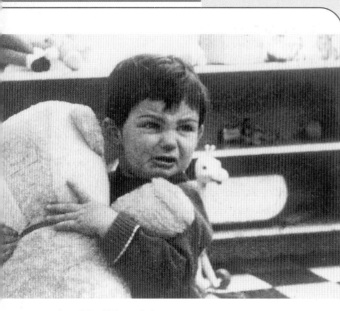

John (17 months)

Day 6: His father visited again (after missing two days). John pinched and smacked him. He brightened up, thinking that his father was going to take him home. John gave his father an angry look as he left without him. He sat alone clutching his blanket.

Days 7–8: John was in despair. He didn't play or eat, and made few demands. When a nurse tried to cheer him up, he hardly responded. He lay on the floor for long periods in apathetic silence, his head on the giant teddy. After his father's visit, he was inconsolable.

Day 9: When his mother arrived to take him home, he started throwing himself around and crying loudly. When she attempted to put him on her lap, John struggled and screamed, ran away from her towards Joyce Robertson. She managed to calm him down, and finally passed him back to his mother. He lay quietly on her lap, but never once looked at her. His father arrived later. John struggled away from his mother, and lay quietly in his father's arms. When he eventually looked at his mother, 'it was a long, hard look'. According to his mother, 'he has never looked at me like that before'.

Conclusions (AO1)

John's distress was caused largely by *bond disruption.* He was, obviously, very attached to his mother. But in her absence, there was no opportunity for a continuing, intense, personal interaction with the same individual (nurse). Because of how the nursery was run, he couldn't predict who'd care for him at any particular time. He couldn't *rely* on anyone, as he'd always been able to rely on his mother. There was no one to take his mother's place.

Criticisms (AO1/AO2)

✔ **The Robertsons recorded their observations in a systematic way:** They provided clear evidence that a young child's separation from his mother sets in motion a sequence of psychological reactions likely to have long-term effects (Robertson & Roberson, 1989).

✖ • ✔ **Theoretical importance:** The study both supports *and* challenges Bowlby's MDH. John's reactions to separation illustrate very clearly what Bowlby called *distress* (see page 43). But Bowlby and the Robertsons differ in their interpretations of what causes distress. Bowlby believes that it's *loss of the mother(-figure)* that's crucial. But according to the Robertsons, what was so distressing for John was that there was no one to replace his mother (*bond-disruption*).

✔ **Subsequent research:** Largely as a response to John's experience, the Robertsons made film records of four other children: Jane (17 months), Lucy (21 months), Thomas (28 months), and Kate (29 months). In each case, the mother went into hospital for the birth of their second child. But the Robertsons themselves acted as foster parents for these children. Joyce Robertson gave each child her full-time care, and tried to preserve the mother's methods as far as possible. The degree of disturbance was far less than it was for John. But the Robertsons concluded that however good the substitute mothering, separation is always dangerous and should be avoided if at all possible.

✔ **Practical influence:** The Robertsons' films helped change hospital policies. At the time, visiting hours were restricted, and parents had no special access to their sick children. Now, it's taken for granted that parents can stay in hospital with their children. This is due largely to the Robertsons' research.

THE COMPONENTS OF DISTRESS

- **Protest:** The immediate reaction involves crying, screaming, kicking, and generally struggling to escape, or clinging to the mother to prevent her from leaving. This is an *outward*, direct expression of the child's anger, fear, bitterness, and confusion.

- **Despair:** The struggling and protest are eventually replaced by calmer behaviour. The child may seem apathetic, but still feels all the anger and fear etc. *inwardly*. It keeps these feelings 'locked up', and may no longer expect the mother to return. S/he hardly reacts to other people's offers of comfort. Instead, the child prefers to comfort itself, by rocking, thumb-sucking, and so on.

- **Detachment:** If the separation continues, the child begins to respond to people again. But it tends to treat everyone alike, and rather superficially. When reunited with the mother, the child may have to 'relearn' its relationship with her. The child may even 'reject' her – as she 'rejected' him/her.

FACTORS INFLUENCING DISTRESS

Separation is likely to be most distressing:

- between the ages of 7/8 months (when attachments are beginning to develop) and three years. There's a peak at 12–18 months (Maccoby, 1980)

- for boys, although there are also individual differences *within* each gender

- if there have been any behaviour problems (such as aggression) prior to the separation

- if the relationship with the mother has been too close

- if the child has never been separated from the mother before

- if there aren't other attachment figures who can provide love and care in the mother's absence.

Long-term deprivation includes the permanent separation resulting from the *death* of a parent. Children are also increasingly likely to be separated from one of their parents through *divorce*.

THE EFFECTS OF DIVORCE

- According to Schaffer (1996), nearly all children are adversely affected by parental divorce, at least in the short term. This is true regardless of age, but especially true of boys.

- But most children are resilient enough to adapt to their parents' divorce eventually (Hetherington & Stanley-Hagan, 1999).

- The nature, severity, and duration of the effects are influenced by several factors. These include (a) continuity of contact with the non-custodial parent; (b) the financial status/lifestyle of the custodial parent; (c) whether the custodial parent remarries and the nature of the resulting step-family.

- The effects include (a) lower levels of academic achievement and self-esteem; (b) higher incidence of anti-social and delinquent behaviour; (c) a tendency in young adulthood to more frequent job changes, lower socioeconomic status, and depression (Hetherington & Stanley-Hagan, 1999; Richards, 1995).

One important effect of long-term deprivation is what Bowlby called **separation anxiety**. This is the fear that separation will occur again in the future. It may express itself as:

I BLAME MY POOR ACADEMIC ACHIEVEMENT ON THE DISCONTINUITY OF CONTACT WITH MY NON-CUSTODIAL PARENT

EXAM tips BOX

To what extent does psychological research show that deprivation is harmful to children's development? (18 marks)

● You could structure your answer in terms of three paragraphs, all about 100–130 words long.

● *Remember that 'research' refers to both theory and studies. So, it's perfectly acceptable to include some of the material you might have used to answer the previous question on Bowlby's MDH. But this is a much broader question, and so your answer shouldn't be limited to an answer on Bowlby's research.*

● The first paragraph could include a *definition* of deprivation, perhaps saying how it's different from privation, distinguishing between short- and long-term deprivation, and giving examples of each. You might also indicate *how* deprivation is supposed to be harmful. (AO1, worth 6 marks).

● In the second paragraph, you could *analyse and evaluate* the evidence which shows that deprivation *is* harmful. You might concentrate on studies of children experiencing brief and/or longer-term/permanent separations (including day care).

● In the third paragraph, you could *analyse and evaluate* the evidence which shows that deprivation *isn't always or inevitably* harmful. Again, you might consider studies of brief and/or longer-term/permanent separations. (AO2, worth 12 marks).

Try to write a suitable answer in about 300–350 words.
As with all questions, there's no single correct way of answering it. The above are just pointers. There's a sample answer at the end of the book. Try not to look at it until you've had a go at doing it yourself.

● increased aggressive behaviour, and greater demands made on the mother

● clinging behaviour: the child won't let the mother out if its sight

● detachment: the child becomes apparently self-sufficient (s/he cannot afford to be let down again)

● psychosomatic reactions (physical symptoms associated with/caused by stress and anxiety).

Another example of long-term deprivation is *day care*. The effects of day care are discussed in the Critical issue below (pages 47–50).

The effects of privation

As we noted earlier, privation is the failure to develop an attachment to any individual. The child's first relationship acts as a model or *prototype* of relationships in general. So, failure to develop an attachment of any kind is likely to negatively affect all later relationships.

AFFECTIONLESS PSYCHOPATHY

● According to Bowlby, maternal deprivation in early childhood causes **affectionless psychopathy**. This is the inability to care and have deep feelings for other people, combined with the inability to experience guilt.

● Bowlby *et al* (1956) studied 60 children, aged 7–13 years, who'd spent between five and 24 months in a tuberculosis (TB) sanatorium at various ages up to four years. About half had been separated from their parents before their second birthday. They were compared with a group of non-separated (control) children from the same school classes. The sanatorium group was more likely to display signs of emotional disturbance. But these children *weren't* more likely to show affectionless psychopathy. Also, it made no difference when they were separated (before or after two years).

● Bowlby admitted that part of their emotional disturbance was due to factors *other than separation*. These included illness and death in their families.

● The study provides very little evidence for a link between affectionless psychopathy and deprivation/separation. But some of the sanatorium children may have suffered *privation*.

According to Rutter (1981), privation is likely to lead to: (a) an initial phase of clinging, dependent behaviour; (b) attention-seeking, and indiscriminate friendliness; and (c) lack of guilt, an inability to follow rules, and an inability to form lasting relationships.

Are the effects of privation reversible?

Some of the main kinds of study which show that it's possible to undo the effects of early privation include:

● Studies of *late adoption*. Children raised in institutions are adopted after Bowlby's critical period for attachment (12 months for most children, up to two-and-a-half/three years for the rest). Studies include those of Tizard and her colleagues (e.g. Hodges & Tizard, 1989: see Essential Study 2.4 below).

● *Case studies* of children who've endured *extreme* early privation. This has often involved almost complete isolation. Examples include the Czech twins (Koluchova, 1972, 1991: see below).

Studies of late adoption

Hodges & Tizard's (1989) **study of Teenagers Raised in Orphanages** (TRIO)
●●●

Aim (AO1)

This is the latest in a series of reports on the development of several children who spent at least the first two years of their lives in institutions. They subsequently grew up in family situations. They were first studied at age 4 (Tizard, 1977), then at age 8 (Tizard & Hodges, 1978). This study reports on these children at age 16.

This 'progress report' is common in *longitudinal studies*, in which the same group of people is followed up over a period of time (usually several years). This represents an overall *approach* within developmental psychology. The aim is to study *change over time*.
●●●

Procedures (AO1)

Hodges and Tizard collected their data through interviews and questionnaires, with the participants (the 16-year-olds), their parents, and teachers. They refer to the study as a form of 'natural experiment'. Something changes in the natural course of events (being raised in institutions, then living in a family situation – the *independent variable*). The effect of this change on the child's development (social relationships – the *dependent variable*) can then be investigated.

The children left care between the ages of 2 and 7 years. They were either adopted, or returned to their own (biological) families. The children whose environment changed (the *ex-institution group*) were compared with similar children raised from birth by their natural parents (*matched controls*).
●●●

Findings (AO1)

The institutions they grew up in provided good physical care. They also appeared to offer adequate intellectual stimulation. But staff turnover was high, and they discouraged the formation of strong attachments between staff and children. As a result, the children had little opportunity to form close, continuous relationships with adults. This opportunity only arose when they left care to live with a family.

By age 8, most of the adopted children had formed close attachments to their adoptive parents. But only some of those who'd returned to their biological families had formed attachments. The ex-institution group as a whole didn't have more problems than the control group (according to their parents). But their teachers thought they were attention-seeking, restless, disobedient, and had poor peer relationships.

At age 16, most of the adopted children had mutually satisfying family relationships. In this respect, they were very similar to the control group. But those who'd returned to their biological families still had poor family relationships. They had difficulty showing their

ESSENTIAL STUDY 2.4

parents affection (as did their parents towards them). Their parents reported feeling closer to their other children.

But *outside* the family, *both* the adopted and returned children were:

- still more likely to seek adult affection and approval
- still more likely to have difficulties in their peer relationships
- less likely to have a special friend, or to see peers as sources of emotional support
- more likely to be friendly to any peer, rather than choosing their friends.

Conclusions (AO1)

Children who don't enjoy close, lasting relationships early on in life *can* still make attachments later on. The adopted children managed to form close attachments to their adoptive parents. They became as much part of the family as any other child. This is contrary to Bowlby's MDH. But these attachments don't develop simply by being placed in a family. They depend on the adults concerned, and how they nurture such attachments. Adoptive parents very much wanted a child, while many of the biological parents seemed reluctant to have their children back.

But *all* the ex-institution children had difficulties in their *peer* relationships. This suggests that their early privation left its mark. This is consistent with Bowlby's MDH.

Criticisms (AO1/AO2)

✓ **Theoretical implications:** The data both support and contradict Bowlby's MDH. This makes the findings 'theoretically rich'. For example, they suggest that there may be a critical period for forming attachments with peers later in life. But there may *not* be one for forming attachments with adults.

✗ **Methodological problems:** How was it decided which children would be adopted, and which would return to their biological families? It could have been based on certain characteristics of the children themselves. For example, the more socially responsive may have been chosen for adoption. If so, the participants wouldn't all have had an equal chance of being allocated to one or other of the experimental conditions. This *random* allocation to conditions is required in a *true* experiment. But this was a natural experiment, so there are many extraneous variables that couldn't be properly controlled (see the Evaluation of Bowlby's MDH above, pages 39–40).

✗ **The problem of 'drop-out' rate:** This is a major problem associated with longitudinal studies. Of the 51 ex-institution children studied at age 8, nine were unavailable (for various reasons) at age 16. So, how representative of the original institutionally reared children was the sample of 16-year-olds?

✗ **The reliability and validity of the data:** Was there any independent check on the accuracy of the answers given in the interviews and questionnaires? How objective can parents be about their children, or children about their parents? How objective could the teachers be, since they knew which pupils were from institutions?

● Chisolm *et al* (1995) studied Romanian orphans, adopted by Canadian families between the ages of 8 months and 5 years, 6 months. They were reared in extremely poor conditions in large-scale institutions. This early privation seemed to have some negative impact on the children's relationships with adoptive parents. For example, their behaviour was often described as *ambivalent*. That is, they both wanted contact and resisted it (see Essential Study 2.1, pages 32–4). Also, they weren't easily comforted when distressed.

● Follow-up is needed to see if life in a loving family can eventually overcome these difficulties. Based on their intellectual recovery, there are good reasons for being optimistic (Schaffer, 1998).

STUDIES OF EXTREME PRIVATION

What happens to children who suffer extreme privation, but are then 'rescued' and enjoy much improved conditions?

● Koluchova (1972, 1991) studied identical twin boys, born in 1960 in the former Czechoslovakia. Their mother died shortly after their birth. When they were about 18 months old, they went to live with their father who'd remarried. The stepmother treated them very cruelly. They spent much of the next five-and-a-half years locked in the cellar, and they were harshly beaten.

● The twins were discovered in 1967, and were legally removed from their parents. They were very short in stature, and had rickets (due to lack of calcium). They had no spontaneous speech, and communicated largely by gesture. They were terrified of many aspects of their new environment.

● They spent some time in a school for children with learning difficulties, after which they were adopted by two women.

● By age 14, they showed no signs of psychological abnormality or unusual behaviour. They went on to further education.

● They both had very good relationships with their adoptive mothers, their adopted sisters, and the women's relatives. They both later married and had children. At the age of 29, they were entirely stable, without abnormalities, and enjoying warm relationships.

● Clearly, the twins' experience of prolonged early privation didn't predestine them to a life of severe handicap (Clarke & Clarke, 2000).

EXAM tips BOX

Consider psychological research into the effects of privation on children's development. (18 marks)

● You could structure your answer in terms of three paragraphs, all about 100–130 words long.

● *Remember that 'research' refers to both theory and studies. So, it's perfectly acceptable to draw on both theoretical accounts of the effects of privation (such as Bowlby's MDH) and the findings of studies. But the former on its own would not be sufficient.*

● The first paragraph could include a *definition* of privation, with some examples. Because the effects of privation are long-term (such as affectionless psychopathy), you could say that much research has been concerned with whether or not the effects are *reversible*. You could also indicate the *kinds* of studies which are relevant to the question of reversibility, and *describe* some of the research findings. (AO1, worth 6 marks)

● In the second paragraph, you could *analyse and evaluate* the evidence which demonstrates the effects of privation. The study by Bowlby *et al* (1956) is relevant here, even though he discussed it in relation to 'deprivation'. Hodges & Tizard (1989) provide some evidence for the irreversibility of the effects of being raised in an institution.

● In the third paragraph, you could *analyse and evaluate* the evidence which suggests that the effects of privation *can* be reversed/undone. Remember, the Hodges and Tizard study provides evidence for *both* arguments. (AO2, worth 12 marks).

Try to write a suitable answer in about 300–350 words.
As with all questions, there's no single correct way of answering it. The above are just pointers. There's a 'sample answer' at the end of the book. Try not to look at it until you've had a go at doing it yourself.

CRITICAL ISSUE: DAY CARE

What is day care?

Day care includes all varieties of non-maternal care of children who normally live with their parent(s) or close relatives (Scarr, 1998). So, it *excludes* foster care, and institutional (residential) care. It *includes:*

● crèches, day nurseries, childminders (called 'home-based day care' in the US), and other 'out-of-home' facilities

● nannies, (non-resident) grandparents, and other 'in-the-home' arrangements.

Attitudes towards day care

● Most children are cared for by their own mothers. So, child care provided by anyone other than the child's mother is *non-normative*. (This view partly reflects the influence of Bowlby's theory of attachment.)

● But most modern British and American mothers with school-age children (or younger) go out to work. So, shared child care is actually a normative experience.

● Child care has *always* been shared (usually among female relatives), in *all* cultures (Scarr, 1998).

● Mothers' employment outside the home has made it necessary for there to be a variety of non-maternal care.

● But many people still believe that women are 'meant to be' mothers (the *motherhood mystique/mandate*). This belief affects our attitudes about working mothers (Kremer, 1998). Whether or not working mothers have pre-school children is still a significant factor shaping these attitudes.

Measuring the quality of day care

● Much of the research into the *effects* of day care has centred on its *quality*.

● There's widespread agreement about the criteria used to assess quality (Scarr, 1998). These include:

   (i)   health and safety requirements
   (ii)   responsive and warm interaction between children and staff
   (iii)   developmentally appropriate curricula
   (iv)   limited group size
   (v)   age-appropriate caregiver–child ratios
   (vi)   adequate indoor and outdoor space
   (vii)   adequate staff training
   (viii) low staff turnover (as a measure of the *stability* of care).

The effects of poor quality day care

● Studies have found that poor quality care puts children's development at risk:

   (a)   they're likely to obtain lower language and cognitive scores
   (b)   they're also likely to be rated lower on social and emotional development.

● But the quality of care chosen by parents is correlated with their personal characteristics or circumstances. For example, children from families with single working mothers or low income are more likely to experience low quality care.

● So, we can't be sure whether it's the quality of day care or parental characteristics which influences children's development. This confusion between the two variables has led to an *overestimation* of the effects of day care (Scarr, 1998).

The effects of day care on children's social development: Attachment

● According to Bowlby, a child whose mother goes out to work suffers *maternal deprivation.*

● If this happens *before* an attachment has formed (during the child's first year), s/he may fail to form an attachment at all (remember, strictly this is *privation*). If it happens *after* an attachment has formed, the child will be distressed, may experience separation anxiety etc (see page 43).

● Research evidence shows that the daily separations involved in day care *don't* weaken attachment to the mother. Provided the day care is *stable* and of a reasonable *quality*, children don't suffer any ill effects. They might actually benefit from day care (Schaffer, 1996).

● But Belsky & Rovine (1988) reported that day care *can* adversely affect attachments. Babies who'd been in day care for (a) at least four months before their first birthday and (b) more than 20 hours per week, were more likely to develop *insecure attachments* than 'home-reared' babies.

● Belsky and Rovine's findings were based on the Strange Situation. But this is an *inappropriate* technique to use with children in day care. It assumes that repeated separations from the mother are stressful for the child. But day-care children are *used* to such separations. So, they may not find them stressful. They might appear to be indifferent to the mother's return. But this may really be independence and self-reliance (Clarke-Stewart, 1989).

● In the US, 36% of babies with working mothers are classified as *insecure* (22% Type A, 14% Type C). This is almost identical to the overall percentages for worldwide studies, based on almost 2,000 children of mainly *non-working* mothers (van Ijzendoorn & Kroonenberg, 1988).

● Several studies have shown that children who were in day care as babies are as self-confident and emotionally well-adjusted as those who weren't (Clarke-Stewart, 1989).

The effects of day care on children's cognitive development

● According to Scarr (1998), *high quality* day care:

(i) *benefits* children from low-income families. They do better academically at school, and show more socialised behaviour in later years, than similar children without day care experience.

(ii) provides learning opportunities, as well as social and emotional support, that many wouldn't enjoy at home.

(iii) for middle class and high income families, the long-term picture is far less clear.

● Clarke-Stewart (1991) found that 150 two-to-four-year-olds who'd attended day care centres had better intellectual (and social) development than those who'd received home care (either with mothers or childminders).

EXAM tips BOX

'*While going out to work may benefit mothers of young children, the children themselves may suffer compared with those whose mothers stay at home.*'

To what extent does psychological research support this view of the effects of day care on children's social development? (18 marks)

● You could structure your answer in terms of three paragraphs, all about 100–130 words long.

● The first paragraph could include a *definition* of day care (and one or two examples, perhaps), and social development (here, it means, essentially, the development of attachments). You could also briefly *describe* one piece of research which supports, and one which challenges, the view of the effects of day care expressed in the quote (AO1, worth 6 marks).

Note that the question refers to the quote when it says '…this view of the effects of day care…'. So, you need to make it clear what 'this view' is (probably in the first paragraph).
Note also that 'research' refers to both 'studies' and 'theories'.

● In the second paragraph, you could *analyse and evaluate* research which *supports* the view that day care may be harmful to children's social development. For example, you could look at how Bowlby's attachment theory has influenced attitudes towards day care, as well as studies which support this theory (other than the one you described in the first paragraph). An important point to bear in mind is the reliance of such studies on the Strange Situation.

● In the third paragraph, you could *analyse and evaluate* research which *contradicts* the view that day care may be harmful. In both this and the second paragraph, you should bear in mind the issue of quality of day care, the link between this and family circumstances, and the difficulty of generalizing from the results of (mainly) American studies. (AO2, worth 12 marks).

Try to write a suitable answer in about 300–350 words.
There's a 'sample answer' at the end of the book, but try not to look at it until you've had a go at answering the question yourself.
Note that you could be asked a very similar question that refers to' 'cognitive development' (or to 'social and/or cognitive development').

● But Baydar & Brooks-Gunn's (1991) study of over 1100 children presented a more negative picture. They compared children whose mothers went out to work *before* they were one year old with those whose mothers started work later. The former were worse off, both cognitively and behaviourally.

● Scarr & Thompson (1994) made a similar comparison with 1100 children in Bermuda. Teachers rated the children at ages five, six, seven, and eight. There were *no* differences in cognitive (or socio-emotional) development between those who'd started day care before or after the age of one. Nor did it make any difference how many hours per week they spent there.

EVALUATION OF RESEARCH INTO THE EFFECTS OF DAY CARE

❌ Much of the research into the effects of day care has been conducted in the US. The conclusions from these studies may not apply to other societies and cultures. Patterns of maternal, and paternal, employment differ between cultures. The contribution of mothers and fathers to child care at home may also vary.

✓ Mooney and Munton (in Judd, 1997) reviewed 40 years' research. They concluded that there's *no* evidence that working mothers stunt their children's emotional or social development. Even poor quality care may make no difference to a child from a stable family. Good quality care may provide real benefits.

❌ • ✓ We shouldn't be discussing the rights and wrongs of working mothers. What's important is providing enough good child care. As Clarke-Stewart (1989) says:

> 'Maternal employment is a reality. The issue today, therefore, is not whether infants should be in day care but how to make their experiences there and at home supportive of their development and of their parents' peace of mind.'

SUMMARY

The development and variety of attachments

Attachments are intense emotional relationships, which endure over time. They develop through a series of **phases**.

The **Strange Situation** is the most widely used observational method used to study attachments. It comprises eight episodes involving the baby, its mother, and a female stranger. Most attention is given to the baby's **reunion behaviours**.

Ainsworth *et al* classified 15% of their sample as **anxious-avoidant (Type A)**, 70% as **securely attached (Type B)**, and 15% as **anxious-resistant (Type C)**. The baby's attachment type is related to the mother's **sensitivity**.

There are also important **cultural variations** (both **within** and **between** cultures). But the Strange Situation may not be equally valid in Western and non-Western cultures.

Bowlby's attachment theory rejects **cupboard love** accounts (such as **learning theory**). He was influenced both by Harlow's research with rhesus monkeys, and Lorenz's study of **imprinting** in goslings.

Bowlby argued that newborn humans are **genetically programmed** to behave in ways that ensure their survival. This is coupled with **monotropy**. There's a **critical period** for attachment formation.

Bowlby's **maternal deprivation hypothesis (MDH)** was based largely on studies of children raised in institutions. But Bowlby failed to distinguish between **deprivation** and **privation**.

Deprivation and privation

Deprivation refers to the loss, through separation, of an attachment figure.

A typical response to **short-term deprivation** is **distress**. This was demonstrated in the Robertsons' study of John. Distress comprises **protest**, **despair**, and **detachment**. It can be influenced by a number of factors, including the child's age and gender.

Divorce, the **death** of a parent, and **day care**, are all examples of **long-term deprivation**.

While almost all children are adversely affected by divorce, most children adapt eventually. A crucial factor is continuity of contact with the non-custodial parent.

One important effect of long-term deprivation is **separation anxiety**.

Privation is the failure to develop an attachment to any individual. A major effect of privation is **affectionless psychopathy**.

Studies of late adoption and **case studies of extreme early privation** suggest that the effects of privation are **reversible**.

Hodges and Tizard's study of children raised in institutions offers some support for Bowlby's MDH. But it also shows that attachments can be formed with adults long after the critical period.

Critical issue: Day care

Day care includes all varieties of non-maternal care of children who normally live with their parent(s) or close relatives.

Much of the research into the **effects** of day care has centred on its **quality**. An important feature of quality is **stability**.

It's difficult to know whether the negative effects of poor quality day care are due to the quality of care itself, or the parental circumstances/characteristics that are correlated with it.

Research evidence using the Strange Situation both supports and contradicts the claim that children in day care are more likely to develop **insecure attachments**. But this may not be an appropriate way of assessing attachments in day-care children.

Day care may improve the **cognitive development** of children from low-income families. The picture is much less clear for children from middle class and high-income families.

Findings from US-based research may not apply to other societies and cultures.

The issue isn't about whether or not mothers of young children should go out to work, but rather providing enough good quality day care.

Self-assessment questions

These are some example Part a and Part b questions (worth 40% of your exam.) Part c questions (worth 60%) have been dealt with throughout the chapter in the Exam Tips Boxes and in the Sample Answers (SAs) at the end of the book.

1a. What is meant by the terms 'attachment', 'deprivation', and 'privation'?
(2 + 2 + 2 marks)

b. Outline conclusions from research into the effects of day care on social development. (6 marks)

2a. Describe *two* ways in which the child's response to separation can be modified. (3 + 3 marks)

b. Outline findings from research into the effects of day care on cognitive development. (6 marks)

3a. Outline the main features of *one* theory of attachment. (6 marks)

b. Explain what is meant by the terms 'secure' and 'insecure attachment' and give *one* difference between them. (2 + 2 + 2 marks)

4a. Describe the procedure and findings of *one* study of privation. (3 + 3 marks)

b. Outline the findings of *one* study of deprivation and give *one* criticism of this study. (3 + 3 marks)

5a. Describe Bowlby's maternal deprivation hypothesis. (6 marks)

b. Outline *two* factors that can influence children's response to deprivation. (3 + 3 marks)

ESSENTIAL STUDY SUMMARY

Topic	Research study	Researcher date	Page
Secure/insecure attachments	Strange Situation study of Attachments (SSoA)	Ainsworth *et al* (1971, 1978)	32
Cultural variations in attachment	Review of Patterns of Attachment (RPA)	Van Ijzendoorn & Kroonenberg (1988)	35
Individual differences	SSoA or RPA		
Effects of deprivation/ separation	Case study of John	Robertson & Robertson (1969)	41
Effects of privation	Teenagers Raised in Orphanages (TRIO)	Hodges & Tizard (1989)	45

Physiological Psychology

10.3

What's covered in this chapter?

STRESS

a. **Stress as a bodily response**
- The body's response to stressors, including the General Adaptation Syndrome (Selye).
- Research into the relationship between stress and physical illness, including cardiovascular disorders and the effects of stress on the immune system.

b. **Sources of stress**
- Research into sources of stress, including life changes (e.g. Holmes & Rahe), and workplace stressors (e.g. work overload, role ambiguity).
- Individual differences in modifying the effects of stressors, including the role played by personality (e.g. Friedman & Rosenman), culture, and gender.

CRITICAL ISSUE: STRESS MANAGEMENT
- Methods of managing the negative effects of stress, including physiological (e.g. drugs, biofeedback) and psychological approaches (stress-inoculation, increasing hardiness).
- The role of control in the perception of stress.
- The strengths and weaknesses of methods of stress management.

STRESS AS A BODILY RESPONSE

What do we mean by stress?

Stress can be defined in three main ways:

- stress as a **stimulus**. This refers to the characteristics of an environmental event or situation, and is basically something that happens *to* us. *Sources of stress* ('stressors') include life changes and workplace stressors.

- stress as a **response**. This refers to what happens *within* us as a result of environmental events or situations. In particular, it refers to the physiological/bodily responses, such as the General Adaptation Syndrome (Selye, 1956). This relates to *stress as a bodily response*.

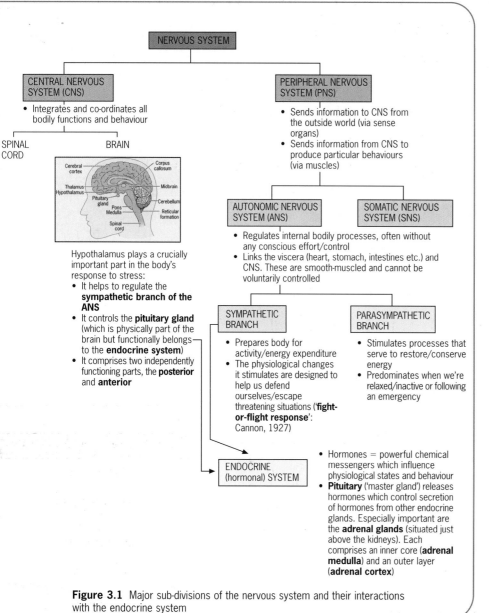

Hypothalamus plays a crucially important part in the body's response to stress:
- It helps to regulate the **sympathetic branch of the ANS**
- It controls the **pituitary gland** (which is physically part of the brain but functionally belongs to the **endocrine system**)
- It comprises two independently functioning parts, the **posterior** and **anterior**

NERVOUS SYSTEM

CENTRAL NERVOUS SYSTEM (CNS)
- Integrates and co-ordinates all bodily functions and behaviour

SPINAL CORD   BRAIN

PERIPHERAL NERVOUS SYSTEM (PNS)
- Sends information to CNS from the outside world (via sense organs)
- Sends information from CNS to produce particular behaviours (via muscles)

AUTONOMIC NERVOUS SYSTEM (ANS)
- Regulates internal bodily processes, often without any conscious effort/control
- Links the viscera (heart, stomach, intestines etc.) and CNS. These are smooth-muscled and cannot be voluntarily controlled

SOMATIC NERVOUS SYSTEM (SNS)

SYMPATHETIC BRANCH
- Prepares body for activity/energy expenditure
- The physiological changes it stimulates are designed to help us defend ourselves/escape threatening situations ('**fight-or-flight response**': Cannon, 1927)

PARASYMPATHETIC BRANCH
- Stimulates processes that serve to restore/conserve energy
- Predominates when we're relaxed/inactive or following an emergency

ENDOCRINE (hormonal) SYSTEM
- Hormones = powerful chemical messengers which influence physiological states and behaviour
- **Pituitary** ('master gland') releases hormones which control secretion of hormones from other endocrine glands. Especially important are the **adrenal glands** (situated just above the kidneys). Each comprises an inner core (**adrenal medulla**) and an outer layer (**adrenal cortex**)

Figure 3.1 Major sub-divisions of the nervous system and their interactions with the endocrine system

● stress as **interaction** between an individual and his/her environment. We experience stress when we believe we don't have what's needed to meet the demands of a particular situation. But people differ in what makes them feel stressed, how much stress they feel, and how they try to deal with it. This relates to *stress management.*

According to Selye (1956), 'Stress is the non-specific response of the body to any demand made upon it'. Selye observed that all hospital patients display the same pattern of symptoms (or syndrome), regardless of their particular illness. These included:

● a loss of appetite

● an associated loss of weight and strength

● a loss of ambition

● a characteristic facial expression.

After examining extreme cases in more detail, Selye concluded that this non-specific response in turn reflected the *General Adaptation Syndrome* (GAS).

SELYE'S GAS

According to Selye, GAS represents the body's defence against stress. The body responds in the same way to any stressor, whether it's environmental or arises from within the body itself. Environmental stressors may include insulin, excessive heat or cold, X-rays, sleep and water deprivation, and electric shock. Selye defined stress as:

'... the individual's psychophysiological response, mediated largely by the autonomic nervous system and the endocrine system, to any demands made on the individual.'

To understand GAS, we must have a working knowledge of the **nervous system** and the endocrine system. We also need to understand how they *interact* with each other. These are summarised in Figure 3.1.

THE THREE STAGES/PHASES OF GAS

Alarm reaction

When a stimulus is perceived as a stressor, there's a brief, initial *shock phase.* Blood pressure (BP) and muscle tension drop. Resistance to the stressor is reduced. But this is quickly followed by the *countershock phase.* The hypothalamus activates the sympathetic branch of the ANS. This, in turn, stimulates the *adrenal medulla* to secrete increased levels of adrenaline and noradrenaline (*catecholamines*).

Table 3.1 Major sympathetic reactions associated with the 'fight-or-flight response' (FOFR)

Organ or function involved	Sympathetic reaction
Heart rate	Increases
Blood pressure	Increases
Secretion of saliva	Suppressed (dry mouth)
Pupils of eye	Dilate (to aid vision)
Limbs (and trunk)	Dilation of blood vessels of voluntary muscles (e.g. to help us run faster)
Peristalsis (contraction of stomach and intestines)	Slows down (we don't feel hungry in an emergency)
Galvanic skin response (GSR) (measure of skin's electrical resistance)	Decreases (due to increased sweating associated with increased anxiety)
Bladder muscles	Relax (there may be temporary loss of bladder control)
Breathing rate	Increases (through dilation of bronchial tubes)
Liver	Glucose (stored as energy) released into bloodstream to increase energy
Emotion	Experience of strong emotion (e.g. fear)

The catecholamines (or 'stress hormones'):

● mimic the activity of the sympathetic branch of the ANS, and so are called *sympathomimetics*

● trigger and maintain increased levels of physiological activity, which are collectively called the *fight-or-flight response* (FOFR) (Cannon, 1927). These changes are summarised in Table 3.1 and Figure 3.2.

For all these reasons, the alarm reaction is associated with the *sympatho-adrenomedullary axis* (SAA).

Resistance

If the stressor isn't removed, sympathetic activity *decreases*. But output from the other part of the adrenal gland (the *adrenal cortex*) *increases*. The adrenal cortex is essential for the maintenance of life, and its removal causes death. It's controlled by how much *adrenocorticotrophic hormone* (ACTH) there is in the blood. ACTH is released from the *anterior pituitary*. In turn, the anterior pituitary is controlled by the hypothalamus.

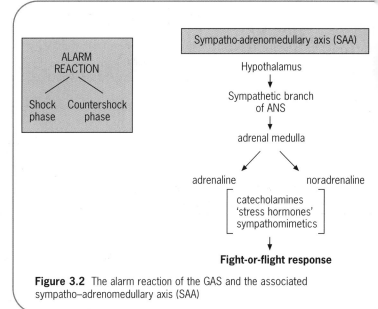

Figure 3.2 The alarm reaction of the GAS and the associated sympatho–adrenomedullary axis (SAA)

ACTH stimulates the adrenal cortex to release *corticosteroids* (or *adrenocorticoid hormones*). One group of adrenocorticoid hormones are the *glucocorticoid hormones*, which include corticosterone, cortisol, and hydrocortisone. These regulate the amount of glucose in the blood (*glucogenesis*). This helps to resist all kinds of stress.

The glucocorticoids:

● convert protein into glucose

● make fats available for energy

● increase blood flow

● generally stimulate behavioural responsiveness.

In this way, the *hypothalamic-pituitary-adrenal axis* (HPAA) contributes to the fight-or-flight response.

Exhaustion

Once ACTH and corticosteroids are circulating in the bloodstream, they tend to inhibit more ACTH being released from the pituitary. If the stressor is removed during the resistance stage, blood sugar levels will gradually return to normal. But if the stressful situation continues, so will the pituitary-adrenal excitation. By this time:

● the body's resources are becoming depleted

● the adrenals can no longer function properly

● blood glucose levels drop. In extreme cases, hypoglycaemia could result in death

● *psychophysiological disorders* develop. These include high BP (hypertension), coronary artery disease (CAD), coronary heart disease (CHD), asthma, and peptic (stomach) ulcers. Selye called these the *diseases of adaptation.*

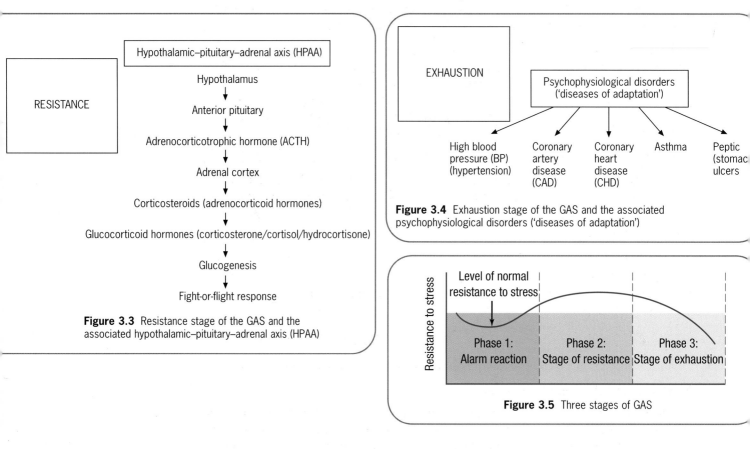

Figure 3.3 Resistance stage of the GAS and the associated hypothalamic–pituitary–adrenal axis (HPAA)

Figure 3.4 Exhaustion stage of the GAS and the associated psychophysiological disorders ('diseases of adaptation')

Figure 3.5 Three stages of GAS

E V A L U A T I O N   O F   T H E   G A S

✓ It helps account for the physiology of stress.

✗ Not all stressors produce the same pattern of physiological activity.

✗ Research into the GAS involved mainly rats' responses to stressors.

✗ Selye largely ignored the psychological aspects of stress. A stressor must first be *perceived* as a stressor before any physiological changes occur. It's almost as though he left the person out of the picture by focusing on the body's responses.

How does stress make us ill?

CARDIOVASCULAR DISORDERS

The GAS provides a general answer to the question: why does stress makes us ill? For more specific, detailed answers, we need to consider other research.

An evolutionary perspective:

- represents a general way of trying to understand why stress is bad for us

- provides some important links with research into the cardiovascular effects of stress (such as heart disease, and circulatory disorders).

Box 3.1. The evolutionary explanation of how stress makes us ill

The sympathetic branch of the ANS responds as a unit. This causes a state of generalised arousal, which is pretty much the same whatever the stressor might be. This was probably crucial in our evolutionary past, when our ancestors were commonly faced with life-threatening dangers. This is exactly what the FOFR is for.

For example, increased heart rate supplies more blood to the muscles, which is a good idea when faced with a hungry sabre-toothed tiger. But most everyday stressors involve a much greater *psychological* element and *aren't* life-threatening. Yet our nervous and endocrine systems have evolved in such a way that we typically react to everyday stressors as if they *were*. What may have been *adaptive*, advantageous, responses for our ancestors have become *maladaptive* today.

So, what happens to all that internal, physiological activity?

- Chronic (long-term, ongoing) stress involves repeated episodes of increased heart rate and BP. This, in turn, increases plaque formation within the cardiovascular system.

- Adrenaline and noradrenaline contribute to increases in blood cholesterol levels. Cholesterol particles clump together, leading to clots in the blood and the artery walls. The arteries become thickened.

- In turn, raised heart rate is linked to a more rapid build-up of cholesterol on artery walls.

- High BP results in small lesions on the artery walls, where cholesterol gets trapped.

Friedman and Rosenman's research

Friedman and Rosenman (two American cardiologists) concluded that some men are more prone to CHD, because they typically respond to stressful situations in a particular way. So, their research is just as relevant to understanding the factors which mediate the effects of stressors (see pages 68–9).

In the late 1950s, Friedman and Rosenman found that American men were far more susceptible to CHD than American women, despite the similarity of their diets. A subsequent questionnaire study suggested that job-related stress may have been the crucial factor. They followed this up by monitoring the *blood-clotting speed* and *serum cholesterol levels* of 40 tax accountants over a period of several months. These are two warning signs of CHD. As the deadline for submitting tax returns approached, the two measures rose alarmingly. But they soon returned to normal levels following the deadline.

ESSENTIAL STUDY 3.1

Friedman and Rosenman's (1974) Study of Type A Behaviour (STAB)

Aims (AO1)

Friedman and Rosenman wished to find evidence for the role of *non-physiological* factors in CHD. In particular, they were interested in the role of *individual differences* in men's ways of dealing with stressful situations.

Procedures (AO1)

Starting in 1960–61, 3,000 American men, aged 39–59, were followed for a period of over eight years. So, it was a *longitudinal* study. They were all well when the study began.

How they dealt with stressful situations was assessed in two ways:

- a *structured interview*, which involved pre-determined, open-ended questions
- a pencil-and-paper *self-assessment* test, consisting of several multiple-choice questions.

Based on these two measures, the men were classified as displaying either Type A behaviour (TAB) or Type B (non-Type A) behaviour (TBB):

- *Type A* behaviour involves a chronic sense of time urgency, excessive competitiveness, and a generalised (but well controlled) hostility. These men are always setting themselves deadlines, suffer from 'hurry sickness', cannot bear waiting their turn (in queues), and have to do several things at once. They're also insecure about their status, and need to be admired by their peers to feel good about themselves.
- *Type B* behaviour may involve the same degree of ambition, but these men seem to be steadied by it. They're much more self-confident, relaxed and easy-going, not driven to achieve perfection, and much less hostile.

Findings (AO1)

Type A men were more than twice as likely to develop CHD than Type B men. After taking risk factors into account (e.g. age, smoking, blood cholesterol, BP, family history of heart disease), they were still *twice* as likely to suffer heart attacks.

Conclusions (AO1)

A man's personality can make it more likely that he will develop CHD, over and above the effects of smoking and other ('traditional') risk factors. In this sense, personality can be regarded as a risk factor.

In a more general sense, the harmful effects of stressors can be mediated through psychological factors. In other words, stressors aren't harmful *in themselves*. It's how people perceive and react to them that's (potentially) dangerous for health.

Criticisms (AO1/AO2)

✓ **Substantial study:** It was a long-term study involving a very large sample.

✓ **Mind–body interaction:** It showed how *psychological* factors (in this case, personality) can produce *physiological effects* (CHD).

✓ **Well-designed study:** Since all the men were free of heart disease at the start, the results weren't contaminated. In other words, those who developed heart disease did so during the course of the study.

✔ **Separation of variables:** Friedman and Rosenman were able to separate out the effects of risk factors from the effects of personality.

✘ **Unreliability of measures:** The measures used to assess TAB/TBB have been criticised. For example, interviewers require special training, which is expensive and time-consuming. Also, the men's scores on one measure didn't always match their scores on the other. This means they might have been measuring *different things*.

✘ **Biased sample:** The sample was all male. Although there were good reasons for this, it means we cannot generalise the results to women.

EVALUATION OF FRIEDMAN AND ROSENMAN'S RESEARCH

✔ **Replication of findings:** Their basic findings have been replicated in several countries (in Europe, Canada, and New Zealand).

✘ **Relative risks:** The greater risk of CHD faced by Type As is only *relative.* The vast majority of Type As *don't* develop CHD, while many Type Bs *do*.

✘ **Is TAB a distinct risk factor?** Most studies have found that TAB assessed immediately following a heart attack *doesn't* predict future attacks. This suggests that it's *not* a distinct risk for CHD in those already at risk (Penny, 1996).

✘ • ✔ **Does TAB cause CHD?** Friedman and Rosenman see personality as playing a *causal* role in CHD. But their evidence is merely *correlational*. All we can say for sure is that Type A men are *more likely* to develop CHD. TAB might be a *response* to high BP and other increased physiological activity, rather than a cause. Some people may be *predisposed* to react to stressors with raised BP etc. They may learn to *cope* with these physiological changes by developing more hostile, competitive, 'driven' behaviours.

THE EFFECTS OF STRESS ON THE IMMUNE SYSTEM

What is the immune system?

● The *immune system* is a collection of billions of cells which travel through the bloodstream. They're produced mainly in the spleen, lymph nodes, thymus, and bone marrow.

● These cells move in and out of tissues and organs, defending the body against foreign bodies or *antigens* (such as bacteria, viruses, and cancerous cells).

● The major type of cell are white blood cells (*leucocytes*), of which there are many types.

● Some immune cells produce and secrete *antibodies*. These bind to antigens and destroy them.

EXAM tips BOX

To what extent does stress play a role in cardiovascular disorders? (18 marks)

● You could structure your answer in terms of three paragraphs, all about 100–130 words long.

● In the first paragraph you could briefly *describe* what's meant by the term stress, say what's meant by cardiovascular disorders, and give some examples. You could then outline some of the evidence relating to the role of stress in cardiovascular disorders. This could include more general explanations (such as Selye's GAS, and the evolutionary perspective) *and/or* studies which have looked more directly at the role of stress in cardiovascular disorders. (AO1, 6 marks).

● In the second paragraph, you could *analyse and evaluate* the more general explanations of the physiological effects of stress.

● In the third paragraph, you could *analyse and evaluate* research that has looked more directly at the role of stress in cardiovascular disorders, such as that of Friedman and Rosenman. You need to point out some of the strengths *and* limitations of their research. *Remember, merely* describing *the findings of such research will only count as AO1.* (AO2, worth 12 marks).

● A word of warning: *This isn't a question about the GAS (or the evolutionary perspective). So, you must emphasise only those aspects of these explanations which are relevant to the question.*

Try to write a suitable answer in about 300–350 words.
As with all questions, there's no single correct way of answering it. The above are just pointers. There's a sample answer at the end of the book. Try not to look at it until you've had a go at doing it yourself.

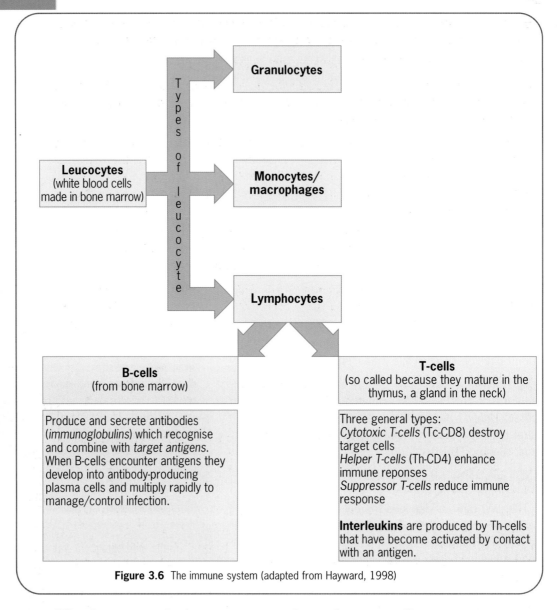

Figure 3.6 The immune system (adapted from Hayward, 1998)

What happens to the immune system when we're stressed?

● The immune system's ability to fight off antigens is reduced. This is why we're much more likely to pick up infections when we're 'under stress' (we often talk of being 'run down').

● But this doesn't mean that stress actually *causes* infections. Stress makes us more susceptible to infectious agents by temporarily suppressing immune function (the **immunosuppressive effects** of stress). Stressors that seem to have this effect include exams (e.g. Kiecolt-Glaser *et al*, 1984: see Essential Study 3.2 opposite), and the death of a spouse (e.g. Schliefer *et al*, 1983: see below).

● Our bodies produce more corticosteroids when we're under stress (see page 55). Intermittent production of corticosteroids doesn't do much harm to the immune system. But if they're produced *continuously* (as in the GAS), they can interfere with leucocyte activity and the production of antibodies.

● Stressful events have been linked to various infectious illnesses. These include influenza, herpes, and the Epstein-Barr virus (associated with extreme tiredness).

Research that demonstrates the immunosuppressive effects of stress

● Riley (1981) created stress by placing mice on a turntable rotating at 45 rpm. He found a marked decrease in their lymphocyte count over a five-hour period. In other words, their immune response was suppressed.

● In a later study, Riley studied the link between stress and tumour growth. He implanted cancer cells in two groups of mice. Group 1 had 10 minutes of rotation per hour for three days (*high-stress condition*). Group 2 had no rotation at all (*no stress control condition*). As expected, Group 1 developed large tumours, while Group 2 showed no tumour growth.

● There are always important ethical issues raised by such experiments with non-humans. But there are scientific issues too. In particular, what can studies of mice tell us about the immunosuppressive effects of stress in humans?

● There are human studies that support Riley's findings. For example, Schliefer *et al* (1983) investigated the immune system of men whose wives had died from breast cancer. Their immune systems functioned less well after their wives had died than before.

Kiecolt-Glaser *et al's* (1984) **study of Immunosuppression in Medical Students** (ISMS)

Aims (AO1)

The researchers wanted to study the 'competence' of the immune system in people facing stressful situations (medical students facing important exams).

Procedures (AO1)

Kiecolt-Glaser *et al* took blood samples from 75 first-year medical students (49 males, 26 females). They all volunteered to take part. The samples were taken (a) one month before their final exams, and (b) on the first day of the exams (after they'd sat two papers). The blood samples were analysed for the amount of leucocyte activity. Specifically, how much *natural killer cell* activity was there? These help fight off viruses and tumours.

Findings (AO1)

As predicted, natural killer cell activity was greatly reduced in the second sample compared with the first.

The students were also given questionnaires to assess psychiatric symptoms, loneliness, and life events (all potential sources of stress: see below, pages 63–5). Immune responses were weakest of all in those students who reported feeling most lonely. It was also weakest for those who were experiencing other stressful life events and psychiatric symptoms (such as depression and anxiety).

Conclusions (AO1)

Stress is associated with reduced immune function. That is, Kiecolt-Glaser *et al* found evidence for the immunosuppressant effects of stress. They also showed that these effects can be increased when individuals are exposed to particular kinds of stressors.

ESSENTIAL STUDY 3.2

Criticisms (AO1/AO2)

✓ **The study was a natural experiment.** That is, the researchers didn't decide what stressors the students would be exposed to. Their exams would have happened anyway, and the researchers took the opportunity to measure their immune function in response to these stressors.

✓ **Participant variables controlled.** The students were being compared *with themselves* on the two occasions the blood samples were taken. This controls important *participant variables*, such as personality.

✗ **Not all environmental variables controlled.** Strictly, we can't be sure that it was the stressors (and only the stressors) which caused the change in immune function. Other variables which weren't controlled (as would happen in a true experiment) might have played a part.

EXAM tips BOX

Consider research into the effects of stress on the immune system. (18 marks)

● You could structure your answer in terms of three paragraphs, all about 100–130 words long.

● In the first paragraph, you could give a brief *description* of the immune system, and briefly summarise some findings of research into the effects of stress on the immune system. (AO1, worth 6 marks).

● In the second paragraph, you could look at studies of non-human animals. You could *analyse and evaluate* these in terms of (i) their relevance to human beings; and (ii) their ethical acceptability.

● A word of warning: *You must address these issues in a way that's relevant to the question. If you make your points in a very general way, you'll gain very few marks.*

● A word of advice: *the question doesn't actually refer to human beings. So, it would be perfectly acceptable to include studies of non-human animals (in addition to/instead of humans). But it's also ok for you to write just about human research.*

● In the third paragraph, you could look at studies involving human beings. You could *analyse and evaluate* these in terms of (i) whether or not the evidence really shows that stress *causes* decreased immune function; (ii) how valid are the definitions/measures of stress used; and (iii) the possible practical benefits of such research. *Remember, merely describing research findings will only count as AO1.* (AO2, worth 12 marks).

Try to write a suitable answer in about 300–350 words. As with all questions, there's no single correct way of answering it. The above are just pointers. There's a sample answer at the end of the book. Try not to look at it until you've had a go at doing it yourself.

● Cohen *et al* (1991) gave participants nasal drops containing cold viruses. Stress was defined as (a) the number of life changes an individual had recently experienced; and (b) how 'out of control' they felt. Those participants with the highest stress levels were almost *twice* as likely to develop colds as those with the lowest levels.

● *Interleukin-b* (see Figure 3.7, page 60) is produced soon after tissue damage. It helps to remodel connective tissue in wounds, and to form collagen (scar tissue). Kiecolt-Glaser *et al* (1995) compared the rate of wound healing in two groups: (a) a group of 'high-stress' women, caring for relatives with Alzheimer's disease; and (b) a 'stress-free' matched control group. On average, it took 9 days longer for group (a)'s wounds to heal than (b)'s.

SOURCES OF STRESS

In the previous section, we've mentioned a variety of stressors. These include insulin, electric shock, excessive heat or cold, exams, and death of spouse. The last of these is an example of a major life change. In this section, we concentrate on these and workplace stressors.

Life changes

ESSENTIAL STUDY 3.3

Holmes & Rahe's (1967) Social Readjustment Rating Scale (SRRS)

Aims (AO1)

The main aim of this study was to construct an instrument for measuring stress. Holmes and Rahe defined stress as the amount of *change* an individual has had to deal with during a particular period of time. They claimed that the degree of stress is related to both physical and psychological illness. People are more likely to show symptoms following periods of stress. The greater the stress, the more serious the illness.

Procedures (AO1)

Holmes and Rahe examined the medical records of 5,000 patients. They also compiled a list of 43 life events, which seemed to cluster in the months prior to the onset of their illness.

They told 100 people ('judges') that 'marriage' had been assigned an arbitrary value of 500. The judges then had to assign a number to each of the other life events, indicating how much readjustment they'd involve *relative to marriage.*

So, death of spouse was judged (on average) to require *twice* as much readjustment as marriage. The average (mean) of the numbers assigned to each event was then divided by 10. The resulting values became the weighting (numerical value) of each life event. For example, the weighting for death of spouse was 100 (1,000, divided by 10). A sample of the 43 life events is shown in Table 3.2 on page 64.

The amount of life stress a person has experienced in a given period (say, 12 months) is measured by the total number of **life change units** (LCUs). These units are calculated by adding the mean values (in the right-hand column of Table 3.2) associated with the events the person has experienced during that time (the middle column). The ranks (left-hand column) simply denote the order in which the life events appear in the SRRS. When participants are given the SRRS, they're presented *only* with the list of life events (without mean values). They're simply asked to tick the ones that apply to them.

Findings (AO1)

Most life events were judged to be *less* stressful than getting married. But six (including death of spouse, divorce, and personal injury or illness) were rated as *more* stressful.

Holmes and Rahe found that people with high LCU scores for the preceding year were likely to experience some sort of physical illness the following year. For example, someone scoring over 300 LCUs had about an 80% chance of becoming ill. Health problems included sudden cardiac death, non-fatal heart attacks, tuberculosis (TB), diabetes, leukaemia, accidents, and sports injuries.

Conclusions (AO1)

Holmes and Rahe concluded that stress could be measured objectively as an LCU score. This, in turn, predicts the person's chances of becoming ill (physically and/or mentally) following the period of stress. Stress and illness aren't just correlated. Stress actually makes us ill.

Criticisms (AO1/AO2)

✓ **Landmark study.** This was the first major attempt to measure stress objectively and to examine its relationship to illness.

✂ **Are all changes equally stressful?** The SRRS assumes that *any* change is, by definition, stressful. But the *undesirable* aspects of events are at least as important as the fact that they change people's lives. Table 3.2 suggests that life changes have a largely *negative* feel about them (especially those with the highest LCU scores). So, the SRRS may be confusing 'change' with 'negativity'.

✂ **Ambiguity.** Some of the life events are *ambiguous.* For example, those that refer to 'change in . . . ' could be positive or negative.

✂ **Missing life events.** The list of life events is *incomplete.* For example, there's no reference to the problems of old age, natural or 'man-made' disasters (Lazarus, 1999).

✂ **Change or uncontrollable change?** It may not be change as such that's stressful, but change that's *unexpected*, and in this sense, *uncontrollable*. When people are asked to classify the undesirable life events on the SRRS as either 'controllable 'or 'uncontrollable', only the latter are correlated with later illness.

✂ **Not everyday occurrences.** By definition, most of the 43 life events aren't everyday occurrences. Kanner *et al*'s (1981) **hassles scale** includes losing weight, traffic jams, bad weather, arguments, and financial and family worries (see opposite).

Table 3.2 A selection of life events from the Social Readjustment Rating Scale (SRRS)

Rank	Life event	Mean value
1.	Death of spouse	100
2.	Divorce	73
3.	Marital separation	65
4.	Jail term	63
5.	Death of close family member	63
6.	Personal injury or illness	53
7.	Marriage	50
8.	Fired at work	47
10.	Retirement	45
11.	Change in health of family member	44
12.	Pregnancy	40
13.	Sex difficulties	39
16.	Change in financial state	38
17.	Death of close friend	37
18.	Change to different line of work	36
23.	Son or daughter leaving home	29
27.	Begin or end school	26
38.	Change in sleeping habits	16
42.	Christmas	12
43.	Minor violations of the law	11

EVALUATION OF STUDIES USING THE SRRS

✓ **Support using large sample.** 2,500 navy personnel from three US navy cruisers completed the SRRS before they left for a six-month tour of duty. While they were away, a health record was kept for each participant by the ships' doctors. As predicted, LCUs were positively correlated with illness (Rahe *et al*, 1970).

✗ • ✓ **Results open to interpretation.** Instead of life events *causing* illness, it could be the other way round. Some life events (such as 8, 13, and 38: see Table 3.2) might be early signs of an illness that's already developing (Penny, 1996). This is because studies like Rahe *et al*'s are *correlational* (see Chapter 6, pages 132–3).

✗ **Unreliable data.** Many studies are *retrospective.* People are asked to *recall* both their illnesses and the stressful life events that occurred during, say, the previous 12 months. This is likely to produce unreliable data. For example, if you're under stress (for whatever reason) you may focus on minor physiological sensations and report them as 'symptoms of illness' (Davison & Neale, 2001).

✗ **Life events may mean different things to different people.** On the SRRS, particular events give a pre-determined LCU score. But individuals can experience the 'same' life event very differently. For example, divorce may mean release from an unhappy, stressful, situation, and so may be a very *positive* event. (Also, what's a hassle one day may not be the next – and vice-versa: see below).

✗ **Hassles are more stressful.** Kanner *et al* (1981) studied 100 men and women over a 12-month period. They confirmed their prediction that hassles were correlated with undesirable psychological symptoms. Also, hassles were a more powerful predictor of symptoms (both physiological and psychological) than the SRRS life events. Delongis *et al* (1982) compared the hassles scale and a life events scale as predictors of later health problems. They also wanted to study the effect of 'uplifts'. These are events that make you feel good (the opposite of hassles).
100 participants, aged 45–64, completed questionnaires, once a month, over the course of a year. Both the frequency and intensity of hassles were significantly correlated with overall health status and physical symptoms. There was *no* relationship between life events and health during the course of the study itself. But there was for the 2–3 years *prior* to the study. Daily uplifts had little effect on health.
These findings confirm Kanner *et al*'s conclusion that daily hassles are a better predictor of health problems than life events. But this may partly reflect the time period for which life changes are recorded. In other words, it may take longer than 12 months for (certain) life events to have their effects on health.

EXAM tips BOX

Consider psychological research into the role of life events as a source of stress. (18 marks)

● You could structure your answer in terms of three paragraphs, all about 100–130 words long.

● The first paragraph could include some examples of life events, and a brief *description* of evidence for the role of life events as a source of stress. This is likely to focus on Holmes & Rahe's (1967) Social Readjustment Rating Scale (SRRS) study and related research. (AO1, worth 6 marks).

● In the second paragraph, you could *analyse and evaluate* Holmes and Rahe's research. Remember, this was an attempt to *construct an instrument for measuring stress.* So, you could consider the strengths and weaknesses of the SRRS as a way of measuring stress. You could also compare the SRRS with other attempts to measure stress.

● In the third paragraph, you could *analyse and evaluate* studies which have used the SRRS and/or other measures of stress in relation to physical and/or mental illness. (AO2, worth 12 marks).

● Remember, merely describing research findings will only count as AO1. You must evaluate (AO2) the research findings in order to answer the question.

Try to write a suitable answer in about 300–350 words. As with all questions, there's no single correct way of answering it. The above are just pointers. There's a sample answer at the end of the book. Try not to look at it until you've had a go at doing it yourself.

Workplace stressors

ARE SOME OCCUPATIONS MORE STRESSFUL THAN OTHERS?

Four of the most stressful occupations are nursing, social work, teaching, and the emergency services (police, ambulance, fire etc.). In *nursing*, for example, certain sources of stress are part-and-parcel of the job. These include:

- dealing constantly with patients' pain, anxiety, and death

- giving emotional support to relatives, often with little appropriate training

- having to maintain high levels of concentration for long periods (as in ITU/intensive care)

- being in the 'front line' when major disasters occur (such as the 1989 Hillsborough football disaster).

More recently, nurses and others working in healthcare have become the victims of violence.

THE EFFECTS OF BEING IN CONTROL: GOOD OR BAD?

Executives (in industry and business organisations) are another occupational group that face above-average stress levels. They constantly have to make important decisions, and they're responsible for their outcomes. This is very stressful ('executive stress').

In a famous early study, Brady placed monkeys in 'restraining chairs' and conditioned them to press a lever. They'd receive an electric shock every 20 seconds if they didn't press the lever within that interval. But many of the monkeys died suddenly, and the experiment had to be abandoned. Post-mortem examinations showed that the monkeys had raised levels of gastrointestinal hormones. The cause of death was ulcers. Other monkeys had been restrained for up to six months without any ill effects. So, the ulcers had been caused *either* by the electric shocks *or* the stress of having to press the lever to avoid them.

ESSENTIAL STUDY 3.4

Brady's (1958) **Executive Monkey Experiment** (EME)

Aims (AO1)

This was a follow-up to the earlier experiment described above. Brady was trying to test the relationship between (a) high stress levels and (b) increased hormone production and the development of ulcers. He was primarily interested in the effects of stress in business executives.

Procedures (AO1)

Brady tested monkeys *in pairs*. The experimental 'executive' was responsible for pressing the lever. A 'yoked control' received the shocks, but couldn't control the lever. So, only the executive monkey was stressed, but both monkeys received the shocks. This occurred at 20-second intervals, for six hours at a time, over a three-week period.

Findings (AO1)

The executive monkeys developed severe ulcers and eventually died. The yoked controls showed no apparent ill effects. The executive's stomach acidity was greatest during the rest period.

Conclusions (AO1)

Brady concluded that it was stress, not the shocks, that caused the ulcers. The most dangerous time was when the sympathetic arousal *stopped* (during the rest period). The stomach became flooded with digestive hormones (a 'parasympathetic rebound'), and this produced the ulcers.

Criticisms (AO1/AO2)

✓ **Direct test of how stress can induce physical illness** (see the last bullet point).

✓ **Contradicts other studies:** Brady's conclusion seems to contradict other research (involving humans), which shows that *control* helps to *reduce* stress (see pages 74–5).

✗ **Biased results:** Brady's monkeys *weren't* randomly assigned to the executive/yoked control conditions. They were allocated according to how quickly they learned to avoid shock. This makes his conclusions less valid than they'd otherwise be.

✗ **The importance of a warning signal:** Weiss (1972) used rats in a partial replication of Brady's experiment. The shock was preceded by a *warning signal* for the executives, who were far *less* likely to develop stomach ulcers than the yoked controls. This suggests that what's stressful is having to be *constantly vigilant.* Without any warning signal, Brady's executive monkeys could never be sure whether they'd manage to avoid the *next* shock. But Weiss's rats could rely on the warning signal.

✓ **Constant vigilance is stressful:** Human executives, and air-traffic controllers, have the highest incidence of stomach ulcers of any US occupational groups. The latter especially have to be constantly vigilant.

✗ **Generalising from non-humans to humans:** Brady's and Weiss's results can only *suggest* why stress is harmful for humans. It's always dangerous to generalise research findings from one species to another.

✗ **Unethical:** Brady's experiments have been criticised for being unethical. Clearly, such experiments involving human participants wouldn't be allowed. But it's always controversial to deliberately expose members of *any* species to high stress levels (see Chapter 5, pages 122–6).

Other evidence suggests that people low down on the occupational ladder (that is, those who *lack* control) are most susceptible. For example, Marmot *et al* (1997) found that men and women in the lowest grade jobs (within the civil service) were four times more likely to die of a heart attack than those in the most senior positions. They were also more likely to suffer from cancers, strokes, and gastrointestinal disorders.

This study (and others) suggests that having *too little* stress can damage your health (e.g. low self-esteem, anxiety, depression, apathy, exhaustion, CHD). In practice, this may mean:

- having little control over your work situation
- being unable to make decisions that affect you
- having little responsibility (and, therefore, status).

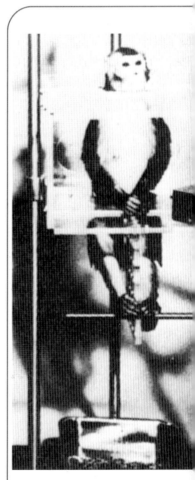

An 'executive monkey'

Brady's EME, on the other hand, suggests that having *too much* stress can damage your health (e.g. peptic ulcers). In practice, this may involve:

- having to be constantly 'in charge' and making important decisions

- being mainly or exclusively responsible for a section or department.

Weiss's replication of Brady's EME suggests that control is harmful if it involves:

- having to be constantly vigilant.

OTHER SOURCES OF WORKPLACE STRESS

- **Work overload/underload** can be quantitative or qualitative (see Table 3.3 below).

- **Role ambiguity** refers to an employee's confusion about his/her role in an organisation ("what exactly is my job?"). This is associated with frustration and anxiety.

- **Role conflict** occurs when an employee is asked to perform two incompatible roles or tasks. For example, s/he may have two bosses, who both want something done *now*. This is associated with cardiovascular disorders and peptic ulcers.

Quantitative overload	**Qualitative overload**
Too much to do; having to be excessively quick or productive. Associated with anxiety and frustration.	The work is too difficult or demands excessive attention. Associated with anxiety and frustration.
Quantitative underload	**Qualitative underload**
Not having enough to do. Associated with boredom, frustration, low job satisfaction, and lack of commitment.	Under-using your skills and abilities. Associated with boredom, frustration, low job satisfaction, and lack of commitment.

Table 3.3 Examples of quantitative and qualitative work overload and underload.

- **Job insecurity/redundancy** are both associated with anxiety.

- **Lack of career structure** (poor promotion opportunities) is associated with poor physical health.

- **Poor interpersonal relations/support** is associated with anxiety and low job satisfaction.

- **Bullying** and **violence** at work are associated with absenteeism and poor mental health.

Modifying the effects of stressors: Individual differences

When discussing Friedman & Rosenman's (1974) STAB earlier in the chapter (see Essential Study 3.1, pages 58–9), several important points emerged:

- Stressors don't exist 'objectively'. Something only qualifies as a stressor if an individual perceives it as a stressor.

- So, we must take psychological (and other non-physiological) factors into account if we're to understand properly what stressors are and how they affect people. (One criticism of Selye's GAS is that he focused exclusively on physiological factors: see pages 56–7).

● One major kind of psychological factor is personality, or characteristic patterns of behaviour.

● TAB describes a typical way of reacting to life in general, and work-related situations in particular. According to Friedman and Rosenman, people who display TAB have a greater chance of developing CHD than other 'types'.

But personality is only *one* way in which people differ. Other individual differences include gender and culture.

PERSONALITY

● Recent research has focused on *specific Type A characteristics*. In particular, *hostility* seems to be the best single predictor of CHD. It's a better predictor than TAB as a whole. But this doesn't mean that hostility *causes* CHD (just as we can't claim that TAB as a whole does).

● *Type C personalities* are cancer-prone (Temoshok, 1987). They have difficulty expressing emotion, and tend to suppress or inhibit emotions (especially negative ones, such as anger). It seems likely that these personality characteristics influence the progression of cancer and patients' survival time (Weinman, 1995).

● Women diagnosed with breast cancer showed significantly more emotional suppression than those with non-life-threatening breast disease (Greer & Morris, 1975).

EXAM tips BOX

Consider psychological research into the effects of workplace stressors. (18 marks)

● You could structure your answer in terms of three paragraphs, all about 100–130 words long.

● In the first paragraph, you could give some examples of workplace stressors, and briefly *describe* evidence relating to the effects of workplace stressors. (AO1, worth 6 marks).

● A word of advice: *although we normally associate work with human beings, any studies involving non-human animals can be included, provided they're relevant.*

● In the second paragraph, you could consider what can be learned from studies of executive monkeys and/or rats about human executive stress. There are both specific and more general issues involved here.

● In the third paragraph, you could consider (i) what it is about certain occupations that make them inherently more stressful; (ii) how different studies have defined and measured *control*; and (iii) why both too much and too little stress can be harmful. (AO2, worth 12 marks).

● *Remember, merely* describing *research findings will only count as AO1. You must* analyse and evaluate *(AO2) the research findings in order to answer the question.*

Try to write a suitable answer in about 300–350 words.
As with all questions, there's no single correct way of answering it. The above are just pointers. There's a sample answer at the end of the book. Try not to look at it until you've had a go at doing it yourself.

Greer *et al's* (1979) Beating Breast Cancer study (BBC)

Aims (AO1)

To investigate the psychological aspects of cancer. In particular, to understand how women with breast cancer use *coping mechanisms* to reduce their stress levels.

Procedures (AO1)

Greer *et al* interviewed women who'd recently been diagnosed with breast cancer. They were mainly concerned with the women's attitudes towards their diagnosis.

Findings (AO1)

Based on their replies, Greer *et al* identified four types of attitude. These attitudes indicate the women's coping strategies:

● *denial* (e.g. "I'm being treated for a lump, but it's not serious")

ESSENTIAL STUDY 3.5

- *fighting spirit* (e.g. "This is not going to get me")
- *stoic acceptance* (e.g. "I feel an illness is God's will ... ")
- *giving up* (e.g. "Well, there's no hope with cancer, is there?").

Women in the first two categories were significantly more likely to be free of cancer five years later than women in the second two. A follow-up at 15 years (Greer *et al,* 1990) confirmed the improved prognosis.

Conclusions (AO1)

The findings lend scientific support to the advice to 'think positive'. We're better off adapting to, rather than giving in to, severe threats to our well-being. It might even be possible to teach such strategies to people who either don't possess or don't use them (Hegarty, 2000).

Criticisms (AO1/AO2)

✅ **Personality defined in terms of coping strategies:** This allows it to be measured in a reasonably simple way. By implication, Type C women are more likely to use *stoic acceptance/giving up.*

✅ **Longitudinal (follow-up) study.** Participants were compared with themselves over a 15-year period. In relation to breast cancer, this is a substantial period. It allows us to see the role played by personality/coping strategies very clearly.

✖ **Indirect effect of personality on cancer.** It's now widely believed that cancer is a disorder of the *immune system* (see pages 59–62). If a Type C woman is under severe stress, her immune system might become so suppressed that cancer cells could start growing into a tumour. For example, Cooper & Faragher (1993) found that experiencing a major stressful event was a crucial predictor of breast cancer. This was especially so in women who used denial as their main coping mechanism.

Culture

- Western culture seems to encourage and value many of the components of TAB. For example, competitiveness and striving for achievement are common goals in capitalist societies. This is much less true of non-Western, more traditional societies (Penny, 1996).

- The SRRS has been criticised for not taking account of cultural and ethnic differences. What count as (potentially) stressful life changes differ between cultures. Even where a life event is common to all cultures (such as marriage), its meaning differs. Clearly, many of the 43 life events on the SRRS don't apply at all in many cultures. (Try to identify those life events which clearly reflect the American society of the mid-1960s in which the scale was devised.)

- Both the physical and mental health of African Americans is worse than that of whites. African Americans are especially likely to have AIDS and hypertension. This is partly caused by the direct negative effects of poverty, such as poor diet, low levels of education, and poor medical care. But there are also many psychological and social stressors involved. Blacks in North America and Europe face a unique kind of stress, namely *racial discrimination* (Cooper *et al,* 1999).

Gender

- From a purely biological perspective, females are the stronger sex. For example, more male foetuses are spontaneously aborted, stillborn, or die of birth trauma.

• This *biological vulnerability* of males persists throughout life. For example, women's average life expectancy exceeds men's by 7–8 years. Males are also more susceptible to various diseases, including convulsions, viral infections, ulcers, CHD, and some kinds of cancer.

• The smaller male Y chromosome seems to account for much of this vulnerability. (Males have one X and one Y, while females have two Xs.)

• But women have higher *morbidity rates*, that is, they're more likely to suffer generalised poor health and specific diseases. For example, women have higher rates of diabetes, gastrointestinal problems, and rheumatoid arthritis. They visit their GPs more often, and use more prescribed drugs.

• There's some evidence that females produce less adrenaline in response to stressors compared with males (Frankenhauser, 1983). Over the course of a lifetime, this may prove to be a protective factor.

• Women are less likely than men to display TAB. They're also less hostile than men. TAB might reflect the male gender role. This could help explain why men are more vulnerable to cardiovascular disorders.

• But the gap between the sexes for deaths from cardiovascular disorders has closed over the last 30 years or so. This could be due to *lifestyle changes*, with women smoking and drinking more than they used to (Davison & Neale, 2001).

EXAM tips BOX

To what extent have the effects of stressors been shown to be modified by personality? (18 marks)

• You could structure your answer in terms of three paragraphs, all about 100–130 words long.

• In the first paragraph, you could briefly say what's meant by personality, then go on to briefly *describe* some relevant research into personality's influence on the effects of stress. (AO1, worth 6 marks).

• In the second and third paragraphs, you should *analyse and evaluate* (some of) the research you described in the first paragraph. Here, you're considering how research both supports and challenges the view that personality can modify the effects of stressors. Two important questions to bear in mind are: (i) are there any interactions between personality and other variables, such as gender? (ii) *how* is personality meant to modify the effects of stressors? (AO2, worth 12 marks).

• *Remember, merely* describing *research will only count as AO1. You must* analyse *and* evaluate *in order to answer the question.*

Try to write a suitable answer in about 300–350 words.
As with all questions, there's no single correct way of answering it. The above are just pointers. There's a sample answer at the end of the book. Try not to look at it until you've had a go at doing it yourself. Note: A similar question could be asked about the modifying effects of culture and/or gender.

CRITICAL ISSUE: STRESS MANAGEMENT

Methods of managing the effects of stress

PHYSIOLOGICAL APPROACHES

Psychotherapeutic drugs

• Psychotherapeutic drugs act directly on the ANS. *Anxiolytic* (anxiety-reducing) drugs are commonly used in cases of chronic stress. The *benzodiazepine* group of anxiolytics include *chlordiazepoxide* (*Librium*) and *diazepam* (*Valium*).

• Anxiolytic drugs usually succeed in reducing the physiological effects of stress. But *side-effects* may include drowsiness and lethargy. People may also become *physically dependent* on them. If the drug is stopped, the person may experience insomnia, tremors, and convulsions. These are symptoms of *withdrawal* (or *abstinence syndrome*).

• Anxiolytics are also associated with *tolerance*. That is, an increasing amount of the drug is needed to produce the same, original, effect.

• Physical dependence and tolerance together constitute *drug addiction*.

Biofeedback

Biofeedback

● Patients are given information (via monitors or buzzers) about BP, heart rate, muscle tension or other *autonomic functions*. These are automatically regulated by the ANS, and so we're usually unaware of them and unable to control them. But the feedback provided by the monitor or buzzer allows the patient to bring them under voluntary control. For example, a line on a TV monitor swings to the left or right depending on changes in heart rate. The person is taught to use meditation or muscle relaxation in order to control the movement of the line.

● College students suffering from muscle contraction headaches were given seven 50-minute sessions, twice weekly. They were given feedback about muscle tension (*electromyograph* (EMG) feedback). They also had to practise their newly learned skills at home when free of headaches, and at the first sign of one. A *waiting-list control group* only received treatment when the study was over. In the *placebo condition,* participants engaged in 'pseudomeditation'. Compared with both these groups, the EMG biofeedback produced significant reductions in EMG and tension headaches (in Bradley, 1995).

● Biofeedback requires the use of specialised equipment. This is clearly a disadvantage compared with alternative techniques (such as *progressive muscle relaxation*), which don't. Other techniques may also be just as effective in stress reduction.

● It's unclear exactly how biofeedback works.

● Regular practice is needed if the person is to benefit, especially in the longer term.

● It may not be biofeedback itself which helps in stress reduction. Other factors, such as the person's determination to beat stress, may be crucial.

● Biofeedback is designed to treat the *symptoms* of stress, *not* to tackle the stressor itself.

PSYCHOLOGICAL APPROACHES

Stress inoculation

● **Stress inoculation training** (SIT) is a form of **cognitive restructuring**. This refers to various methods of changing the way people *think* about themselves and their lives. The aim is to change their emotional responses and their behaviour.

● SIT (Meichenbaum, 1976) is an attempt to reduce stress through changing cognitions. It assumes that people sometimes find things stressful because they think about them in *catastrophising ways*. This is another (extreme) example of how stressors aren't stressful in themselves. It's how people interpret or construe events or situations that makes them stressful.

● SIT comprises three stages.

Box 3.2 The three stages of SIT

Stage 1: Cognitive preparation (or conceptualization)

The therapist explores with the person how s/he thinks about and deals with stressful situations. They also discuss how successful these strategies have been. A common response to stressful situations is to make negative self-statements, such as "I can't handle this". This is a *self-defeating internal dialogue*, which makes a stressful situation even more stressful.

Stage 2: Skill acquisition and rehearsal

The therapist helps the person to use *preparation statements* (e.g. "Maybe what you think is anxiety is eagerness to confront it"). These are positive, coping statements that are incompatible with the negative self-statements. The person practices these preparation statements.

Stage 3: Application and follow-through

The therapist guides the person through more and more threatening situations. These are actual stress-producing situations (not role plays). Once the person can cope with a relatively non-threatening situation, they're presented with a more threatening one.

- Meichenbaum (1997) believes that the 'power-of-positive-thinking' approach advocated by SIT can successfully change people's behaviour (see **Essential Study 3.5**, page 69). It's proved particularly successful in reducing exam-nerves and the anxiety associated with severe pain.

Increasing hardiness

- **Hardiness** is really a feature of personality. That is, some people are hardy and others aren't. So, hardiness can help explain individual differences in the ability to resist stress.

- According to Kobasa (1979, 1982), 'hardy' and 'non-hardy' individuals differ in three main ways:

Box 3.3 The three Cs of hardiness

Hardy people:

- are highly **committed**. They're deeply involved in whatever they do, and approach life with a sense of curiosity and meaningfulness.

- view change as a **challenge**. They regard change (rather than stability) as normal. Change is an opportunity for personal growth and development, rather than a threat to security.

- have a strong sense of being **in control**. In Rotter's (1966) terms, they have a *high internal locus of control* (see page 74).

- Presumably, stress could be reduced if hardiness could be increased. So, can a person learn to become hardier?

Box 3.4 Three ways of increasing hardiness

- **teaching** people to identify the physical signs of stress (e.g. tenseness). We can't deal with a stressor unless we first identify it. Kobasa called this **focusing**. But identifying a stressor doesn't by itself guarantee that we'll deal with it in an appropriate or beneficial way.

- **reconstructing stressful situations** is an attempt to make a more realistic assessment of different stressors. This involves considering how a past stressful experience could have been dealt with more or less effectively.

- **compensation through self-improvement** is related to Kobasa's claim that what we believe about our abilities to bring about change has important effects on our capacity to withstand stress. When we can't avoid a stressor's effects, or deal with it in some other way, we should take on some other challenge which we *can* meet. In this way, we experience the *positive* aspects of coping with a stressor. This allows us to 'bounce back' more easily after things have gone wrong. As a result, we'll experience stressors as less stressful.

The role of control in the perception of stress

- When discussing the SRRS (see Essential Study 3.3, pages 63–4), we noted that it's only those life events classified as 'uncontrollable' that are correlated with later illness.

- We also noted the importance of control in Brady's executive monkey experiment (EME: see Essential Study 3.4, pages 66–7).

- One of the three Cs of Kobasa's hardiness is control (see Box 3.4). We noted that this corresponds to a *high internal locus of control* (Rotter, 1966).

Box 3.5 Locus of control (Rotter, 1966)

Locus of control refers to our perceived sense of control over our behaviour. It's measured on a scale that runs from *high internal* to *high external control*. If you have high *internal* locus of control (as hardy people do), you:

- take responsibility for your actions

- view yourself as being in charge of what happens to you.

If you have high *external* locus of control, you:

- tend to see your fate as out of your own hands

- attribute both your successes and failures to outside forces.

Life events stress was found to be more closely related to depression and anxiety among people with high external locus of control (Johnson & Sarason, 1978).

- Locus of control is related to **learned helplessness** (Seligman, 1975). This refers to the belief that nothing we do will make any difference to our situation.

- Seligman strapped dogs into harnesses and gave them a series of electric shocks. They couldn't escape the shocks. Later, they had to jump a barrier within 10 seconds of a warning signal (an avoidance response). Otherwise, they'd receive a painful shock. About two-thirds of these dogs failed to learn the avoidance response. They seemed passively resigned to suffering the shock. A control group of dogs (which hadn't been subjected to the unavoidable shock) learned the avoidance response easily.

- A similar effect has been shown using human participants (Miller & Norman, 1979).

- Maier & Seligman (1976) have tried to explain human depression in terms of learned helplessness.

STRESS MANAGEMENT

The term *stress management* (SM) has two main meanings:

- In a *formal* sense, SM refers to a range of techniques (both physiological and psychological) used deliberately, by professionals, to help people reduce their stress levels. These can be used singly or in combination. Major examples include *anxiolytic drugs, biofeedback, cognitive restructuring* (such as Meichenbaum's SIT), and Kobasa's attempts to increase hardiness. Others include progressive muscle relaxation, meditation, and hypnosis (all used to induce a state of relaxation). (See pages 71–4.)

- In an *informal* sense, SM refers to what we all do quite spontaneously on a day-to-day basis. In this sense, we all 'manage our stress, more or less effectively'. A major way in which we achieve this is through the use of **coping strategies/mechanisms.**

- These are conscious attempts to adapt to stress in a positive and constructive way. They involve cognitive and behavioural efforts to meet those external and/or internal demands which stretch our capacities and resources.

- Cohen & Lazarus (1979) classified all the coping strategies we might use into five general categories.

Box 3.6 Cohen & Lazarus's (1979) five Categories Of Coping (COC)

- **direct action response:** we try to change or manipulate our relationship to the stressful situation. For example, we try to escape from it or remove it

- **information seeking:** we try to understand the situation better, and to predict future events associated with the stressor

- **inhibition of action:** we do nothing. This may be the best course of action if the stressor looks like being temporary

- **intrapsychic (palliative) coping:** we reassess the situation (for example, through the use of defence mechanisms) or change the 'internal environment' (through drugs, alcohol, or relaxation)

- **turning to others:** for help and emotional support.

These five categories overlap with the distinction between *problem-focused* and *emotion-focused* coping.

Self-assessment questions

These are some example Part a and Part b questions (worth 40% of your exam). Part c questions (worth 60%) have been dealt with throughout the chapter in the Exam tips Boxes and in the Sample Answers (SAs) at the end of the book.

1a. What is meant by the terms 'stress', 'stress management', and the 'immune system'? (2 + 2 + 2 marks)

b. Outline conclusions from research into the role of personality in modifying the effects of stressors. (6 marks)

2a. Describe *two* methods of managing the negative effects of stress. (3 + 3 marks)

b. Outline findings from research into life changes as a source of stress. (6 marks)

3a. Outline the main features of the General Adaptation Syndrome (Selye). (6 marks)

b. Explain what is meant by physiological and psychological approaches to stress management and give *one* difference between them. (2 + 2 + 2 marks)

4a. Describe the procedures and findings of *one* study of stress as a bodily response. (3 + 3 marks)

b. Outline the findings of *one* study of the sources of stress and give *one* criticism of this study. (3 + 3 marks)

5a. Describe *one* account of the body's response to stressors. (6 marks)

b. Outline *two* factors that can modify the effects of stressors. (3 + 3 marks)

ESSENTIAL STUDY SUMMARY

Topic	Research study	Researcher date	Page
Stress as a bodily response	Study of Type A Behaviour (STAB)	Friedman & Rosenman (1974)	58
..	Immunosuppression in Medical Students (SMS)	Kiecolt-Glaser *et al* (1984)	61
Sources of stress	Social Readjustment Rating Scale (SRRS)	Holmes & Rahe (1967)	63
..	'Executive Monkey' Experiment (EME)	Brady (1958)	66
Modifying the effects of stress	Beating Breast Cancer study (BBC)	Greer *et al* (1979)	69

AS Module 2:
Individual Differences
Abnormality 11.2

What's covered in this chapter?

DEFINING PSYCHOLOGICAL ABNORMALITY

Abnormality is a difficult term to define, because abnormal behaviour can take many different forms, and involve different features. There's no single feature that distinguishes between abnormal and normal behaviour. Despite this, attempts have been made to define abnormality.

'Statistical infrequency' definition

By definition, abnormality means *'deviating from the norm or average'*. Statistically infrequent behaviour is regarded as abnormal, whereas frequent behaviour is normal. Individual characteristics can be measured (e.g. mood, intelligence) and the distribution of these characteristics within the population can be graphed. The normal distribution curve shows the majority of people as being in the middle. These people are defined as 'normal'. Relatively few people fall at either end. These people are 'abnormal' (see normal distribution, Figure 4.1).

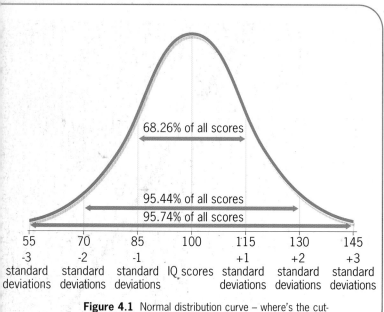

Figure 4.1 Normal distribution curve – where's the cut-off between normal and abnormal?

In the figure: 68.26% of all scores; 95.44% of all scores; 95.74% of all scores

IQ scores: 55 (-3 standard deviations), 70 (-2 standard deviations), 85 (-1 standard deviations), 100, 115 (+1 standard deviations), 130 (+2 standard deviations), 145 (+3 standard deviations)

LIMITATIONS

● **Fails to take account of desirable behaviour:** The term 'abnormal' is usually used in a negative sense. However, being 'abnormal' according to a statistical definition would include very gifted people (e.g. Mozart, Beckham). Such people wouldn't be classified as abnormal or as having a psychological disorder. Indeed, these people are usually respected and admired.

● **Abnormality is statistically common:** Up to 50% of the American population have a mental disorder at some time during their life (depression, anxiety and/or phobias are most common). These behaviours are therefore statistically frequent, but undesirable.

● **Not applicable to mental disorders:** The definition *can* be applied to abnormality, but not to mental disorders. Psychiatrists diagnose on the basis of symptoms, *not* the prevalence of the illness in society.

● **Gender and mental illness:** Men are less likely to consult their doctor about mental problems than females. Thus, women may be over-represented in mental illness statistics compared to men. This statistical difference doesn't accurately portray prevalence rates, merely reported rates.

● **Difficult to measure all behaviours:** Some behaviours (e.g. anxiety or mood disorders) aren't easily measured, nor do they conform to a normal distribution.

● **The 'cut-off' point?** How far from the norm (2 or perhaps 3 standard deviations?) do you have to be to be classified as abnormal? The setting of a 'cut-off' point is arbitrary. Indeed, different IQ tests have different standard deviations.

CULTURAL RELATIVISM

● **Under-reporting of mental illness:** Depression is rarely reported in Asian cultures, and mental illness is rarely diagnosed in China (Rack, 1982). These contrast a lot with the American figures reported above. There are different attitudes towards reporting and diagnosing various conditions within these cultures. The 'statistically infrequent' definition cannot account for such cultural differences.

● **No universal statistical measures of behaviour:** Statistical standards are set within specific populations or cultures. These may not be appropriate for different populations or cultures. For example, Lee (1969) found that many Zulu women report screaming to themselves for days or weeks as a response to unhappiness. Such behaviours would be statistically infrequent and abnormal in our society, but entirely appropriate for Zulu women.

'Deviation from social norms' definition

Society sets norms or unwritten rules for acceptable behaviour. Behaviour that deviates from these norms is considered abnormal. Abnormal behaviour is therefore whatever violates social norms. This approach takes into account the *desirability of behaviour*, as social norms identify those behaviours that are desirable for both the individual and society.

LIMITATIONS

● **Subjective:** The norms defined by society are subjective. They're often based on the opinions of elites within society rather than the majority opinion.

LOOK AT THAT ODD PERSON

- **Change over time:** The norms defined by society are often related to moral standards that vary over time as social attitudes change. For example, the wearing of trousers by women and views on homosexuality.

- **Human rights abuse:** The use of this definition has allowed serious abuse of human rights. According to Szasz (1962) the term 'mental illness' is a form of social control, a subjective concept that is used to label those who don't conform to the norms of society. Those seen as abnormal are labelled and discriminated against. For example, in the Soviet Union after WW II, political dissenters were frequently classified as mentally ill and sent to mental hospitals.

- **Value of breaking social norms:** It can be beneficial to break social norms. Suffragette campaigners for women's votes broke many norms and this led to electoral reform. But, deviating from social norms doesn't necessarily have any consequences. For example, naturists don't harm anyone but, nevertheless, do break social norms.

- **'Conforming neurotics':** These are people who conform strictly to social norms, and this is their problem. They've such a fear of rejection that they adhere to all of society's norms. Such cases aren't included within this definition.

CULTURAL RELATIVISM

- **Cultural differences:** Norms vary across cultures. There's no universal agreement as to what's normal or abnormal behaviour.

- **Ethnocentric bias in diagnosis:** In the West, the social norms that are adopted reflect behaviours of the majority 'white'

Oscar Wilde (1854–1900) the Irish writer, was imprisoned for homosexuality in 1895

population. Deviation from these norms by ethnic groups means that ethnic minorities are more likely to be over-represented in the mental illness statistics. This is supported by Cochrane (1977). He found that African-Caribbean immigrants are far more likely to be diagnosed as schizophrenic than whites or Asians. Of course, this might reflect the true incidence of schizophrenia in these groups. However, the high schizophrenia rate for African-Caribbean immigrants is *only* found in the UK, not in other countries. It's suggested that this reflects a cultural bias (or blindness) in diagnosis amongst British psychiatrists.

'Failure to function adequately' definition

This means that a person is unable to live a normal life. Such people don't experience a 'normal' range of emotions or participate in a 'normal' range of behaviours. People's behaviour is considered abnormal if it causes great distress and torment in them leading to dysfunction. That is, their behaviour disrupts their ability to work and/or conduct satisfying relationships with people. They cannot cope with day-to-day life.

Rosenhan & Seligman (1989) suggested that the concept of dysfunction includes:

- **Personal distress:** this is a key feature of abnormality. This would include depression and anxiety disorders.

- **Maladaptive behaviour:** behaviour that stops individuals from attaining satisfactory goals, both socially and occupationally.

- **Unpredictability:** behaviour that wouldn't be expected given the particular circumstances (e.g. trying to commit suicide having failed a driving test).

Dr Harold Shipman: a serial killer while working as a GP

- **Irrationality:** behaviour that cannot be explained in a rational way.

- **Observer discomfort:** behaviour that causes distress or discomfort to others.

- **Violation of moral and ideal standards:** behaviour that doesn't fit in with society's standards.

The more of these indicators that are present, the more abnormal an individual is considered to be.

This approach does recognise the *subjective experience* of the individual.

LIMITATIONS

- **Abnormality isn't always accompanied by dysfunction:** People with anti-social personality disorders (psychopaths) have been known to commit murders and still continue to lead a 'normal' life (e.g. Jeffrey Dahmer, Harold Shipman). Such people must be classified as abnormal in the absence of *'a failure to function adequately'*. In addition, some schizophrenics aren't aware or deny that they have a problem.

- **Subjective nature of Rosenhan and Seligman's components:** There are problems in defining some of Rosenhan and Seligman's components. For example, how is personal distress measured? People are likely to differ in their subjective experience. Similarly, there are people who experience mania (unbounded joy). Their behaviour doesn't appear to cause them distress, but would count as evidence for a psychological disorder. It would also appear to be abnormal *not* to suffer personal distress at various points during one's life, say when a close relative dies.

CULTURAL RELATIVISM

Explains higher incidence of mental illness in sub-cultures: The 'failure to function adequately' definition might explain why certain groups or sub-groups in the population are over-represented in the mental illness statistics (see Cochrane, 1977 above). This could be due to the extra stress and pressures associated with moving to a different culture. Alternatively, it could be due to the amount of racism or prejudice experienced by such minority groups (this might include bias in psychiatric diagnosis).

'Deviation from ideal mental health' definition

This approach concentrates on defining the 'normal' characteristics people should possess. Abnormality is seen as a deviation from these ideals of mental health. Jahoda (1958) identified six criteria relating to ideal mental health. These factors are required for 'optimal living' (*'living life to the full'*):

- **Positive attitude towards oneself:** This is shown by having a fairly high self-regard (self-esteem).

- **Potential for growth and development:** This is shown by self-actualisation. Maslow (1968) defines this as *'becoming everything that one is capable of becoming'*. The more things you do, the healthier you are (psychologically).

- **Autonomy:** Being able to make decisions on our own and not being dependent on other people.

- **Resistance to stress:** Being able to cope with anxiety-provoking situations.

THAT MAN HAS NO IDEA OF THE SOCIAL NORMS EXPECTED ROUND HERE

QUEUE HERE

- **Accurate perception of reality:** Having an objective and realistic view of the world. For example, not being too pessimistic or optimistic.

- **Environmental mastery:** Being able to meet the demands of any situation, and being flexible enough to adapt to changing life circumstances.

The further people are from these ideals, the more abnormal they are.

LIMITATIONS

- **Over-demanding criteria:** Most people don't meet all these ideals. For example, self-actualisation is achieved by very few people. Therefore, according to this definition, most people could be classified as abnormal. If most people are abnormal, then according to the statistical definition, abnormality would actually become the norm! In addition, Harold Shipman might also have scored highly on these six criteria!

- **Subjective criteria:** Many of the concepts aren't clearly defined. Measuring physical health is more of an objective science using well-established methods such as X-rays and blood tests. Diagnosing mental health is far more subjective, and relies to a large extent on patient self-reports. Some of these patients may actually be mentally ill, and so may not be particularly reliable!

- **Contextual effects:** As with some of the other definitions, mental health criteria can be affected by context. Stripping naked in your Psychology lesson may be a sign of mental illness (try it and see!) whereas remaining fully clothed on a nudist beach might appear strange.

- **Changes over time:** Mental health criteria also change over time. In thirteenth century Europe, seeing visions was a sign of religious fervour, now it would be seen as a sign of schizophrenia.

CULTURAL RELATIVISM

- **Mental health criteria vary across cultures:** Many studies have found that 'being mad' can vary across cultures (Berry *et al*, 1992). For example, *Koro* refers to an acute anxiety reaction whereby a man fears his penis is retracting into his abdomen and a woman that her breasts are retracting into her body. This disorder is reported in South East Asia and is an example of a **culture-bound syndrome**. It's assumed that the Western concept of mental disorder is culture-free, but this may not be the case.

- **Collectivist societies:** Collectivist societies that emphasise co-operation amongst their members would reject the importance of individual autonomy as a criterion for mental health. Nobles (1976) claimed that African people have a sense of 'we' instead of the 'me' view common in the West. Western cultures tend to be more concerned with individual attainment and goals.

Diagnosing mental health relies on patient self-reports

EXAM **tips** BOX

Briefly describe definitions of abnormality and assess to what extent they have taken into account cultural differences. (18 marks)

- You have 18 minutes to answer this question and you should aim to write at least 300–350 words in this time. Think of it as writing three paragraphs, each about 100–130 words.

- The first paragraph could involve a short *description* of some of the definitions of abnormality. Since the answer asks for 'definitions' (plural) you must cover at least two, but you *could* cover all four of the definitions covered in this chapter. Examiners will recognise the 'trade-off' between depth and breadth in your choice. This paragraph will mainly comprise description (AO1– 6 marks).

- The final two paragraphs will comprise the *analysis and evaluation* (AO2 – 12 marks) component. Here, you should deal with each of the definitions covered and discuss whether they do or do not take account of cultural differences. You could include contextual effects, different societal and cultural values, ethnocentric bias and the under-reporting of mental illness in groups and sub-groups. You should also *analyse and evaluate* studies that support these points.

There's a sample answer at the end of the book. Try not to look at it until you've had a go at doing it yourself.

Conclusion

It's extremely difficult to produce a culture-free definition of abnormality. What constitutes abnormal behaviour differs between cultures. This suggests that the concept of abnormality is a social construction. It's difficult enough to define abnormality *within* a culture without trying to produce one to use *between* cultures. As a result, definitions of abnormality, diagnosis and classification of mental illness must be treated with caution.

BIOLOGICAL AND PSYCHOLOGICAL MODELS OF ABNORMALITY

The biological (medical) model

ASSUMPTIONS/CAUSES

This is the most widely used approach to the causes and treatment of mental illness in the West. It was developed by the medical profession, hence its name.

The medical model has a number of key assumptions:

● **Similar to a disease, a physical cause:** Abnormal behaviour may be compared with a disease. It's assumed that all mental illnesses have a physiological cause related to the physical structure and/or functioning of the brain. A distinction is made between 'organic' and 'functional' disorders. Organic disorders involve obvious physical brain damage and/or disease (say, a brain tumour), whereas functional disorders don't have an obvious physiological cause (e.g. depression).

● **Symptoms:** In medicine, physical illnesses have clear-cut symptoms. Doctors diagnose using well-established criteria. Psychiatrists also use diagnostic manuals for mental illness and compare symptoms with set classifications of illnesses. There are slight differences between ICD-10 (International Classification of Diseases 10th ed, 1992) and DSM-IV (Diagnostic Statistical Manual 4th ed, 1994). Brain scans can be used to help with the diagnosis, particularly with organic disorders.

● **Genetic inheritance:** It's assumed that genes have a major effect on the likelihood of developing a mental illness. People have a genetic predisposition to certain psychological disorders. Twin and family resemblance studies have shown that some mental illnesses 'run in the family'. Kendler *et al* (1985) found that relatives of schizophrenics were 18 times more likely to develop the illness than a matched control group.

● **Bio-chemistry:** Chemical imbalances in the brain may be involved in certain mental illnesses. Neurotransmitters (chemicals in the brain) play an important part in behaviour, and an excess of dopamine has been detected in the brains of schizophrenics. However, such findings involve correlations and don't prove cause and effect. For example, it might be the schizophrenia itself that's causing the dopamine excess, rather than the other way round.

● **Infection:** This is a common cause of physical illness, but has also been found with some mental illnesses. Barr *et al* (1990) found increased levels of schizophrenia amongst mothers who had flu whilst they were pregnant, suggesting a possible link with the disorder.

TREATMENT

Treatment based on the medical model involves invasive, physical intervention. It's assumed that there's a physiological cause, and so a physiological treatment is used. There are three main somatic (soma = 'body' in Greek) therapies:

- **Psychotherapeutic drugs (chemotherapy):** By far the most widely used treatment for mental illness. Drugs have the benefit of having been tested (for safety and effectiveness) in scientific trials. In addition, they're relatively cheap and quick to administer. However, drugs may merely reduce the symptoms and not tackle the actual cause of the disorder. Drugs can also cause side-effects, and physiological and psychological dependence. For example, the anti-depressant Prozac, although effective in 70% of cases, can cause insomnia and headaches.

- **ECT (electro-convulsive therapy):** Here, an electric current is passed through the brain to cause a small seizure or convulsion. Although the original theoretical basis for this is discredited, it's believed that it helps reset brain neurotransmitter levels. It appears to help in 75% of cases of severe depression (Fink, 2002). However, there's no agreed way to assess this success. It's even been measured as the number of patients who don't subsequently commit suicide in a set period! In 2001, there were 13,000 treatments per week in England. In about 10% of cases it's administered involuntarily (Pippard, 1992). Other ethical issues concern ECT's disputed benefits and the procedure itself (sometimes called 'barbaric').

- **Psychosurgery:** This is primarily used for severe depression. It's extremely rare in Britain, with only 7 operations in 1999 and 2 operations in 2000. Typically, electrodes are inserted into the brain and heated to destroy the brain tissue. The theoretical basis for this is unclear but it's thought that other areas of the brain may take over the function of any destroyed tissue. There are ethical concerns with psychosurgery. Some people see it as a beneficial 'last resort' for seriously ill patients with a 75% success rate (Cobb 1993). Others see psychosurgery as 'partially killing' the person. Of 42 patients with data available, 34 showed some improvement. However, MIND are not happy with its continued use without proper and rigorous assessment (MIND, 2002).

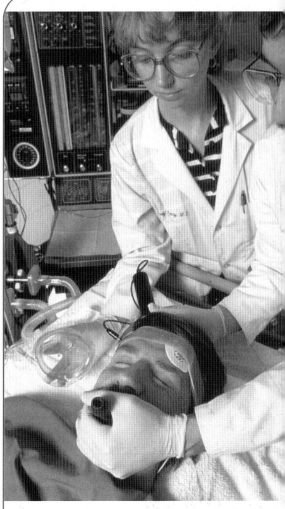

A patient undergoing ECT for depression

EVALUATION OF MEDICAL APPROACH

✓ **Humane approach:** The medical approach attaches no blame to the mentally ill individual. People with a mental illness are just unlucky to develop it, in the same way that someone might catch an illness such as measles. This is a humane approach since mental illness, in practice, often invokes fear and stigma.

✓ **Effective treatments:** Carefully controlled studies demonstrate the effectiveness of drugs. Possible side-effects don't outweigh the benefits. The case is less clear-cut for ECT and psychosurgery. However, patients are often pleased to have tried these 'last-ditch' treatments even if they haven't been successful.

✓ **Physiological evidence, well-established scientific principles:** The increased use of brain scans and post mortems adds to the growing body of physiological evidence supporting the medical approach.

✗ • ✓ **Reliability of diagnosis:** Two reliability measures can be used. Different psychiatrists can be given the same patients to diagnose (*inter-rater reliability*) and the same patients can be assessed at different times by the same psychiatrist *(test-retest reliability)*. Both types of reliability have increased since the introduction of the newest classification systems (post-1980). Pre-1980 diagnosis was not so accurate (see Rosenhan study below).

'Being insane in sane places': Rosenhan (1973) sent participants to mental hospitals where they claimed to be hearing voices. They were admitted and then behaved entirely normally. Much of their subsequent behaviour was interpreted by staff as being indicative of mental illness. Some were detained for up to 50 days. In a follow-up study, Rosenhan told hospitals in a different area that he would replicate the study to see if they could detect the sane from the insane. 41 patients were turned away in the following six months, despite the fact that Rosenhan did not send any participants! Rosenhan concluded that psychiatric diagnosis was unreliable. However, since this study diagnostic procedures have been improved, and psychiatrists don't expect to be deliberately misled or lied to by patients.

✗ • ✓ **Validity of diagnosis:** This refers to whether the diagnosis is measuring what it's supposed to be measuring (i.e. is there an actual underlying illness called schizophrenia?). Research shows that diagnosis is valid for the general categories of mental disorder, but not for the sub-categories of disorders. However, the same could be said of physical illness diagnosis.

✓ **Animal research support:** Many experiments carried out on animals lend weight to the biological approach to abnormal behaviour.

✗ **Reductionist approach:** The medical approach reduces the diagnosis of mental illness to lists of physical symptoms. Greater emphasis should be placed on a patient's personal feelings, and experiences.

✗ **Animal studies:** Ethical and methodological issues arise with animal experiments. Is it reasonable to exploit animals for the (possible) benefit of humans (so-called 'speciesism')? In addition, researchers cannot be certain that animals that display abnormal behaviours are experiencing a mental disorder in the same way that humans do.

✗ **Responsibility denied:** People aren't held responsible for their actions or their treatment. They become 'patients'. Responsibility for the therapy is 'passed over' to the 'great expert' (the psychiatrist). Therapy works best when people take more responsibility for their treatments and behaviour. (The same is true of physical illness!)

✗ **Relies on self-report, not objective tests:** Unlike doctors, psychiatrists have few objective tests for mental illnesses. Instead, they rely on patient self-reports. This has led to cases where people have successfully pretended to be mentally ill, which challenges the accuracy of mental illness diagnosis (see Rosenhan above).

✗ • ✓ **Treats symptoms, not causes:** Physiological treatments alleviate the symptoms, but don't treat the root cause. Symptoms recur when physiological treatments stop. This leads many patients to be re-admitted to hospitals, the so-called 'revolving door' syndrome. However, if the main symptom of depression is the feeling of depression and drugs stop this, then perhaps the medical approach has succeeded. Indeed, the original cause of the depression may not be worth pursuing, since the main problem (feeling of depression) no longer exists. The root cause may also be impossible to detect.

✗ **Cause and effect problem:** It's not clear whether some physiological abnormalities are the cause of the illness or one of its effects. For example, does excess dopamine in the brain cause schizophrenia, or is it merely the effect?

✗ **Culture-bound syndromes:** Not all mental illnesses are universal. Those which only occur in particular cultures are called 'culture-bound syndromes' (as explained above). Such syndromes aren't easily explained by the medical model.

✗ **The myth of mental illness:** Szasz (1962) was a leading member of the so-called anti-psychiatry movement. He believed that since the mind doesn't exist as a physical organ, it can't be diseased. Abnormal behaviours are thus viewed as 'problems in living'. Szasz believed that diagnosis of mental illness is used as a form of 'social control'. Laing (1959) also controversially viewed mental illness as a sane response to an insane world.

✗ **Labelling and stigma:** The medical approach tends to lead to labelling of patients. Labels are definitions which when applied to people identify what they are. Mental illness terms often identify the whole person ('schizophrenics' rather than a person with schizophrenia). This doesn't occur to the same extent with physical illnesses. Labelling may lead to a *self-fulfilling prophecy*, whereby a person identified as mentally ill *actually* becomes mentally ill. Once labelling has occurred, stigma can result. Stigma is a 'mark' that sets people apart on the basis of an undesirable characteristic. The mentally ill often suffer from such stigma.

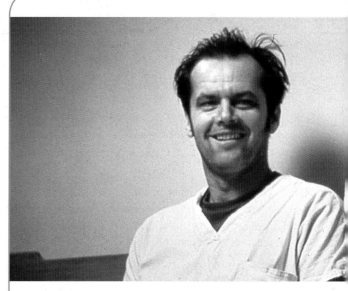

One Flew Over the Cuckoo's Nest explored the treatment of mental illness as a form of social control

Psychodynamic model
ASSUMPTIONS/CAUSES

The psychodynamic approach explains the forces or dynamics that determine behaviour. The best known example of this was proposed by Sigmund Freud. Although subsequently developed by others, there are some commonly agreed key assumptions:

- **Mental illness is psychological in origin:** The psychodynamic approach suggests that abnormality occurs as a result of psychological, not physical problems (in contrast to the medical approach).

- **The importance of the unconscious:** Although, by definition, the unconscious isn't accessible to the conscious mind, it plays a major role in determining behaviour. The term 'dynamic unconscious' is used to explain why people don't know the reasons for their behaviour. There's an assumption that abnormal behaviours occur due to unconscious problems or forces.

- **Three components to the personality: id, ego, superego:** Freud stated that there were three components to the personality or psyche. The *id* is present at birth. This represents a person's instinctual, basic drives related to sex and aggression. Later, people are socialised into the moral standards of their culture and develop a *superego*. This represents their conscience. These two parts of the personality are in conflict and therefore need to be managed by the third part of the personality, the ego. When this balance isn't achieved, abnormal behaviour may result. For example, anxiety disorders may occur from an over-developed superego (conscience). Since these processes occur at an unconscious level, people aren't aware of them.

- **Importance of childhood experiences:** Freud argued that childhood experiences play a crucial part in adult development. Particularly distressing events in childhood may also become part of the unconscious. Although unconscious, they may be expressed in later abnormal behaviours.

The conflict between the superego and the id

EXAM tips BOX

Briefly describe and evaluate the biological (medical) approach to abnormality. (18 marks)

● Again, the three-paragraph approach could be employed. You'll have to briefly *describe* the biological (medical) approach in the first paragraph. This could include details of the assumptions of, and treatments used within the approach (AO1–6 marks).

● In the second paragraph, you could *analyse and evaluate* material that *supports* the biological approach. These include the humane nature of the approach, supporting physiological evidence, and studies that demonstrate the effectiveness of biologically based treatments.

● In the final paragraph you could analyse and evaluate material that *criticises or rejects* the approach. The validity of diagnosis, the reductionist nature of the approach, the denial of responsibility, and the treatment of symptoms could be included (AO2 – 12 marks).

● Examiners will be expecting an answer about 300–350 words long.

There's a 'sample' answer at the end of the book. Try not to look at it until you've had a go at doing it yourself.

● **Psychosexual developmental stages:** Freud argued that children pass through a number of psychosexual stages. Conflicts that occur during these stages can affect later behaviour. The stages are:

● **Oral stage (0–1 year):** The primary source of pleasure is the mouth and sucking.

● **Anal stage (1–3 years):** The primary source of pleasure involves the membranes of the anal region.

● **Phallic stage (3–6 years):** The primary source of pleasure comes from the genitals.

● **Latency stage: (6–12 years):** The development of other activities means less concentration on sexual areas.

● **Genital stage (puberty onwards):** The primary source of pleasure is through heterosexual relationships.

Freud believed that people can become stuck or 'fixated' at any of these stages. This will also affect later behaviour. For example, someone who smokes is described as having an 'oral' personality, since they gain pleasure through the mouth. Someone who is excessively tidy and obsessive might be described as having an 'anal' personality.

● **Defence mechanisms:** Childhood conflicts cause anxiety, and the ego uses a number of defence mechanisms to keep these thoughts in the unconscious. *Repression* is the major defence mechanism, whereby traumatic events are forced into the unconscious (see page 18). Defence mechanisms help to reduce anxiety, but don't resolve deep psychological problems.

TREATMENT

● The main therapeutic goal is to make the 'unconscious conscious', in order to reveal the true cause of any psychological problems.

● Patients are encouraged to develop 'insight' (enhanced self-knowledge and understanding) in order to deal with their problems.

● Patients try to regress back to their childhood in order to re-experience feelings and conflicts.

● Therapeutic techniques to help this include:

  ● Dream interpretation: Freud believed that dreams represented the disguised fulfilment of suppressed wishes, and that the latent (or hidden) content of dreams helped to uncover the unconscious.

  ● Free association: involves the patient talking freely without prompting or interruption. Hence, this therapy is often called 'the talking cure'.

● The analyst also takes note of non-verbal (or para-linguistic) communication, such as hesitations, slips of the tongue (Freudian slips) or even silence about a particular subject. All this information provides clues about what's happening in the unconscious.

● The analyst interprets what the patient says or does and makes use of symbolism (one thing representing another). For example, a dream about 'climbing the stairs' might be interpreted as symbolic of sexual intercourse.

Psychodynamic therapies remain controversial:

● They're expensive and are usually long-term. Indeed, patients can become dependent on their therapist.

● Its effectiveness is also questioned. Eysenck (1952) reviewed 7000 cases and claimed it doesn't work and can be detrimental to patients since it might 'reveal' disturbing repressed thoughts. Such thoughts can be viewed as possible 'side-effects' of psychodynamic therapy.

EVALUATION OF PSYCHODYNAMIC APPROACH

Sometimes in psychodynamic therapy, silence speaks louder than words

✔ **Psychological factors:** Freud was the first to stress the importance of psychological factors causing abnormal behaviour. He argued that psychological problems can result in physical symptoms – an accepted viewpoint today. However, physiological factors are largely ignored.

✘ • ✔ **Importance of childhood:** Most psychologists would accept that childhood is an important, influential factor in future adult development. Indeed, many people suffering from psychological problems can recount childhood difficulties. However, the original model over-emphasised childhood influences and ignored the everyday problems faced by the adult patients. Current psychodynamic therapy recognises this.

✔ **Importance of the unconscious:** Many people would agree that unconscious processes do have an effect on human behaviour.

✔ **Influential theory:** Freud remains the best known psychologist of all time and psychoanalysis the most influential theory. His ideas appear strange to some whilst others pay for therapy based on them. Freud's ideas have found expression in many other domains including art, film, literature and so on. An unimportant theory would have been dismissed years ago. In addition, Freudian terminology has been adopted into everyday language and conversation.

✘ **Problems validating the theory:** It's impossible to scientifically test some of the model. The subtlety and complexity of the theory means it's not suited to empirical research. The strength of the evidence remains variable. Sometimes, interpretation plays a major part in the theory. For example, if a patient 'uncovers' painful childhood memories this can be taken as a cause of any later abnormal behaviour. If they don't uncover or recall anything, it can be claimed that they still happened but remain hidden in their unconscious. Both interpretations can be used to support the model!

✘ **Poor methodology:** The dominant use of case studies in psychodynamic therapy is unscientific. Evidence produced by therapists is subjective and biased. Indeed, Freud was accused by his own patients of exaggerating the effectiveness of his therapy (Woods, 1990). Freud's patients were mainly middle class, Viennese women. Whether findings from such a sample can be generalised into a universal theory is open to question.

Give a brief account of the psychodynamic approach to abnormality and assess its strengths and limitations. (18 marks)

● A very straightforward question. The only difficulty here is that there is so much information that could be included on the psychodynamic approach. Your answer can follow the structure used with the biological approach question above.

● You'll have to briefly *describe* the psychodynamic approach in the first paragraph (AO1 – 6 marks).

● In the second paragraph, you could *analyse and evaluate* material that supports the psychodynamic approach. In the final paragraph you could analyse and evaluate material that criticises or rejects the approach (AO2 – 12 marks).

There's a 'sample' answer at the end of the book. Try not to look at it until you've had a go at doing it yourself (300–350 word minimum).

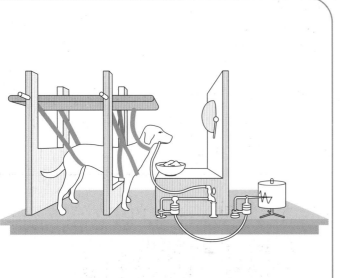

Figure 4.2 The apparatus used by Pavlov in his experiments on conditioned reflexes

✖ **Over-emphasis on sexual factors:** Freud believed that sexual factors were a major cause of abnormal behaviour. Nowadays, other factors such as social relationships are recognised as important. Indeed, it's argued that inadequate inter-personal relationships can also cause sexual problems. Freud's ideas on sexual repression may be less relevant in today's sexually permissive society.

✖ **Blames parents:** Since people cannot really influence their own personality, it's assumed that people aren't to blame for their illness. However, given the importance of childhood conflicts, parents might feel the blame for any subsequent abnormal behaviour in their children. The individual is seen as the result of their parenting. Child abuse cases are cited as evidence to support this, although so-called 'recovered memory syndrome' has been questioned (see page 18).

Behavioural model
ASSUMPTIONS/CAUSES

The behavioural model concentrates on observable behaviour, not on physical or psychological processes. It's associated with maladaptive behaviour, not mental illness.

● **All behaviour is learnt:** All behaviour (both normal and abnormal) is learnt through the processes of classical and operant conditioning.

Classical conditioning is 'learning through association'. It was first proposed by Ivan Pavlov who noticed that his laboratory dogs had learnt to salivate to the sound of the footsteps of the man who fed them. They'd learnt to associate the footsteps with food. Later, Pavlov classically conditioned the dogs to salivate to the sound of a bell that he rang before giving them their food (see Figure 4.2).

Classical conditioning can apply to abnormal behaviour. For example, a phobia may develop when children see the fear of their parents when confronted by a spider. They learn to associate the fear with the spider.

Operant conditioning is 'learning through the consequences of behaviour'. If a behaviour is rewarded (reinforced) then it will be maintained or increase. If it's punished, then it will cease. Skinner investigated operant conditioning using pigeons and rats in a laboratory.

Again, operant conditioning can apply to abnormal behaviour. For example, adolescents who are criticised or ridiculed (punished) for being fat, may stop eating to reduce their weight and develop an eating disorder.

● **Abnormal behaviour can be unlearnt using the same learning (conditioning) principles:** The case study of Little Albert demonstrates how a phobia can be acquired through classical conditioning. Watson & Raynor (1920) proposed to rid Little Albert of his fears through counter-conditioning. They planned to do this by pairing a pleasurable stimulus or reward (e.g. a sweet) with the sight of the rat. Unfortunately, they didn't get the chance when Albert was withdrawn from the study. The ethics of this study left a lot to be desired!

In an experiment that would today be regarded as unethical, Watson & Rayner (1920) classically conditioned a fear response in a young child called Albert. According to Jones (1925):

'Albert, eleven months of age, was an infant with a phlegmatic disposition, afraid of nothing "under the sun" except a loud noise made by striking a steel bar. This made him cry. By striking the bar at the same time that Albert touched a white rat, the fear was transferred to the white rat. After seven combined stimulations, rat and sound, Albert not only became greatly disturbed at the sight of the rat, but this fear had spread to include a white rabbit, cotton wool, a fur coat and the experimenter's [white] hair. It did not transfer to wooden blocks and other objects very dissimilar to the rat.'

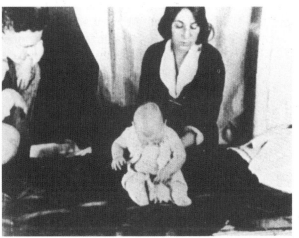

A very rare photograph of John Watson and Rosalie Rayner during the conditioning of Little Albert.

TREATMENT

● The aim of therapy is to change maladaptive behaviour by replacing it with appropriate learnt behaviour.

● According to behaviourist theory, abnormal behaviours can be objectively measured and therapies can be planned to modify them using conditioning principles. They fit into two types:

   ● **behaviour therapy** based on classical conditioning principles
   ● **behaviour modification** based on operant conditioning principles.

● *Systematic desensitisation* is an example of behaviour therapy. This might involve a phobic (person with a phobia) confronting a feared object (e.g. spider) in a relaxed situation and associating these calm feelings with the object.

● *Token economies* are examples of behaviour modification. This involves the reinforcement of appropriate behaviour through the use of tokens that can be exchanged for privileges. For example, anorexics who eat all their meals might be given tokens that can be exchanged for rewards, such as home visits away from the hospital.

● Behaviourists seek to treat the symptoms, not the causes of abnormal behaviour. They believe that the symptoms are the problem, and that searching for the causes is likely to be fruitless. After all, if you can alleviate the symptoms of depression, what does it matter what the underlying causes are? Critics claim that symptoms are merely the 'tip of the ice-

Arachnophobia can be successfully treated using systematic desensitisation

berg', underlying causes remain, and 'symptom substitution' will occur. That is, other abnormal symptoms will replace the symptoms which have been removed.

EXAM tips BOX

Give a brief account of the behavioural model of abnormality and consider its strengths and limitations. (18 marks)

● Follow the answer structure suggested with the other approaches above.

● You'll have to briefly *describe* the behavioural approach in the first paragraph (AO1 – 6 marks).

● In the second paragraph, you could *analyse and evaluate* the model by outlining the strengths of the behavioural approach. In the final paragraph you could *analyse and evaluate* by presenting material that shows limitations of the model (AO2 – 12 marks).

There's a 'sample' answer at the end of the book. Try not to look at it until you've had a go at doing it yourself.

EVALUATION OF BEHAVIOURAL APPROACH

✔ **Experimentally tested:** The principles of learning have been, and continue to be, tested empirically in the laboratory. The concentration on observable behaviour means it can be objectively measured.

✔ **Present, not past:** The behavioural approach concentrates on the 'here and now' rather than delving into the past. This is advantageous since many people don't know the past causes for their abnormal behaviour and it's more important to sort out present symptoms. But it's also important to try to uncover the causes, otherwise the abnormal behaviour may reappear.

✔ **Effective treatments:** Behavioural treatments are effective for certain disorders, such as obsessive-compulsive disorders and phobias. They are less effective for more serious disorders, such as schizophrenia.

✔ **Accounts for cultural differences:** The behavioural model recognises the importance of the environment in shaping behaviour. Thus, it does take into account cultural differences.

✘ **Simple, mechanistic model:** The behavioural approach suggests that humans are simple mechanisms at the mercy of stimulus-response behaviours. The approach ignores people's complex thought processes. This is a reductionist, dehumanising approach.

✘ **Animal studies:** The principles of learning have been tested mainly on animals and such findings may not be totally applicable to more complex human behaviour.

✘ **Ethical treatment?** Some behavioural treatments are used without the consent of patients. In addition, certain treatments use punishments to change behaviour, and these can cause pain or discomfort to patients. Behaviourists would agree that this is undesirable, but necessary. Behavioural techniques can be used as a form of 'social control' to manipulate people's behaviour.

Cognitive model

ASSUMPTIONS/CAUSES

Inevitably, the cognitive model concentrates on the individual's thought processes. The disturbed individual is affected by disturbed thoughts. This approach sees the individual as an active processor of information. It's the way individuals perceive, anticipate and evaluate events, rather than the events themselves, which have the greatest impact on behaviour. Psychologists most associated with this approach are Beck and Ellis.

● **Cognitions affect behaviour:** Behaviour is primarily affected by an individual's thoughts and cognitions. Healthy cognitions lead to normal behaviour, whereas faulty cognitions lead to abnormal behaviour. Beck (1967) called these irrational thoughts 'cognitive errors'.

● **Cognitive errors:** Individuals try to make sense of their world through cognitive processes. *Automatic thoughts* are thoughts that occur without thinking. People with psychological problems tend to have more negative automatic thoughts. *Attributions* refer to people's attempts to make sense and explain their own and others' behaviour. People with psychological problems may make more inaccurate attributions. For example, they may attribute a failed relationship to their own lack of social skill. In addition, people suffering from psychological problems may have inaccurate *expectations*. For example, they may *expect* their relationships to end in failure. Such expectations will make it more likely to happen in reality – *a self-fulfilling prophecy*. In effect, people with psychological problems may lack confidence in their own ability to achieve the goals they want to in life. These illogical thoughts may not reflect reality. Nevertheless, these negative thoughts will adversely affect their behaviour.

● **Cognitive processes can be faulty in many ways:** These include:

(a) *Over-generalisation*: a conclusion is reached on the basis of one event or incident. For example, missing a penalty at football means you're completely useless in life.

(b) *Magnification and minimisation*: This involves magnifying failures and minimising successes. The glass is half-empty rather than half-full.

Our own interpretation of events can affect future outcomes

● **Cognitions can be monitored and altered:** It's assumed that all biased cognitions can be replaced by more appropriate ones (see treatment below).

● **Cognitive change will lead to behaviour change:** It's assumed that changing faulty thinking will lead to a change in behaviour.

TREATMENT

● Cognitive therapy involves *cognitive restructuring*. This refers to techniques used to make a patient's irrational and negative thoughts more rational and positive. The therapist's aim is to challenge the patient's thinking and to show how irrational their thoughts are. Patients are taught to monitor negative automatic thoughts and examine the evidence that supports them. In this way, patients may learn to see why they hold distorted thoughts.

● Cognitive therapy depends on an individual being able to talk about their thought processes lucidly. Hence, the method doesn't work for particularly severe mental disorders such as schizophrenia.

● Beck's cognitive therapy is often used for depression. Beck proposed the *cognitive triad*, where a patient has negative thoughts about themselves, about the world, and about the future (these form the triad). Therapy is a collaborative process between the patient and therapist. The first step involves identifying the problem and the desired goal. The next step involves challenging negative thoughts associated with the depression. The patient may be asked to undertake 'homework' between sessions to test these thoughts. For example, recording the number of times someone is rude to them. They may be pleasantly surprised that people aren't 'always nasty' to them as they thought. The last step involves the patient monitoring their own perceptions accurately.

Beck's Cognitive Triad

EVALUATION OF COGNITIVE MODEL

✔ **Concentrates on current cognitions:** The cognitive model doesn't delve into the past to try to sort out problems. It concentrates on the individual's current thought processes.

✔ **Research evidence:** Many people suffering from anxiety disorders and/or depression do appear to report irrational thought processes.

✔ **Influential and popular model:** Currently, the cognitive approach seems to be favoured in many fields of psychology. The cognitive approach to abnormality is no different, and many cognitive therapists practice successfully within the NHS.

✔ **Empowers the individual:** The individual is given responsibility to change their cognitions. As such, it presents a positive view of humankind.

✘ **Underplays physiological and environmental influences:** Evidence suggests that physiological factors and past events can affect an individual's behaviour. These social aspects are largely ignored with this approach. This (over) emphasis on cognitive processes has led to criticisms that the cognitive model is reductionist and mechanistic.

✘ **Unscientific:** Since thoughts can't be observed or measured, it's been claimed that the cognitive approach is unscientific.

Sometimes being depressed is entirely rational

✘ **Cause and effect problem?** It's uncertain whether irrational beliefs cause the anxiety disorder/depression, or whether they are merely a by-product (effect) of the disorder.

✘ **Individual blame:** Since disorders result from an individual's faulty thinking, it's clear that any blame for the disorder rests with the individual. This can have the unfortunate side-effect of making the disorder worse. It might also be unfair, since factors beyond the individual's control might be seen as contributory factors to their mental disorder.

✘ **Is thinking irrational?** There are two associated problems with questioning someone's thought processes. Firstly, given some people's lives, is their thinking so irrational? Depression may be a rational response to one's (miserable) life. It's been claimed that many depressives have a more realistic view of life than 'normal' people. Viewing the world through rose-coloured spectacles might be equally irrational yet psychologically healthy! Secondly, should a therapist argue that someone is thinking irrationally when their life circumstances appear to support that pessimistic view?

CRITICAL ISSUE: EATING DISORDERS – ANOREXIA NERVOSA (AN) AND BULIMIA NERVOSA (BN)

Increasing numbers of sufferers from eating disorders have been reported in the last 20 years. The two most common eating disorders are anorexia nervosa (AN) and bulimia nervosa (BN).

Clinical characteristics of anorexia nervosa (AN)

There are estimated to be 70,000 people with AN in Britain. AN literally means *'nervous loss of appetite'*.

- AN is primarily a female disorder, which usually (but not exclusively) occurs during adolescence.

- There is a refusal to maintain normal body weight. Individuals have to weigh less than 85% of their normal body weight to be diagnosed as anorexics.

- Anorexics have an intense fear of being over-weight. This continues even when their actual body weight is extremely low. This distorted body image is not evident to anorexics themselves.

- There's a general physical decline. This can include cessation of menstruation (amenorrhoea), low blood pressure, dry, cracking skin, constipation and insufficient sleep. Depression and low self-esteem are also common, and approximately 6% of AN cases are fatal (ANAD, 2003).

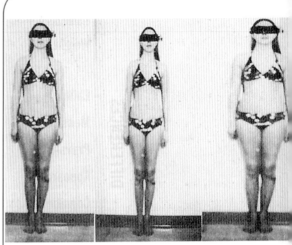

Body dysmorphia: most anorexics perceive themselves to be larger than they actually are (shown by their choice of adjusted photos)

Clinical characteristics of bulimia nervosa (BN)

BN can be viewed as a variation of AN. BN is more common than AN, affecting as much as 5% of the population. BN literally means *'ox hunger'*.

- BN is characterised by periods of binge eating, frequently followed by purging. Binge eating involves the rapid consumption of large amounts of high calorific foods. Purging involves the expulsion of the food through the use of laxatives or vomiting. Sometimes coloured 'marker' foods are consumed, so the bulimic will recognise when all food has been purged.

- Bulimics have an intense fear of fatness, and are pre-occupied with their body weight and shape. The discrepancy between actual body size and desired body size is considerable.

- Bulimics feel guilt about their binge/purge episodes, and are aware of their problem.

- Bulimics tend to try to keep their disorder a secret. This is often successful, since the physical effects of the disorder are less obvious than with AN.

- Physical effects of BN include: a swollen face, deterioration of tooth enamel, and digestive tract damage. These are caused by stomach acids during vomiting. Sleep problems, anxiety and depression are also common.

In a 1995 Panorama interview, Princess Diana admitted to being bulimic, a fact she'd managed to keep secret for many years

ESSENTIAL STUDY 5.1

Asch's (1951) **Comparison-Of-Lines Experiment** (COLE)

Aims (AO1)

Asch criticised an earlier study by Sherif (1935). Sherif claimed that when people are unsure about the answer to a question, they use others' answers to guide them. He gave his participants an *ambiguous* task. (This involved estimating how far a light moved that actually didn't move at all, as when you look at a lighted cigarette in a completely dark room.) So, there couldn't be any right or wrong answers.

Asch argued that Sherif hadn't demonstrated conformity at all. The true test of conformity is to see if people will agree with others when the experimental task is *unambiguous*.

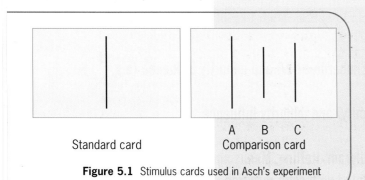

Standard card

A B C
Comparison card

Figure 5.1 Stimulus cards used in Asch's experiment

Procedures (AO1)

Asch showed participants two cards (as in Figure 5.1).

He then asked them to say which of the comparison lines was the same length as the standard line. This was repeated 17 times (making 18 trials altogether). On every trial, the correct answer was obvious to anyone with normal eyesight. This happened in groups of 7–9 people, but only *one* participant was naïve. The others were **stooges** (or accomplices). Asch had briefed them beforehand about what answers to give on particular trials. The stooges gave their answers, in turn, and the naïve participant was the last (or last-but-one) to answer.

On the first two trials, the stooges gave the correct answer (*neutral trials*). But on the third trial, all the stooges gave the same wrong answer (*critical trial*). There were 11 more critical trials (making 12 in all), and four more neutral trials (six in all) between the critical trials.

Findings (AO1)

The crucial measure was how often naïve participants gave the same wrong answer as the stooges on the critical trials. This was a measure of conformity. Overall, there was a 32% conformity rate. In other words, participants agreed with the wrong answer on about a third of the critical trials. But there were important *individual differences*. For example, no one conformed on all the critical trials, and about 25% didn't conform even once. About 75% conformed at least once.

A minority of one faces a unanimous majority

Conclusions (AO1)

Because the answers on the critical trials were obviously incorrect, Asch's study shows the impact that a majority can have on an individual. However, the majority doesn't have the same impact on every individual. In fact, Asch was interested in the social and personal conditions that help individuals *resist* group pressure.

ESSENTIAL STUDY

Criticisms (AO1/AO2)

✓ **The task was unambiguous.** Control participants who performed the line-matching task individually hardly ever made mistakes. Therefore, conformity rate could be measured in an objective way.

✗ **Participants were stressed.** Some participants reported getting quite stressed when the stooges gave the wrong answer on critical trials. This could be considered unethical. Also, they were clearly deceived about what was really going on.

✗ **The artificiality of COLE.** In everyday life, we're unlikely to disagree with other people so fundamentally about the 'correct' answer. Real-life situations are rarely as clear-cut as this.

EVALUATION OF ASCH'S CONFORMITY RESEARCH

✓ **The Asch paradigm.** Asch's method for studying conformity has been adopted by many other researchers. It's a 'way of doing' conformity research.

✗ **It's uneconomical and time-consuming.** Only one naïve participant is tested at a time. Crutchfield (1954) tested participants in separate booths. Each booth had a panel of lights, which supposedly showed other participants' answers. This way, he was able to test several participants at once.

✓ **Majority size or unanimous majority?** In later experiments, Asch found that it wasn't the size of the majority that mattered. The crucial factor was whether or not the stooges agreed with each other (that is, were they *unanimous*). So, if one stooge gave a different answer from the rest (there was a *dissenter*), naïve participants were more likely to give the correct answer. That is, they were more likely to resist group pressure. The dissenting stooge seems to give the naïve participant moral support ("If he disagrees with them, why shouldn't I?").

✓ **Task difficulty.** In another experiment, Asch made the comparison lines more similar (making the task more ambiguous and consequently more difficult). This increased conformity.

✗ **Replication of Asch's findings.** Other American (and British) researchers have not always replicated Asch's findings. For example, some have found *lower* conformity rates than Asch. But others have found similar rates to Asch. This suggests that conformity in experiments may reflect current social and political conditions.

✗ **Cross-cultural studies.** Generally, people in Western cultures (such as the US and the UK) are *less* likely to conform than people in non-Western countries (such as Japan and Africa).

✗ **Who's the real minority and majority?** The numerical majority (the stooges) actually represent an unorthodox, unconventional (*minority*) viewpoint. The numerical minority (the naïve participants) represent the conventional, traditional (*majority*) 'truth'. This minority influenced the majority a third of the time (Moscovici & Faucheux, 1972: see Essential Study 5.3, pages 112–13).

ESSENTIAL STUDY 5.2

Zimbardo *et al's* (1973) **Prison Experiment** (PE)

Aims (AO1)

The study is relevant to understanding obedience (see pages 115–122), as well as conformity. It also demonstrates the *power of social situations* on people's behaviour. Specifically, Zimbardo *et al* were testing (and trying to find evidence against) the **dispositional hypothesis**. According to this, the dehumanising effects of the prison system are due to prisoners' antisocial attitudes and behaviour, and guards' sadism and insensitivity.

Participants were carefully selected for *not* displaying any of these characteristics. They were randomly assigned to the role of prisoner or guard. This meant that any antisocial behaviour or sadism they showed was caused by the prison conditions, not by participants' personal characteristics.

A mock (**simulated**) prison was deliberately created (in the basement of the Stanford University psychology department). Hence, the study is often called the 'prison simulation experiment' (or the 'Stanford prison study'). Zimbardo *et al* wished to create a prison-like environment, which was as psychologically real as possible.

Procedures (AO1)

Participants were recruited through newspaper advertisements asking for male student volunteers for a two-week study of prison life. From 75 volunteers, 24 were selected. They were judged to be emotionally stable, physically healthy, and of 'normal to average' personality. They also had no history of psychiatric problems, and had never been in trouble with the police. They were all white, middle-class students from across the US.

Those allocated to the prisoner role were arrested by the local police. They were charged with a felony, read their rights, searched, handcuffed, and taken to the police station to be 'booked'. After being fingerprinted, each prisoner was taken blindfold to the basement prison. On arrival, they were stripped naked and issued with a loose-fitting smock. Their ID number was printed on the front and back, and they had a chain bolted around one ankle. They wore a nylon stocking to cover their hair, were referred to by number only, and were allocated to 6 x 9 ft 'cells' (three to a cell).

The guards wore military-style khaki uniforms and silver reflector sunglasses (making eye contact impossible). They carried clubs, whistles, handcuffs, and keys to the cells. There were guards on duty 24 hours a day, each working eight-hour shifts. They had complete control over the prisoners, who were confined to their cells around the clock – except for meals, toilet privileges, head counts, and work.

Findings (AO1)

An initial 'rebellion' by the prisoners was crushed. After this, they began to react passively as the guards stepped up their aggression. They began to feel helpless and no longer in control of their lives. Every guard at some time or another behaved in an abusive, authoritarian way. Many seemed to really enjoy the new-found power and control that went with the uniform.

After less than 36 hours, one prisoner had to be released because of uncontrolled crying, fits of rage, disorganised thinking, and severe depression. Three others developed the same symptoms, and were released on successive days. Another prisoner developed a rash over his whole body. They became demoralised and apathetic, and started to refer to themselves (and others) by their numbers.

Zimbardo *et al* intended the experiment to run for two weeks. But it was abandoned after just six days, because of the prisoners' pathological reactions.

Conclusions (AO1)

Zimbardo *et al* rejected the dispositional hypothesis. They argued that their findings supported the **situational hypothesis**. This claims that it's the conditions of prisons (physical, social and psychological) that are 'to blame', *not* the characteristics of prisoners and guards. So, anyone given the role of guard or prisoner would probably behave as Zimbardo *et al*'s participants did. A brutalising atmosphere, like the mock prison, produces brutality. If the roles had been reversed, the prisoners would have abused their power in just the same way. It's the prison environment that makes people act in 'typical guard' or 'typical prisoner' ways.

Criticisms (AO1/AO2)

✓ **High ecological validity.** Both the environment and the behaviour (of guards and prisoners) were 'realistic', and the findings can be applied to real prisons.

✗ **Mere role-playing.** Participants were acting out their prior expectations about how guards and prisoners *should* behave (based on TV, movies etc.). In other words, they were *conforming*, but this wasn't so much yielding to group pressure as trying to be a 'typical' guard or prisoner.

✓ **The reality of roles.** They may have been role-playing at the start. But participants were soon taking their roles very seriously indeed – they became 'real'.

✓ **Relevant to social influence.** The experiment relates to various forms of social influence. These include both conformity and obedience.

✓ **Informed consent.** Participants signed an informed consent form before the experiment began. They were told a great deal about the experiment – its purpose, what was likely to happen and so on. But they *weren't* told about how they'd be arrested (see **Critical Issue** pages 122–6).

✗ **Zimbardo's loss of objectivity.** Zimbardo *et al* should have stopped the experiment long before six days. Zimbardo admitted that he became too involved in his role as prison supervisor. An outsider had to remind him that he was also the psychologist in charge of the study!

✓ **Practical consequences.** The experiment had practical implications for the welfare of prisoners.

A prisoner in one of the cells, and a guard asserting his authority over a prisoner

Minority influence

We usually interpret the findings from Asch's experiments as showing how a powerful majority influences an isolated individual. In other words, conformity involves majority influence (see pages 107–10). But is the numerical majority always more powerful? Even in Asch's original experiment, there was *no* conformity on two-thirds of the critical trials. What's more, the numerical minority can sometimes change the views of the majority (minority influence).

ESSENTIAL STUDY 5.3

Moscovici *et al's* (1969) **Green Colour Slide Experiment** (GCSE)

Aims (AO1)

Moscovici *et al* were trying to demonstrate minority influence. The experimental task involved naming the colour of slides. The task was an objective one (there was a right and wrong answer, as in Asch's experiment). Consequently, it might seem very unlikely that a minority could persuade the majority to give the wrong answer. But Moscovici *et al* predicted that a minority could exert influence over a majority if it *consistently* called a green slide blue.

Procedures (AO1)

Moscovici *et al* used groups of six participants, of whom four were naïve and two were stooges. The stooges played the role of the minority. Before the experiment began, Moscovici *et al* tested all the participants' colour vision. They all passed the test! This meant that the naïve participants couldn't explain the stooges' wrong answers by claiming they were colour blind. All the participants gave their answers aloud. The stooges sat either in the first and second position, or first and fourth.

On 36 separate trials, a slide that was clearly blue was presented on a screen. In the *consistent condition,* the stooges called it green *every time.* In the *inconsistent condition*, they answered 'green' 24 times and 'blue' 12 times. There was also a *control condition*, where the groups consisted of six naïve participants.

Findings (AO1)

In the *control condition*, there were fewer than 1% green responses. This showed how obvious the correct response was. In the *inconsistent condition*, 1.25% of responses were green. In the *consistent condition*, green responses were made over 8% of the time. This was significantly more than in the other two conditions. 32% of naïve participants gave at least one green response.

Moscovici *et al* found that there were really two types of group. In one type, nobody was influenced by the minority. In the other, several were influenced. Where the stooges sat made no difference.

Conclusions (AO1)

The experiment clearly showed that a consistent minority can affect the judgements made by the majority. Although the minority doesn't have a numerical advantage, their consistent behavioural style makes them influential. In conformity experiments, the influence of the majority is evident from the start. In contrast, minority influence only begins to show after a while.

ESSENTIAL STUDY

Criticisms (AO1/AO2)

✓ **Important early study.** This was one of the first attempts to demonstrate *minority influence*.

✗ **Ethical issues.** Naïve participants couldn't give their *informed consent*. As with any study involving stooges, participants were deceived as to the true purpose of the experiment.

✗ **Artificiality.** As with Asch's experiments, the experimental task was very artificial. So, the experiment may lack *ecological validity*.

No consistency: no minority influence

Consistency doesn't necessarily have to involve repeating the same response, as in the Moscovici *et al* experiment. This was demonstrated by Nemeth *et al* (1974).

● This was basically a replication of Moscovici *et al*'s (1969) experiment. But Nemeth *et al* added two conditions, in which the stooges said 'green' on half the trials and 'green-blue' on the other half.

● In the *random condition*, the green and green-blue responses were randomly distributed across the trials (there was *no* consistency in their responses). In the *correlated condition*, the stooges said green to the brighter slides and green-blue to the dimmer slides (or vice-versa). Whether they said green or green-blue depended on the brightness of the slide. So, there was a clear *pattern* to their responses.

● Compared to a no-influence *control condition*, the *random condition* had no effect. But in the *correlated condition*, almost 21% of the responses were wrong (minority) answers. Where stooges consistently repeated the green response, there was *no* minority influence. This contrasts with Moscovici *et al*'s findings.

● Nemeth *et al* showed that there's *more* to minority influence than just consistency. It also matters how the majority interprets the minority's answers. They must relate to the stimulus in some predictable way. Here, it was the brightness of the slide that counted.

🔍 **EXAM tips BOX**

Consider psychological research into majority influence (conformity). (18 marks)

● You could structure your answer in terms of three paragraphs, all about 100–130 words long.

● In the first paragraph, you should say what's meant by majority influence (conformity). You could then briefly *describe* some of the research findings using the *Asch paradigm*. (AO1, worth 6 marks).

● In the second paragraph, you could consider some of the strengths of this research. One way of doing this is to consider replications, as well as alternative ways of investigating majority influence.

● In the third paragraph, you could consider some of the limitations of this research. One way you could do this is to consider how Asch's findings have been reinterpreted by Moscovici in terms of *minority influence*. (AO2, worth 12 marks).

Remember that here you're analysing and evaluating the findings, rather than describing them. Try to write a suitable answer in about 300–350 words.

As with all questions, there's no single correct way of answering it. The above are just pointers. There's a sample answer at the end of the book. Try not to look at it until you've had a go at doing it yourself. Note that you could get a similar question on minority influence.

Why do people conform?

Deutsch & Gerard (1955) distinguished between informational social influence (ISI) and normative social influence (NSI). They felt this distinction was crucial for understanding majority group influence.

INFORMATIONAL SOCIAL INFLUENCE (ISI)

● We all have a basic need to be confident that our ideas and beliefs are correct (a need for certainty). This makes us feel in charge of our lives and in control of the world. This is the motive underlying **ISI**. When we're unsure about something, we tend to seek other people's opinions. If we know what they think, we're in a better position to form our own opinions. This is more likely to happen in situations we're not familiar with, or in ambiguous situations. For example, if you're voting in an election for the first time, you may be unsure which candidate to vote for. So, you may ask your friends who *they're* voting for to help you make up your own mind. This is **ISI**.

● The participants in Sherif's experiment were unsure how far the light moved (with good reason – it wasn't actually moving at all!). Similarly, when Asch made the comparison lines more similar the situation became more ambiguous – the correct answer was now much less obvious.

● If we conform because of ISI, it's very likely that we *really* believe the opinion we adopt. The whole point is that we're unsure what to believe, which is why we compare our own ideas with others' in the first place. So, we come to share their views (we're 'converted'). When Sherif's participants were later tested individually (away from the group), they stuck to the answer they'd given while in the group. This shows that they genuinely (privately) believed that the group was correct. In other words, they said what they believed and believed what they said. This kind of conformity is called **internalisation** or **true conformity**.

● Other people help us 'define social reality'. But it also matters *who* these other people are (Brown, 1988). We're only likely to be influenced by others' opinions in an ambiguous situation if we see ourselves as sharing important characteristics with them (Abrams *et al*, 1990). For example, you're more likely to internalise the views of other psychology students than those of, say, history students (assuming you're not doing history too).

NORMATIVE SOCIAL INFLUENCE (NSI)

● The motive underlying **NSI** is the need to be accepted by other people. We want others to like and respect us, and rejection is very painful. In these ways, people have the power to reward or punish us. A way of ensuring their acceptance is to agree with them. But this doesn't necessarily mean that we truly believe in what we say.

● For example, many of Asch's participants who'd conformed on the critical trials *knew* the stooges' answer was wrong. But if they gave the correct answer, they risked being laughed at by the majority (a form of rejection). They said things like "I didn't want to look stupid" or "I didn't want to be the odd-one-out". So, what they *said* (publicly) and what they *believed* (privately) were *different*. This kind of conformity is called **compliance**. It represents a compromise in situations where we face a *conflict* between our own and others' opinions. Sherif's participants didn't face any such conflict.

● However, we only experience conflict if we disagree with others whom we see as similar to us in some relevant way. The example above of being amongst other psychology students applies here too.

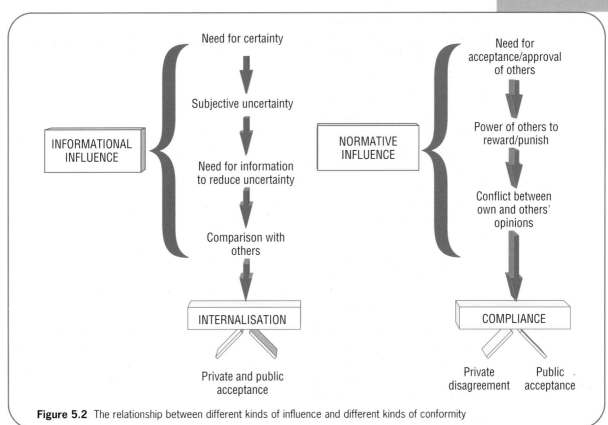

Figure 5.2 The relationship between different kinds of influence and different kinds of conformity

OBEDIENCE TO AUTHORITY

Obedience can be defined as complying with the demands or instructions of an authority figure. The authority figure has greater power and influence in that particular situation.

EXAM tips BOX

Give a brief account of psychological explanations of conformity and consider their strengths and limitations. (18 marks)

● You could structure your answer in terms of three paragraphs, all about 100–130 words long.

● *A word of warning: The question asks for 'explanations of conformity', so you must include at least two. If you wrote about more than two, you wouldn't be expected to give as much detail as for just two.*

● In the first paragraph, you could explain Deutsch & Gerard's (1955) distinction between ISI and NSI. You could also indicate how these are related to different kinds of conformity. (AO1, worth 6 marks).

● In the second paragraph, you could stress the evidence supporting NSI. This is seen most clearly in Asch's experiments. You could draw on some of the limitations of Asch's research when considering the limitations of the NSI explanation. More generally, must we choose between NSI and ISI?

● In the third paragraph , you could stress the evidence supporting ISI. This is seen most clearly in Sherif's experiment. In post-experimental interviews, participants said they didn't feel they'd been influenced by others' judgements. This supports Deutsch and Gerard's distinction between ISI and NSI. Again, you could draw on the limitations of Sherif's experiment when considering the limitations of the ISI explanation. (AO2, worth 12 marks).

Remember that here you're analysing and evaluating the findings, rather than describing them. Try to write a suitable answer in about 300–350 words. As with all questions, there's no single correct way of answering it. The above are just pointers. There's a sample answer at the end of the book. Try not to look at it until you've had a go at doing it yourself.

Table 5.1 Comparison between conformity and obedience

Conformity	*Obedience*
No one tells us what to do. There's no *explicit* requirement to act in a particular way.	The authority figure orders us to do something. So, there *is* an explicit requirement to act in a particular way.
The people who influence us are our *peers*, that is, our *equals*. They influence us by *example*, that is, we tend to behave as they do. In this way, everyone's behaviour becomes more similar.	The person who influences us has greater authority than we do in that particular situation. S/he influences us by *direction*, that is, by giving us orders or instructions. In this way, our behaviour is very different from the authority figure's.
We conform either because we want others to accept us, or because they provide us with important information. But we usually don't like to admit that we've been influenced by them.	We obey because we accept that society is organized in a *hierarchical* way, that is, some people have more power and influence than others. We don't mind admitting that we obey people 'in authority'.

ESSENTIAL STUDY 5.4

Milgram's (1963) 'Shocking Obedience Study' (SOS)

Aims (AO1)

Milgram set out to test the 'Germans are different' hypothesis. This claims that (a) the Germans are a highly obedient nation; and (b) Hitler couldn't have put his plans to exterminate the Jews in the 1930s and 40s into practice unless the German population had co-operated. This American experiment was meant to be a *pilot study*. He was going to carry out the 'real' experiment in Germany.

Procedures (AO1)

Participants volunteered for a study of memory and learning (see Figure 5.3, page 118). This was to take place at the Yale University psychology department. When they arrived, they were met by the experimenter wearing a grey lab coat. They were introduced to a Mr Wallace, who was a stooge pretending to be another participant.

The experimenter told the naïve participant and Mr Wallace that the experiment was about the effects of *punishment* on learning. One of them would be the 'teacher' and the other would be the 'learner'. Things were rigged in such a way that Mr Wallace was always the learner, and the participant the teacher.

The experimenter explained that the punishment was to take the form of electric shocks. All three then went into an adjoining room. There, the experimenter strapped Mr Wallace into a chair with his arms attached to electrodes. The teacher was to deliver the shocks via a shock generator. This was situated in an adjacent room. As the photo on page 118 shows, the generator had a number of switches. Each switch was clearly marked with a voltage level (starting at 15 volts) and a verbal description ('slight shock'). Each switch gave a shock 15 volts higher than the one before. The last switch gave 450 volts.

The teacher was instructed to deliver a shock each time Mr Wallace made a mistake on a paired-associate word task. Mr Wallace indicated his answer by switching on one of four lights located above the shock generator. With each successive mistake, the teacher had to give the next highest shock (that is, 15 volts higher than the one before).

At 300 volts, Mr Wallace kicked against the wall that adjoined the two rooms. After 315 volts, he stopped kicking and also stopped responding to the teacher's questions. The teacher was instructed to keep on shocking if Mr Wallace stopped answering.

Findings (AO1)

Obedience rate was defined as the percentage of participants who kept on giving shocks right up to 450 volts. Obedience rate was 65%. Many showed signs of extreme distress (such as twitching or giggling nervously, digging their nails into their flesh, and verbally attacking the experimenter). Whenever they threatened to pull out of the experiment, the experimenter would 'prod' them by saying:

- "Please continue" (or "Please go on").
- "The experiment requires that you continue".
- "It is absolutely essential that you continue".
- "You have no other choice, you *must* go on".

Conclusions (AO1)

The 'Germans are different' hypothesis was clearly false. Milgram's participants were 40 'ordinary' Americans living in a fairly typical small town. Their high level of obedience showed that we all tend to obey people we regard as authority figures in particular situations. If we had lived in Nazi Germany in the 1930s, we might well have acted just as obediently.

Criticisms (AO1/AO2)

✓ **Famous study:** This is one of the most famous studies in the whole of psychology.

✓ **Milgram paradigm:** It represents the first major attempt to study obedience experimentally, that is, under controlled conditions. Milgram established a basic method (a paradigm) for studying obedience in the lab. This is equivalent to Asch's paradigm for studying conformity.

✗·✓ **Pilot study:** Perhaps it's fairer (and more useful) to consider the research that it stimulated, rather than the study itself. Milgram had expected to find very *low* levels of obedience. So, he conducted several further studies to determine exactly *why* his American participants were so obedient.

✗·✓ **Unethical:** It was condemned for being *unethical* (e.g. Baumrind, 1964). Milgram exposed his participants to high levels of distress, which is ethically unacceptable. This provoked a major debate within psychology about ethics in research (see **Critical Issue**, page 122).

✗·✓ **Cross-cultural replications:** Milgram's experiment has been replicated in several other countries. These include Italy, Australia, the UK, Jordan, and Spain. But methodological differences between these studies make it difficult to compare the results.

ESSENTIAL STUDY 5.5

Public Announcement

WE WILL PAY YOU $4.00 FOR ONE HOUR OF YOUR TIME

Persons Needed for a Study of Memory

*We will pay five hundred New Haven men to help us complete a scientific study of memory and learning. The study is being done at Yale University.

*Each person who participates will be paid $4.00 (plus 50c carfare) for approximately 1 hour's time. We need you for only one hour: there are no further obligations. You may choose the time you would like to come (evenings, weekdays, or weekends).

*No special training, education, or experience is needed. We want:

Factory workers	Businessmen	Construction workers
City employees	Clerks	Salespeople
Laborers	Professional people	White-collar workers
Barbers	Telephone workers	Others

All persons must be between the ages of 20 and 50. High school and college students cannot be used.

*If you meet these qualifications, fill out the coupon below and mail it now to Professor Stanley Milgram, Department of Psychology, Yale University, New Haven. You will be notified later of the specific time and place of the study. We reserve the right to decline any application.

*You will be paid $4.00 (plus 50c carfare) as soon as you arrive at the laboratory.

TO:
PROF. STANLEY MILGRAM, DEPARTMENT OF PSYCHOLOGY, YALE UNIVERSITY, NEW HAVEN, CONN. I want to take part in this study of memory and learning. I am between the ages of 20 and 50. I will be paid $4.00 (plus 50c carfare) if I participate.

NAME (Please Print)...... ....

ADDRESS ....

TELEPHONE NO. .... Best time to call you ....

AGE........ OCCUPATION................... SEX......
CAN YOU COME:

WEEKDAYS .... EVENINGS ......WEEKENDS.........

Figure 5.3 Announcement in a local newspaper to recruit participants

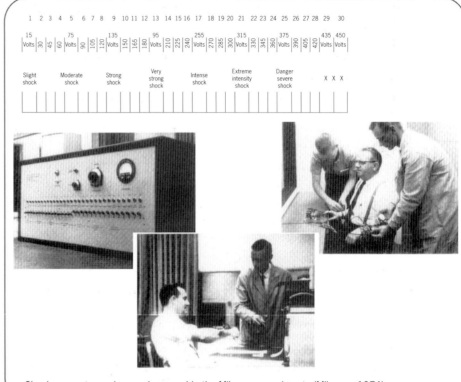

Shock generator and procedure used in the Milgram experiments (Milgram, 1974)

Some of Milgram's (1974) variations on his basic procedure

Aims (AO1)

This was basically the same in all cases, namely to change a *single* variable to see its effect on obedience rate. The *basic procedure* remained the same as in the original experiment (called the **remote victim** experiment).

Procedures (AO1) and Findings (AO1)

Voice feedback (VF)

The teacher heard a series of tape-recorded verbal responses. These were, supposedly, Mr Wallace's spontaneous reactions to the increasing shock levels. At first (75–105 volts), he made a little grunt. At 120 volts, he told the experimenter the shocks were getting painful. He then demanded to be let out, sometimes screaming in agony, sometimes refusing to give any more answers (150–315 volts). After 330 volts, there was silence! *Obedience rate* was 62.5%.

This became the new 'baseline'. In other words, in all the later experiments there was voice feedback, and some *other* variable was changed.

Proximity (P)

The teacher was now in the same room as Mr Wallace. They sat about 1.5 ft/46 cm apart, and the teacher could see as well as hear Mr Wallace's protests and screams. *Obedience rate:* 40%.

ESSENTIAL STUDY

Touch proximity (TP)

The teacher had to help keep Mr Wallace's arms down on the arms of the chair. The electric shock supposedly came through shock plates located on the arms. *Obedience rate: 30%.*

Remote authority (RA)

The experimenter left the room after giving the teacher the essential instructions. He gave all other instructions by phone. *Obedience rate: 20.5%.*

Two peers rebel (TPR)

The teacher was paired with two other (stooge) teachers. One stooge read out the list of word-pairs, while the other told Mr Wallace whether his answer was right or wrong. The teacher delivered the shocks. At 150 volts, the first stooge refused to continue and moved to another part of the room. At 210 volts, the second stooge did the same. The teacher had to take over the stooges' jobs. *Obedience rate: 10%.*

A peer administers shock (PAS)

The teacher was paired with another (stooge) teacher. It was the stooge's job to 'throw the switch'. *Obedience rate: 92.5%.*

Conclusions (AO1)

The 62.5% obedience rate in VF is still frighteningly high. Based on P and TP, it seems easier to resist the demands of an authority figure (disobey) when you can see for yourself the effects your behaviour has on the victim. RA suggests that it's easier to follow the dictates of our conscience when the authority figure isn't around. In TPR, participants see that it's *possible* to disobey and *how* to disobey. Some participants said they didn't realise they *could*. This is a demonstration of *conformity*.

Does Milgram's research have experimental and ecological validity?

✗ According to Orne & Holland (1968), Milgram's experiments lacked **experimental realism/validity.** That is, participants didn't believe that the experimental situation they found themselves in was real. In particular, they didn't think that Mr Wallace was really receiving electric shocks. They were actually responding to the **demand characteristics** of the experiment. That is, they were simply picking up on the cues that showed them how they were *expected* to behave in that situation (see page 131).

✓ But there's good reason to believe that participants *did* take the situation seriously. For example, many showed signs of distress and anxiety (such as nervous laughter and digging their nails into their flesh). According to Orne and Holland, this was a 'pretence'. In post-experimental interviews, participants never indicated that they'd been pretending.

✓ Sheridan & King (1972) found high levels of obedience when participants *must* have believed the situation was real. This involved students training a puppy on a task. Whenever it made a mistake, they punished it with *actual* electric shocks. Although the shocks were small, the students could see and hear the puppy's squeals. 75% of the students delivered the maximum shock.

✔ To criticise Milgram's experiments for being unethical, you must first believe that participants *weren't* pretending. Only if you're convinced his participants were *really* stressed could you condemn Milgram for exposing them to that stress (see Critical Issue, page 122).

✘ Orne and Holland also claimed that Milgram's experiments lacked **mundane realism** (or **ecological validity**). That is, the findings can't be generalised beyond the particular laboratory setting in which they were collected. So, we can't learn from Milgram's research about how people behave in other situations.

However, *naturalistic studies* of obedience suggest otherwise.

● For example, Hofling *et al* (1966) studied 22 nurses working in various U.S. hospitals. A stooge 'Dr Smith of the psychiatric department' instructed them, by 'phone, to give his patient (Mr Jones) 20 mg of a drug called *Astrofen*. Dr Smith was in a desperate hurry, and he'd sign the drug authorisation form later when he came to see Mr Jones.

● *Astrofen* was actually a dummy drug (a harmless sugar pill) invented just for the experiment. The label on the box clearly stated that the maximum daily dose was 10 mg. So, if the nurse obeyed Dr Smith's instructions she'd be giving twice the maximum daily dose. Also, hospital rules required that doctors sign the authorisation form *before* any drug was given. Another rule demanded that nurses should be absolutely sure that 'Dr Smith' was a genuine doctor.

● 21 of the 22 nurses complied without hesitation. A control group of 22 nurses were asked what they *would have done* in that situation. 21 said that they wouldn't have given the drug without written authorisation, especially as it exceeded the maximum daily dose.

● Hofling *et al* concluded that the greater power and authority of doctors seem to influence nurses' behaviour more than those rules do. Also, what people actually *do* in a particular situation and what they *say* they'd do, can be very different.

Why do people obey?

According to Milgram (1974), most of us would have behaved like his obedient participants. So, the explanation for such high levels of obedience lies in aspects of the situation itself, rather than in individual characteristics.

PERCEPTION OF LEGITIMATE AUTHORITY

● Obedient participants seemed to accept the power and status of the experimenter. In the context of the Yale University psychology department, the experimenter was 'in charge'.

● When we obey, we see ourselves as the instrument or agent of the authority figure's wishes (the **agentic state**). We give up personal responsibility for our actions (the **autonomous state**) and transfer that responsibility onto the authority figure. "I was only following orders" was the most common defence given by the Nazi war criminals (including Eichmann, who ran the death camps).

● Once we come to see ourselves in this way, the specific orders are largely irrelevant. In other words, obedience always involves the same mental adjustment (the agentic state); obedience is obedience is obedience.

● Authority figures often possess highly visible symbols of their power and status. These make it much more difficult to disobey them. For example, the experimenter always wore a *grey* lab coat (a white one would have implied 'scientist' rather than 'authority figure'). Zimbardo *et al*'s prison study (see Essential Study 5.2, pages 110–11) also showed the impact of uniforms and other trappings of power and authority.

PERSONAL RESPONSIBILITY

● As we've seen, the agentic and autonomous states are really two sides of a coin. Anything which detracts from the authority figure's power will increase feelings of personal responsibility. This was shown in Milgram's RA (Remote Authority) variation. When the experimenter wasn't in the same room to give his instructions in person, participants were more likely to disobey.

● This was also shown in the P (Proximity) and TP (Touch Proximity) experiments. It's much more difficult to deny responsibility if you're in the same room as Mr Wallace (instead of just hearing his screams etc.). It's even more difficult if you have to physically force him to endure the shocks. In other words, it's easier to disobey when you can see for yourself the effects of your behaviour on the victim (see Conclusions in Essential Study 5.5).

● But when someone else actually 'throws the switch' (as in PAS: A Peer Administers Shock), it's easier to *deny* personal responsibility ("*He* delivered the shock, not *me!*")

THE 'FOOT-IN-THE-DOOR'

● Participants got 'sucked into' a situation which they found very difficult to escape from. They'd volunteered for what seemed like a 'harmless' study of learning and memory. There was no mention in the original ad of punishment, let alone delivering electric shocks to another participant. The first they heard of it was once they'd already made the effort to get to the psychology department.

● Once they were in the experimental situation, it was more difficult to leave. The deeper in you are, the greater the effort you have to make to escape. If the original ad had referred to punishment and/or shock, perhaps fewer volunteers would have come forward. Or perhaps they would have been a more sadistic group of people!

How can we resist obedience?

Anything which *increases* our sense of personal responsibility will also *increase* our resistance to obey. When the experimenter said "You have no other choice, you *must* go on", many participants *stopped* obeying. It brought home to them that they *did* have a choice and *were* responsible.

Milgram himself believed that obedience could be reduced by:

● *educating* people about the dangers of blind obedience

● encouraging them to *question authority*

EXAM tips BOX

Give a brief account of psychological explanations of obedience and consider their strengths *and* limitations. (18 marks)

● You could structure your answer in terms of three paragraphs, all about 100–130 words long.

● *A word of warning: The question asks for 'explanations of obedience', so you must give <u>at least two</u>. But if you give more than two, these won't have to be as detailed. Also, this isn't a 'Milgram question' as such, and you must avoid getting bogged down in the details of particular experiments. Try to bring other researchers into your answer.*

● The first paragraph could describe *one or more* of the specific factors that Milgram investigated in the variations of his original (remote victim) experiment, and/or *one or more* general explanations (such as personal responsibility). (AO1, worth 6 marks).

● In the second paragraph, you could consider some of the strengths and limitations of the studies described in the first paragraph. *Remember, you're not* describing *the findings here. You're* evaluating *these later experiments, drawing out the conclusions, which, in turn, suggest why people obey.*

● In the third paragraph, you could repeat the exercise for perhaps two examples of more general explanations of obedience. The same reminder applies here as for paragraph 2. (AO2, worth 12 marks).

Try to write a suitable answer in about 300–350 words. As with all questions, there's no single correct way of answering it. The above are just pointers. There's a sample answer at the end of the book. Try not to look at it until you've had a go at doing it yourself.

• exposing them to *disobedient models.* This is what happened in *TPR*. Participants were influenced more by *conformity* with the behaviour of peers than by the demands of an authority figure.

CRITICAL ISSUE: ETHICAL ISSUES IN PSYCHOLOGICAL RESEARCH

Ethical issues arising from social influence research

• Most people would agree that it's morally unacceptable (unethical) to harm another person (physically and/or mentally) in everyday life. It may also be illegal. Similarly, if we lie or deceive someone. But until Milgram's initial obedience experiment, psychologists didn't really discuss the ethics of their research in the way they do today.

• The social influence research of Milgram, Zimbardo *et al*, Asch and others have all been criticised for being unethical. But they have also helped to identify the crucial ethical issues that *all* psychologists must consider when planning and conducting their research. Without these social influence studies, there may not be an 'ethics debate' at all.

DECEPTION AND INFORMED CONSENT: MILGRAM'S RESEARCH

• There's no question that Milgram deceived his participants. The original ad stated that the study was concerned with memory and learning. Only after volunteers were already in the experimental situation did the experimenter mention punishment and electric shock.

• Even if the study had actually been about the effects of punishment on learning, Milgram would still have been deceiving his participants. But, of course, it *wasn't.* The more serious deception was that it was really about obedience. This was never mentioned until after the experiment was over. Participants also believed that Mr Wallace was another participant. In fact, he was an actor playing the role of participant. They were also deceived about the electric shocks. Mr Wallace never actually received any!

• What all of this means is that participants couldn't give their **informed consent**. That is, they volunteered for a study without knowing its true purpose or what would happen. Had they known, they might not have volunteered in the first place. You could say that they were tricked into taking part.

DECEPTION AND INFORMED CONSENT: ZIMBARDO ET AL'S RESEARCH

• The prison simulation experiment was advertised as a study of prison life. This was the *true* purpose of the study. In fact, Zimbardo *et al* produced an informed consent contract. This told participants everything that was going to happen to them (as far as this could be predicted). It was signed by every participant. They gave their permission for invasion of privacy, loss of civil rights, and harassment.

• They were only deceived about one thing. They weren't told that the prisoners would be arrested by the local police force. This was partly because the police didn't give their final approval until the last minute. But Zimbardo *et al* also wanted the arrest to come as a surprise. Zimbardo admitted that this was in breach of their own contract.

DECEPTION AND INFORMED CONSENT: ASCH'S RESEARCH

• Asch told his participants that the experiment was concerned with perception. Since it was actually about conformity, they were clearly deceived about its true purpose.

• This means, as with Milgram, that participants couldn't give their informed consent.

And also like Milgram, Asch's participants didn't realise that the other group members were, in fact, stooges.

IS DECEPTION EVER JUSTIFIED?

● Most of Asch's participants were very enthusiastic. In post-experimental interviews, they said how they admired the elegance and significance of the experimental procedure.

● Milgram (1974) defended himself by reporting that he thoroughly *debriefed* his participants. He had a lengthy discussion with each participant individually as soon as the experiment was over (see below). He then sent them a detailed account of the procedure and results of all the experiments. He also sent them a follow-up questionnaire about their experience of taking part.

● Most participants who returned the questionnaire said they were glad or very glad they had taken part. Many said they learned something important about themselves, and there should be more research like it.

● Milgram took this to be *the* crucial justification for deceiving his participants. If *they* didn't object, why should anybody else?

● Participants had to believe they were delivering real shocks, otherwise we couldn't generalise the results to real-life obedience situations. This relates to what we said above about experimental and ecological validity/realism. So, deception was necessary if participants were to behave in a 'realistic' way.

PROTECTING PARTICIPANTS FROM PSYCHOLOGICAL HARM: MILGRAM'S RESEARCH

● Baumrind (1964) accused Milgram of abusing his participants' rights and feelings. She argued that Milgram failed to protect them adequately from stress and emotional conflict.

● Milgram accepted that they did experience stress and conflict. But he argued that Baumrind's criticism assumes that the experimental outcome was *expected*. In fact, Milgram was as surprised as anyone by the high obedience rate. The most distressed participants tended to be those who were the most obedient. So, if Milgram expected very low obedience rates, he certainly didn't expect participants to experience high levels of conflict.

● But shouldn't he have stopped his research as soon as he saw how distressed participants became? Also, the whole set-up was designed to make it difficult for participants to disobey. The experimenter's prods pressurised the participant into obeying. This made **withdrawal from the investigation** extremely difficult. In his defence, Milgram argued that:

(a) At whatever point the participant stopped giving shocks, s/he was reunited with Mr Wallace. The participant could see he was unharmed, and was also informed that the shocks weren't real. Milgram had an extended discussion with each participant individually. He assured obedient participants that their behaviour was completely normal. He supported the disobedient ones in their resistance to the experimenter's demands. This was all part of a thorough **debriefing**, which Milgram had decided would take place as a matter of course. That is, it would have happened anyway, and wasn't a response to any criticisms.

(b) The experimenter *didn't* make the participant shock Mr Wallace (as Baumrind claimed). Indeed, this *couldn't* have happened. Milgram believed that people have free will, and so *choose* to obey or disobey.

Table 5.2 Arguments in Milgram's defence ('for') and criticisms ('against') of his obedience experiments

Consent/informed consent

For	Against
● Participants volunteered	● They volunteered for a study of learning and memory

Deception

For	Against
● Debriefing – as matter of course	● Debriefing only needed because of deception
● Participants accept it	● Prevents informed consent
● The end justifies the means	● Harmful to self-concept

Protection of participants

For	Against
● Results weren't anticipated	● Participants very distressed
● Reunited with unharmed victim	● Debriefing only needed because of participants' distress
● Reassured after the experiment as part of debriefing	
● No evidence of long-term harm	
● Participants have free will	

Withdrawal from the investigation

For	Against
● Participants free to leave at any time	● The whole situation made *resistance* (disobedience) difficult
● 37.5% disobeyed (*voice-feedback condition*)	● 62.5% obeyed (*voice-feedback condition*)

PROTECTING PARTICIPANTS FROM HARM: ZIMBARDO ET AL'S RESEARCH

● Zimbardo believes that the ethical concerns are even greater in his own prison study than in Milgram's research. Volunteer prisoners suffered physical and psychological abuse over several days. Volunteer guards discovered that they enjoyed being powerful and abused this power to make other human beings suffer. Although every participant signed an informed consent form, this couldn't protect the prisoners from the guards' abuse. Nor could it protect the guards from what they learned about themselves. It took Zimbardo *et al* six days to end the experiment that was planned to last for two weeks. Why did it take them so long?

- According to Savin (1973), the practical benefits of the prison study didn't justify the distress, mistreatment and degradation suffered by the participants. That is, the end *didn't* justify the means.

PROTECTING PARTICIPANTS FROM HARM: ASCH'S RESEARCH

- Many of Asch's participants said they only conformed because they didn't want to be laughed at or ridiculed (see page 114). When Asch ran the experiment using several naïve participants and a single stooge, they openly ridiculed him on the critical trials. Other studies have shown that participants' physiological stress levels increase on critical trials.

Dealing with these issues: Ethical guidelines

- An ethics committee of the American Psychological Association (APA) investigated Milgram's (1963) study soon after it was published. The committee eventually judged it to be ethically acceptable. So, even at that time psychologists were aware of ethical issues involved in research with human participants. But it's generally agreed that Milgram's controversial research highlighted these issues and stimulated the 'ethics debate'.

- The major professional bodies for psychologists are the British Psychological Society (BPS) and the APA. Both organizations have published several sets of ethical guidelines. These include the *Ethical Principles for Conducting Research with Human Participants* (BPS, 1993).

WHY DO WE NEED ETHICAL GUIDELINES?

- The introduction to the BPS *Ethical Principles* states that:

  ' . . . for ethical reasons, some areas of human experience and behaviour may be beyond the reach of experiment, observation or other forms of psychological investigation. Ethical guidelines are necessary to clarify the conditions under which psychological research is acceptable'.

- It urges psychologists to encourage their colleagues to follow *the Ethical Principles*. They should be adopted by *anyone* conducting *any* kind of psychological research, including GCSE, and AS/A level students.

- Researchers must consider the psychological consequences of their research *for the participants*. Researchers must ensure that participants' psychological well-being, health, values and dignity aren't threatened in any way.

EXAM tips BOX

To what extent can use of deception in social influence research studies be justified? (18 marks)

- You could structure your answer in terms of three paragraphs, all about 100–130 words long.

- In the first paragraph, you should explain what deception involves/what it means in relation to social influence research, giving one or two examples of how deception has been used in particular experiments. (AO1, worth 6 marks).

- In the second paragraph, you could show how deception and consent/informed consent are related (and explain the difference between consent/informed consent). If you refer to specific studies here, it's to *illustrate this relationship* (*not* to describe the study).

- You're trying to show *how/why* deception may be considered ethically unacceptable.

- In the third paragraph, you could consider, say, *two or more* arguments *against* using deception (one of which is to do with consent/informed consent), then consider *two or more* arguments *in support* of its use. These arguments might centre around the *consequences* of being deceived, including (i) participants' distress, embarrassment etc., (ii) what they learn about themselves as people; (iii) the realistic nature of participants' behaviour. (AO2, worth 12 marks).

- *A word of warning: This question doesn't ask you specifically about Milgram's research, although you're likely to know a lot about it. So, you're free to include other researchers' studies. The 18-mark questions don't ask you to describe the procedures of a study. So, you should only do so when this is relevant.*

Try to write a suitable answer in about 300–350 words. As with all questions, there's no single correct way of answering it. The above are just pointers. There's a sample answer at the end of the book. Try not to look at it until you've had a go at doing it yourself.

MAJOR ETHICAL PRINCIPLES

We've already considered the research of Asch, Milgram, and Zimbardo *et al* in the light of:

● deception

● consent/informed consent

● protection of participants from psychological harm

● withdrawal from the investigation.

If the psychologist decides that deception is necessary, s/he should debrief the participants *as soon as possible* after the experiment. Debriefing is also a major means of protecting participants who've suffered emotional distress.

EXAM tips BOX

To what extent can ethical guidelines ensure that the major ethical issues involved in social influence research are properly dealt with? (18 marks)

● You could structure your answer in terms of three paragraphs, each about 100–130 words long.

● *A word of warning: there's an important distinction between* ethical issues *and* ways of dealing with/trying to ensure they're dealt with properly. *Issues refer to participants' rights and psychologists' responsibilities.*

In the first paragraph, you could briefly *describe* the major ethical issues involved in research with human participants, and *give some examples* of how these issues have been highlighted by social influence research. *Note that while there are several sets of guidelines, it's sufficient for this question just to refer to the BPS Ethical Principles.* (AO1, worth 6 marks).

● In the second paragraph, you could consider the relationship between ethical codes and social influence research. For example, did such codes exist *before* this research took place, and why should social influence research be so central in the 'ethics debate'?

● In the third paragraph, you could consider who publishes ethical guidelines, their main aims and objectives, who's meant to follow the guidelines, and what they recommend psychologists should do in order to achieve the aims and objectives. For example, under what conditions, if any, is deception permissible, and what are the safeguards that help protect participants when deception is used?

● Here, you're *analysing and evaluating* the use of ethical codes as ways of dealing with major ethical issues, rather than saying what they are and giving examples. (AO2, worth 12 marks).

Try to write a suitable answer in about 300–350 words. As with all questions, there's no single correct way of answering it. The above are just pointers. There's a sample answer at the end of the book. Try not to look at it until you've had a go at doing it yourself.

SUMMARY

Conformity and minority influence

Conformity refers to the influence that a group has over an individual **(majority influence)**. This is demonstrated in Asch's experiments, although the **Asch paradigm** has been criticised.

Asch found that it's not the size of the majority that matters, but whether/not the majority is *unanimous*.

Zimbardo *et al*'s prison simulation experiment rejected the **dispositional hypothesis** in favour of the **situational hypothesis**. The study illustrates aspects of both conformity and obedience.

Minority influence was demonstrated by Moscovici *et al*. To be influential, the minority needs to be *consistent*. Consistency doesn't have to involve repeating the same response, provided there's a clear *pattern* in the minority's responses.

The distinction between **informational social influence (ISI)** and **normative social influence (NSI)** is crucial for understanding why people conform. ISI and NSI correspond to **internalisation (true conformity)** and **compliance** respectively.

Obedience

Obedience refers to compliance with the demands/instructions of an **authority figure**. This is one of the important differences between obedience and conformity.

The original idea for Milgram's obedience experiments was the **Germans-are-different hypothesis**. The original **remote-victim** experiment was followed by the **voice-feedback** experiment. Altogether, Milgram conducted 18 experiments. In each one, a different variable was manipulated in order to see its effect on obedience rate.

Orne and Holland criticised Milgram's experiments for their lack of both **experimental realism/validity** and **mundane realism** (or **ecological validity**).

But naturalistic studies suggest that they *do* have mundane realism, and Milgram's findings have been replicated in several cross-cultural studies.

We tend to obey people whom we perceive as a legitimate authority. When they give us orders, our normal **autonomous state** is replaced by the **agentic state**. These are related to our sense of **personal responsibility** for our own behaviour.

Milgram's research suggests ways of resisting obedience.

Critical issue: Ethical issues in psychological research

Social influence research has been criticised for being unethical. But it has also helped identify the ethical issues that lie at the centre of the 'ethics debate' in psychology.

Major ethical issues highlighted by this research include **consent/informed consent, deception, protecting participants from psychological harm,** and **withdrawal from the investigation**.

Ethical guidelines (such as the BPS's *Ethical Principles*) help to define what is acceptable psychological research. Researchers must consider the psychological consequences of their research *for the participants*, whose psychological well-being, health, values, and dignity mustn't be threatened in any way.

For example, if deception is judged to be necessary, the psychologist must **debrief** the participants as soon as possible after the experiment.

Self-assessment questions

These are some example Part a and Part b questions (worth 40% of your exam). Part c questions have been dealt with throughout the chapter in the Exam tips Boxes and in the Sample Answers (SAs) at the end of the book.

1a. What is meant by the terms minority influence, ecological validity, and informed consent? (2 + 2 + 2 marks)

b. Outline conclusions from research into majority influence. (6 marks)

2a. Describe *two* ways in which psychologists deal with ethical issues (such as deception, informed consent, and protecting participants from psychological harm. (3 + 3 marks)

b. Outline findings from research into minority influence. (6 marks)

3a. Outline the main features of *one* explanation of conformity. (6 marks)

b. Explain what is meant by the terms 'conformity' and 'obedience' and give *one* difference between them. (2 + 2 + 2 marks)

4a. Describe the procedure and findings of *one* study of majority influence. (3 + 3 marks)

b. Outline the findings of *one* study of obedience and give *one* criticism of this study. (3 + 3 marks)

5a. Describe explanations of why people obey. (6 marks)

b. Outline *two* factors that can influence obedience to authority. (3 + 3 marks)

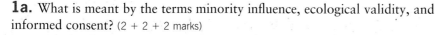

Topic	Research study	Researcher date	Page
Conformity/majority influence	Comparison-Of-Lines Experiment (COLE)	Asch (1951)	108
..	Prison Experiment (PE)	Zimbardo *et al* (1973)	110
Minority influence	Green Colour Slide Experiment (GCSE)	Moscovici *et al* (1969)	112
Obedience	Shocking Obedience Study (SOS)	Milgram (1963)	116
..	Voice Feedback (VF)	.. (1974)	118
..	Proximity (P)	..	..
..	Touch Proximity (TP)	..	..
..	Remote Authority (RA)	..	..
..	Two Peers Rebel (TPR)	..	..
..	A Peer Administers Shock (PAS)	..	..

ESSENTIAL STUDY SUMMARY

AS Module 3:
Social Psychology and Research Methods
Research Methods

12.2

What's covered in this chapter?

QUANTITATIVE AND QUALITATIVE RESEARCH METHODS

The nature and usage of the following research methods and their advantages and disadvantages and how they relate to the scientific nature of psychology:

- Experiments (laboratory, field and natural experiments)
- Investigations using correlational analysis
- Naturalistic observations
- Questionnaire surveys
- Interviews.

The nature and usage of ethical guidelines in psychology.

RESEARCH DESIGN AND IMPLEMENTATION

- Aims and hypotheses (generation of appropriate aims; the formulation of different types of the experimental/alternative hypothesis (directional and non-directional) and the null hypothesis).
- Research designs: experimental (independent groups, repeated measures and matched participants) and the design of naturalistic observations, questionnaire surveys and interviews.
- Factors associated with research design, including the operationalisation of the IV/DV; conducting pilot studies; control of variables; techniques for assessing and improving reliability and validity (internal and external (ecological) validity); ethics.
- The selection of participants (including random sampling).
- The relationship between researchers and participants (including demand characteristics and investigator effects).

DATA ANALYSIS

- Analysis of qualitative data that could be derived from naturalistic observations, questionnaire surveys and interviews.
- Measures of central tendency and dispersion (including the appropriate use and interpretation of medians, means, modes, ranges and standard deviations).
- The nature of positive and negative correlations and the interpretation of correlation coefficients.
- Graphs and charts (including the appropriate use and interpretation of histograms, bar charts, frequency polygons and scattergraphs).

QUANTITATIVE AND QUALITATIVE RESEARCH METHODS

Quantitative research methods allow the numerical measurement of *how much* there is of something i.e. the quantity. Qualitative research methods allow for the measurement of *what* something is like i.e. the quality. An example of **quantitative data** would be the *number* of stressful incidents per day, whereas **qualitative data** would involve a *description* of these incidents.

There are a number of different research methods in psychology. Like the carpenter who selects the most appropriate tool for the job, psychologists choose the most appropriate method for their research. You need to know what these methods are and what their advantages and disadvantages are.

Experiments

An experiment is a research method that helps to discover causal relationships between variables. A variable is any object, characteristic or event that changes or varies in some way. Experiments are the most widely used method in psychology.

The experimenter manipulates an **independent variable** (IV) to see its effect on the **dependent variable** (DV). The IV is the variable that is manipulated or altered by the experimenter to see its effect on the DV. The DV is the measured result of the experiment. Any change in the DV should be as a result of the manipulation of the IV. For example, alcohol consumption (IV) could be manipulated to see its effect on reaction time (the DV).

Extraneous variables are any other variables that may have an effect on the DV. Controls are employed to prevent extraneous variables spoiling the results. Any extraneous variables that aren't controlled can become **confounding variables**. These are so-called because they 'confound' (that is, confuse) the results.

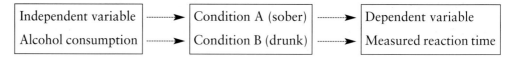

There are several types of experiments:

LABORATORY EXPERIMENTS

The researcher controls as many variables as possible. There's control over the 'who, what, when, where and how'. This is *usually* done in a laboratory using standardised procedures, but can be conducted anywhere provided it's in a controlled environment. Participants should also be randomly allocated to experimental groups.

Advantages:

✔ **High degree of control:** Experimenters can control all variables in the situation. This leads to greater accuracy and objectivity.

✔ **Replication:** Other researchers can easily repeat the experiment and check results.

✔ **Cause and effect:** It's possible to determine the cause and effect relationship between the IV and DV.

✔ **Technical equipment:** It's easier to use complicated technical equipment in a laboratory.

Disadvantages:

✘ **Experimenter bias:** Sometimes an experimenter's expectations about the study can affect results. Participants may be influenced by these expectations.

✖ **Low ecological validity:** The high degree of control can make the experimental situation artificial and not like real life. As such, it may be difficult to generalise results to other settings.

✖ **Demand characteristics:** Sometimes participants try to guess the purpose of the experiment and then act according to the 'demands' of the experiment.

FIELD EXPERIMENTS

An experiment performed in the 'real world' rather than the laboratory. The IV is still manipulated by the experimenter.

NATURAL EXPERIMENTS

Here, the IV occurs naturally, it's not manipulated by the experimenter. The experimenter merely records the effect on the DV. An advantage here is that the effect of an IV can be studied where it would be unethical to manipulate it deliberately e.g. family stress.

Advantages: (can apply to both field and natural experiments)

✔ **High ecological validity:** Due to the 'real world' environment or naturally occurring environment, results are more likely to relate to everyday behaviour and can be generalised to other settings.

✔ **No demand characteristics:** Often, participants are unaware of the experiment, and so there are no demand characteristics.

Disadvantages:

✖ **Less control:** It's more difficult to control extraneous variables, either 'in the field' or in naturally occurring situations.

✖ **Replication:** It's difficult to *precisely* replicate field or natural experiments.

✖ **Ethics:** There are ethical issues (e.g. informed consent, deception) when participants aren't aware of the experiment. This applies more to field experiments, since in natural experiments the independent variable naturally occurs and isn't manipulated by the experimenter.

✖ **Sample bias:** Since participants aren't randomly allocated to groups, there may be some sample bias.

Experimental Research Methods Summary Table

Type of experiment	Variable details	Environment
Laboratory	Manipulation of IV Measure DV	Controlled
Field	Manipulation of IV Measure DV	Real-life
Natural	IV naturally occurs Measure DV	Real-life

Correlations allow you to predict behaviour

Investigation using correlational analysis

This isn't a research method as such, but a method of data analysis. It involves measuring the strength of the relationship between two or more variables (co-variables) to see if a trend or pattern exists between them.

● **A positive correlation:** one variable increases as the other variable increases e.g. ice-cream sales increase as temperature increases.

● **A negative correlation:** one variable increases while the other variable decreases e.g. raincoat sales decrease as temperature increases.

● **A correlation co-efficient:** the number that expresses the degree to which the two variables are related. The measurement ranges from +1 (perfect positive correlation) to –1 (perfect negative correlation). The closer the correlation to a perfect correlation, the stronger the relationship between the two variables. If there's no correlation, the result will be near to zero (0.0) (see scattergram, page 146).

Advantages:

✔ **Allows predictions to be made:** Once a correlation has been found, we can make predictions about one variable from the other e.g. we can predict the number of ice-creams sold on hot days.

✔ **Allows quantification of relationships:** Correlations can show the strength of the relationship between two co-variables. A correlation of +0.9 means a high positive correlation, a correlation of −0.3 indicates a weak negative correlation.

✔ **No manipulation:** Correlations don't require the manipulation of behaviour, and so can be a quick and ethical method of data collection and analysis.

Disadvantages:

✘ **Cause and effect:** It cannot be assumed that one variable caused the other. Interpretation of results is made difficult, since there's no cause and effect in a correlation.

✘ **Extraneous relationships:** Other variables may influence both measured variables e.g. most holidays are taken in the (hot?) summer and people eat ice-creams on holiday. Therefore, the variable 'holiday' is related to both temperature and ice-cream sales.

✘ **Only works for linear relationships:** Correlations only measure linear (straight-line) relationships. The relationship between temperature and aggression is a *curvilinear* relationship (see Figure 6.1). This would be a zero correlation, and yet there's an obvious relationship between these two variables.

Naturalistic observations

This involves the precise (objective) measurement of naturally occurring behaviour. The observation occurs in the participant's own natural environment.

Advantages:

✔ **High ecological validity:** Since observed behaviour takes place in the natural environment, participants behave naturally and results can be generalised to other settings.

Figure 6.1 Scattergraph showing the curvilinear relationship between temperature and aggression

✔ **Practical method:** It can be used in situations where deliberate manipulation would be unethical or impractical (e.g. soccer hooliganism). It's particularly useful for studying animals or children.

✔ **Few demand characteristics:** Participants are often unaware of the observation and so there are few demand characteristics (see page 141).

DISADVANTAGES:

✘ **Cause and effect:** This cannot be inferred, since the variables are only observed, not manipulated.

✘ **Observer bias:** If observers know the purpose of the study, they may see what they want to see.

✘ **Replication:** It's difficult to check the **reliability** and **validity** (see page 139) of observations, since a lack of control means conditions can never be repeated accurately.

✘ **Ethics:** If participants are unaware of being observed, issues of invasion of privacy and informed consent arise.

Questionnaire surveys

A survey is an overall term for questionnaires and interviews. It involves the systematic large-scale collection of data. The National Census is the best-known example of this. Questionnaires are a written method of data collection, where respondents record their own answers to a pre-set list of questions. They're usually concerned with people's behaviour, opinions and attitudes. There are main two types of questions used:

● **Closed questions:** Responses are fixed by the researcher. They usually involve 'tick boxes' (e.g. 'yes' or 'no') or a range of fixed responses (e.g. 'always', 'usually', 'sometimes', 'never'). Such answers are easy to quantify, but restrict participants' answers.

● **Open questions:** Allow participants to answer in their own words. They're more difficult to analyse, but allow freedom of expression and obtain greater depth.

ADVANTAGES:

✔ **Quick and cheap:** A large amount of information can be gathered in a relatively short period of time. As such, they're generally quicker and cheaper in comparison to other methods.

✔ **Large samples:** Questionnaires can be completed without the researcher present. Postal questionnaires can be used to gain very large samples for the cost of a stamp.

✔ **Quantitative analysis:** It's easy to statistically analyse 'closed' questions. Answers can be pre-coded on questionnaires for computer input and almost instant analysis.

✔ **Replication:** Since questionnaires use standardised questions, it's easy to replicate studies.

Naturalistic observation is useful for studying animals and children

Examples of closed and open questions

Victoria Beckham inadvertently revelead her husband's 'Golden Balls' nickname in a Parkinson interview on TV.

DISADVANTAGES:

✗ **Misunderstanding:** Designing a questionnaire is a highly skilled job. Participants may misunderstand or misinterpret questions. For example, what do you mean when you say you 'usually' do your homework?

✗ **Biased samples:** Questionnaires are only suitable for people who are literate and willing and able to spend time filling them in.

✗ **Low response rates:** Some questionnaires have been known to obtain as little as a 5% return rate.

✗ **Superficial issues:** Questionnaires aren't suitable for sensitive issues that require detailed understanding.

✗ **Social desirability:** Participants may present themselves in a positive light. Indeed, they may lie on sensitive issues e.g. sexual behaviour.

Interviews

Interviews involve researchers asking questions in a face-to-face situation. They can be very different but there are two broad types:

- **Structured (or formal) interviews:** A questionnaire is read to participants, and the interviewer writes down the responses. These interviews are identical for all participants and tend to involve more simple, quantitative questions. Interviewers don't need a lot of training, since they're fairly easy to conduct.

- **Unstructured (or informal) interviews:** These are less controlled and involve an informal discussion on a particular topic. Whereas the topic is pre-determined the direction of the interview isn't. This allows the interviewer to explore areas of greatest interest. Friendly rapport between the interviewer and respondent is important in order to gain the required level of detail and understanding. Interviewers need considerable training and expertise to conduct such interviews.

Interviews can combine these two types in semi-structured interviews.

ADVANTAGES:

✓ **Complex issues:** Complicated or sensitive issues are best dealt with in face-to-face interviews. This is particularly true of unstructured interviews where answers can be developed.

✓ **Ease misunderstandings:** Any ambiguity or misunderstanding can be clarified within the interview.

✓ **Data analysis:** The variety and flexibility of interviews allows for the analysis of both quantitative and qualitative data.

DISADVANTAGES:

✗ **Interviewer effects:** Interviewers may inadvertently bias the respondent's answers. This could even occur through the interviewer's appearance. For example, would a white person be less willing to admit to being racist to a black interviewer? Interviews are subject to demand characteristics and social desirability bias.

✗ **Ethical issues:** These can arise when participants don't know the true purpose of the interview. There is also a danger that participants may reveal more than they wish to.

Social desirability: In the 1980s voters were reluctant to admit that they were conservatives – but the Tories kept on winning!

✖ **Respondent answers:** Respondents may be unable to put into words their true feelings about a particular topic.

Summary of ethical issues with different research methods

Research method	Ethical issues
<u>Laboratory experiments</u>	• Participants **feel pressure** to act in a particular way. • Reluctance of participants to exercise their **right to withdraw.** • Experimental situation can be **stressful.**
<u>Field/natural experiments</u>	• **Informed consent** is difficult to obtain. • Participants are unlikely to know of the **right to withdraw.** • **Debriefing** is difficult.
<u>Naturalistic observations</u>	• If participants do not know they are being observed, there are issues of **informed consent, confidentiality and invasion of privacy.**
<u>Correlational analysis</u>	• Interpretation of results: The public may **interpret correlations incorrectly.**
<u>Interviews</u>	• **Confidentiality** must be maintained. • **Right to withhold information** on embarrassing topics.

RESEARCH DESIGN AND IMPLEMENTATION

Aims and hypotheses

An aim is a reasonably precise statement of *why* a study is taking place (e.g. to investigate the effect of alcohol on reaction times). It should include what is being studied and what the study is trying to achieve.

A hypothesis is much more precise and predicts what is expected to happen (e.g. alcohol consumption will significantly affect reaction times). Hypotheses are testable statements. There are two types:

• **Experimental (or alternative) hypothesis:** These predict significant differences in the DV as a result of manipulation of the IV. They predict that any difference or effect found will not be due to chance, e.g. there will be a significant difference in reaction times as a result of alcohol consumption.
(Note: The term 'experimental hypothesis' should only be used with the experimental method. For all other methods, 'alternative hypothesis' should be used.)

• **Null hypothesis:** This is the *'hypothesis of no differences'*. It predicts that the IV will *not* affect the DV. It predicts that results will simply be due to chance, e.g. there will be no (significant) difference in reaction times as a result of alcohol consumption.

One of these hypotheses will be supported by the findings.

(Note: The inclusion of the word 'significant' in the null hypothesis is still being argued about by psychologists.)

There are also two types of experimental (alternative) hypotheses:

- **Directional (also called 'one-tailed'):** These state the direction of the results (e.g. there will be a significant **increase** in reaction times as a result of alcohol consumption) (they'll get slower). They're called one-tailed because they state one direction in which the results can go.

- **Non-directional ('two-tailed'):** These state that there will be a difference but don't state the direction of the results (e.g. there will be a significant **difference** in reaction times as a result of alcohol consumption). In this example, reaction times could either increase *or* decrease, and so they're called 'two-tailed'.

Directional hypotheses are used when previous research evidence suggests that it's possible to make a clear prediction, or when you're replicating a previous study that used a directional hypothesis.

Research designs

INDEPENDENT GROUPS DESIGN

Different participants are used in each of the conditions. Each group of participants is *independent* of the other. Participants are usually randomly allocated to each condition to try to balance out any differences (see page 140).

Advantages:

✔️ **Order effects:** There are *no* order effects (see page 137).

✔️ **Demand characteristics:** Participants take part in one condition only. This means there's less chance of participants guessing the purpose of the study.

✔️ **Time saved:** Both sets of participants can be tested at the same time. This saves time and money.

Disadvantages:

✖️ **More participants:** With participants in only one condition, you need twice as many participants as repeated measures design.

✖️ **Group differences:** Any differences between the groups may be due to individual differences distinct from the IV. This can be minimised by the random allocation of participants to each group.

MATCHED PARTICIPANTS (OR PAIRS) DESIGN

Different, but similar, participants are used in each of the conditions. Participants are matched across the groups on any characteristics judged to be important for that particular study. These are typically age, gender, ethnicity.

Advantages: (see advantages of independent groups design above)

✔️ **Group differences:** Participant variables are more closely matched between conditions than independent groups design.

Disadvantages: (see disadvantages of independent groups design above)

✖️ **Matching is difficult:** It's impossible to match all variables between participants. The one variable missed might be vitally important.

✖️ **Time-consuming:** It takes a long time to accurately match participants on all variables.

REPEATED MEASURES DESIGN

The same participants are tested in the two (or more) conditions. Each participant *repeats* the study in each condition.

Advantages:

✔ **Group differences:** The same person is measured in both conditions, there are *no* individual differences between the groups. Extraneous variables are kept constant (controlled) between the conditions.

✔ **Fewer participants:** Half as many participants are needed as for independent measures design.

Disadvantages:

✗ **Order effects:** When participants repeat a task, results can be affected by order effects. On the second task, participants either:

- do worse due to fatigue or boredom
- improve through practice in the first condition. These can be controlled by *counterbalancing*, where half the participants do condition A followed by condition B and the other half do condition B, then A (ABBA).

✗ **Lost participants:** If a participant drops out of the study, they're 'lost' from both conditions.

✗ **Takes more time:** A gap may need to be given between conditions. This takes time and money.

Did the 1970s Swedish pop band take their name from a counterbalancing technique?

EXPERIMENTAL DESIGN SUMMARY:

Repeated measures: same participants

| Bob, Jane, Tom | ⟶ | Bob, Jane, Tom |
| Condition 1 | ⟶ | Condition 2 |

Independent measures: different participants

| Bob, Jane, Tom | ⟶ | Tina, Kate, Mike |
| Condition 1 | ⟶ | Condition 2 |

Matched pairs: matched participants

| Bob, Jane, Tom | ⟶ | Bob's brother, Jane's sister, Tom's brother |
| Condition 1 | ⟶ | Condition 2 |

Operationalisation of the IV/DV

The term **operationalisation** means being able to define variables simply and easily in order to manipulate (IV) and measure them (DV). Sometimes, this is very easily done.

For example, if we were investigating the effect of alcohol consumption on reaction times we could 'operationalise' the IV as the number of alcohol units consumed and the DV could be the speed of response to a flashing light. However, on other occasions this is more difficult.

For example, how would you 'operationalise' anger or stress levels? There isn't always

Kenrick & McFarlane (1986) operationalised car driver aggression as the time it took for drivers to hoot their horns at a vehicle blocking the road

a 'best way' of operationalising complex variables. The researcher has to make a judgement as to whether they're actually measuring the variables they hope to be measuring and present their arguments to support their decision. A major problem with the operationalisation of complex variables is that they only measure *one* aspect of the variable.

Both IV and DV need to be 'operationalised' accurately and objectively to maintain the integrity of any research study. Without accurate operationalisation, results may not be reliable or valid and certainly cannot be checked or replicated.

Pilot studies

These are small scale 'practice' investigations, where researchers can check all aspects of their research. Changes to the design, method, analysis and so on can be made in the light of this. Pilot studies should improve the quality of the research, help avoid unnecessary work and save time and money. Participants may be able to suggest appropriate changes. For example, participants may admit that they guessed the purpose of the study and acted accordingly (demand characteristics).

The control of variables

In any experiment, the IV is manipulated and the DV is measured. It's assumed that the IV causes any change or effect in the DV. However, there can be other variables that may affect the DV. These are called **extraneous variables**.

Extraneous variables must be carefully and systematically controlled so they don't vary across any of the experimental conditions or, indeed, between participants. When designing an experiment, researchers should consider three main areas where extraneous variables may arise:

- **Participant variables:** participants' age, intelligence, personality and so on should be controlled.

- **Situational variables:** the experimental setting and surrounding environment must be controlled. This may even include the temperature or noise effects.

- **Experimenter variables:** the personality, appearance and conduct of the researcher. Any change in these across conditions might affect the results. For example, would a female experimenter have recorded lower levels of obedience in Milgram's obedience to authority studies? (See pages 116–20.)

Extraneous variables are only a problem if they're not controlled. If they aren't carefully controlled then they may adversely affect or confound the results. They may systematically vary from one condition to another. If this happens we can no longer be sure whether any change in the DV is solely due to the manipulation of the IV or due to the presence of these other 'changing variables'. If this happens, they're called **confounding variables**. The presence of confounding variables minimises the value of any results and are a serious problem.

For example, if researchers wished to investigate the effect of background music (Condition 1) or silence (Condition 2) on homework performance using two classes, they'd have to control a number of possible extraneous variables. These might include: age, homework difficulty and so on. If these were all successfully controlled, then the results would probably be worthwhile. However, if the researchers discovered that those in Condition 1 were considerably brighter than those in Condition 2, then intelligence would be acting as a confounding variable. The researchers could no longer be sure whether any differences in homework performance were due to the presence of the music or due to intelligence levels. Results would be confounded and worthless.

Reliability and validity

Researchers try to produce results that are both reliable and valid. If results are reliable, they're said to be *consistent*. If a study was repeated using the same method, design and measurements, you'd expect to get similar results. If this occurs, the results can be described as reliable.

Reliability in science is essential. If results are unreliable, they cannot be trusted and so will be ignored. However, results can be reliable (i.e. consistent) but still not be accurate. Sometimes measuring instruments may be reliably producing inaccurate results! You may feel this is the case when you consistently get poor marks for your psychology homework! The teacher marks reliably but inaccurately!

Research results must also measure what they're supposed to be measuring (i.e. validity). If they do this and they're accurate, they're said to be valid. In effect, the measures can be described as 'true'. For example, is your teacher measuring your work according to exam board guidelines? If not, then their marking may be reliable but not valid!

It's possible to test both reliability and validity:

- **Internal reliability**: whether a test is consistent within itself. For example, a set of scales should measure the same weight between 50 and 100 grams as between 150 and 200 grams.

- **External reliability**: whether a test measures consistently over time. An I.Q. (intelligence) test should produce roughly the same measure for the same participant at different time intervals. This is called the test–retest method. Obviously, you'd have to ensure that participants don't remember the answers from their previous test.

INTERNAL VALIDITY

This refers to whether the results are valid (see above) and can be directly attributed to the manipulation of the IV. Results are internally valid if they've not been affected by any confounding variables. Are the results valid *within* the confines of the experimental setting? Various characteristics are required in order for an experiment to be internally valid. These are:

- No investigator effects (see page 142)

- No demand characteristics

- Use of standardised instructions

- Use of a random sample (see pages 140–1).

EXTERNAL OR ECOLOGICAL VALIDITY

This refers to whether the results are valid *beyond* the confines of the experimental setting. Can the results be generalised to the wider population or to different settings or different historical times? It's difficult to test whether a study has high ecological validity. It often only becomes clear when research findings are found to either apply or not apply to different situations. Field and natural experiments, and naturalistic observations, are usually regarded as being high in ecological validity. This is because the results can be more easily generalised to other real-life settings. Milgram's obedience experiments have low ecological validity on all three counts outlined above. The sample was predominantly male (cannot be generalised to females); it involved an artificial setting (Yale University laboratory),

EITHER THOSE IQ TESTS WERE UNRELIABLE OR I'VE BECOME A GENIUS IN THE LAST 2 MONTHS

I'M SORRY MR SMITH – THE ELECTRIC SHOCKS WERE ACTUALLY MEANT TO BE FAKE BUT WE WIRED IT UP WRONGLY...COULD YOU RATE ON A SCALE OF 1–10 HOW STRESSFUL YOU FIND THAT NEWS?

Good research means never having to say you're sorry!

and it took place in a different historical time (1960s) to today. Bearing this in mind, are the results still valid today?

Ethics

High quality research should involve good ethical practice. The British Psychological Society (BPS) publishes a code of ethics that all psychologists should follow. Much of this has been covered in the Social Influence chapter (pages 122–6):

- **Informed consent:** should be given by all participants prior to the study. Parental consent should be obtained in the case of children. Consent should also be obtained from children old enough to understand the study.

- **Avoidance of deception:** There may be occasions where some deception is unavoidable. **Presumptive consent** should then be gained from people of a similar background to the participants in the study. If they state that they'd have been willing to participate, it's likely that you'll not upset the actual participants (too much). If deception is used, participants should be told immediately afterwards and given the chance to withhold their data from the study.

- **Adequate briefing/debriefing:** All relevant details of the study should be explained to participants both before and after the study. The debrief is particularly important if deception has been used. Participants should leave the study feeling the same (or better) about themselves as when they started the study.

- **Risk or stress:** Participants should be protected from physical or psychological harm at all times.

- **Right to withdraw:** Participants should always be aware that they can leave the study at any time regardless of whether or not any payment or inducement has been offered. This can be particularly difficult during observations.

- **Privacy:** Participants' data should be treated as confidential and not disclosed to anyone. Numbers should be immediately allocated instead of names, and these should be used by the research team and in any subsequent published articles. It's easy to confuse confidentiality with anonymity. Confidentiality means that data can be traced back to names, whereas anonymous data cannot, since no names are collected by the research team. Confidential data collection is preferable in cases where participants might be followed-up later. Observations should only be made in public places where people might expect to be seen by strangers.

The selection of participants (including random sampling)

Psychological studies usually involve samples drawn from larger populations. Sampling is essential to avoid the need to study entire populations. The selected sample should be representative of this wider population. Representative samples *represent* the target population and should share (some of) the same important characteristics. It's called a target population because this is the group of people whom the researcher is hoping to *target* or generalise the results to. In general, the larger the sample, the better it is. However, the larger the sample, the more costly or time-consuming it is. Psychologists use a number of sampling techniques to try to obtain representative samples:

- **Random sampling:** This is the best known method. It's where every member of the population has an equal chance of being selected. The easiest way to do this is to place all names from the target population in a hat and draw out the required sample number. Computer programs can also generate random lists. This will result in a sample *selected* in an unbiased way. However, it can still result in a biased sample. For example, if 10 boys' and 10 girls' names were placed in a hat, there is a (small) chance that the first 10 names drawn from the hat could be boys. Selection would have been unbiased, but the sample would still be biased! A special form of random sampling involves the random allocation of participants to different conditions in independent groups design (see page 136).

- **Stratified sampling:** With this method, the population is divided into *layers or strata* that are considered important for the particular study. For example, if investigating the effects of age on memory, researchers could identify different age bands (21–30, 31–40, 41–50 etc.) and randomly select people for each band.

- **Quota sampling:** Identical to stratified sampling, except that the participants aren't randomly selected to fit each stratum.

EVALUATION OF THESE TECHNIQUES

✓ The sample is likely to be representative and therefore results can be generalised to the wider population.

✗ It's sometimes difficult to get details of the wider population in order to select the sample.

✗ It's sometimes difficult to decide on the appropriate layers or strata with which to select the stratified sample.

The following two techniques of sampling don't result in representative samples:

- **Opportunity sampling:** Involves selecting participants who are readily available and willing to take part. This could simply involve asking anybody who's passing.

- **Volunteer or self-selected sampling:** Involves people volunteering to participate. They select themselves as participants.

EVALUATION OF THESE TECHNIQUES

✓ They are the easiest, most practical and cheapest ways to get large samples.

✗ The sample is likely to be biased in some (important) way. Thus, the findings may not be generalised to the wider population. Volunteers may be more motivated and thus perform differently than randomly selected participants.

The relationship between researchers and participants

Any social interaction affects people's behaviour. Conducting research is no different. It doesn't take place in a 'social vacuum', and involves some interaction between the researcher and the participant. Such interaction can therefore affect the research findings.

Orne (1962) believed that there are many features in research studies that enable the participants to guess what the study is about and what's expected of them. These demand characteristics can involve participants:

- guessing the purpose of the research and trying to please the researcher by giving the 'right' results.

- guessing the purpose of the research and trying to annoy the researcher by giving them the wrong results. This is called the **'screw you' effect** for obvious reasons!

- acting unnaturally out of nervousness for fear of being thought 'abnormal'

- acting unnaturally in order to 'look good' (**social desirability bias**).

We've previously noted the effect of demand characteristics in different research methods.

I SEE THAT OUR INTERVIEWS LASTED 3 TIMES AS LONG WITH BLONDE SINGLE WOMEN UNDER 30. COULD THIS BE DUE TO EXPERIMENTER EFFECTS...?

A BEAUTIFUL, OAKY BLACKBERRY FINISH

ONLY £4.99 and 12.5% ALCOHOL CONTENT

Qualitative and quantitative analysis of wine!

A technique which reduces demand characteristics is the single blind procedure. This is where participants have no idea which condition of the study they're in. For example, in drug trials, they wouldn't know whether they're being given the real drug or the placebo drug ('sugar pill').

INVESTIGATOR (EXPERIMENTER) EFFECTS

Investigators may inadvertently influence the results in their research. This can occur in a number of ways:

● Certain physical characteristics of the investigator may influence results. Such factors might include age, ethnicity, appearance, attractiveness and so on. For example, white participants may be unwilling to admit their racist views to a black researcher.

● Other less obvious personal characteristics of the investigator such as accent, tone of voice or non-verbal communication (eye contact, smiling) could influence results. Participants may pick up on this and not act as they normally would.

● The investigator may also be biased in their interpretation of the data. This, of course, should never be deliberate. It is claimed that Burt (1955) made up some of his evidence on the influence of heredity on intelligence.

A technique which reduces investigator (experimenter) effects is the double blind procedure. This is where neither the participant nor the investigator knows which condition the participant is in. They are both 'blind' to this knowledge. This prevents the investigator from inadvertently giving the participant clues as to which condition they are in and therefore reduces demand characteristics. Obviously, there is an investigator in overall charge who is aware of the allocation to conditions.

DATA ANALYSIS

Research involves the collection of data. This data can be analysed both quantitatively and qualitatively. Psychologists are still debating the merits of each approach. Generally, qualitative studies produce subjective, detailed, less reliable data whereas quantitative studies produce objective, less detailed, more reliable data. Although all research methods can involve both types of data analysis, there are certain methods that tend to favour the qualitative approach.

General summary of quantitative and qualitative data

Qualitative data	Quantitative data
Subjective	Objective
Imprecise measures used	Precise measures used
Rich & detailed	Lacks detail
Low in reliability	High in reliability
Used for attitudes, opinions, beliefs	Used for behaviour
Collected in 'real-life' setting	Collected in 'artificial' setting

Qualitative data involves people's meanings, experiences and descriptions. It is particularly good for attitudes, opinions and beliefs. Data usually consists of verbal or written descriptions. The qualitative approach suggests that information about human events and experience loses much of its meaning and value when reduced to numerical form (Coolican, 1994).

There is no one agreed way to analyse qualitative data. Each researcher has their own ideas for the best way to do it. The analysis of qualitative data is a fairly new field and new methods are emerging and developing. Some of the ways to analyse qualitative data include:

Content analysis: This is most commonly done within media research. Strictly speaking, it actually involves the quantification of qualitative material. That is, it analyses in a numerical way written, verbal or visual communication. It can involve the analysis of speeches, graffiti, newspapers, TV adverts and so on. Wayforth & Dunbar (1995) analysed the content of Lonely Heart columns to see if men and women were looking for the same things in life.

Sometimes the analysis of content can be very obvious!

Content analysis requires coding units to be developed where analysed material can be categorised. For instance, the number of times women appear as housewives in TV adverts. Analysis can involve words, themes, characters or time and space. The number of times these things do not occur can also be important.

Coding Units for Content Analysis

Unit	Examples
Word	Count the number of slang words used
Theme	The amount of violence on TV
Character	The number of female bosses there are on TV programmes
Time and space	The amount of time (on TV) and space (in newspapers) dedicated to famine in Africa

- **Categorising:** This involves the grouping of common items together. For example, it might be possible to group students' perceptions of their Psychology course into: resources, peer/teacher relationships, teacher knowledge, delivery and so forth. It's often difficult to decide on the categories to use.

- **Quotations:** Word for word quotations are often used to bring the research findings to life. The quotes should 'tell it like it is'. They should typify what others have said during the research.

Qualitative data and naturalistic observations

Observers typically give a running commentary into a tape recorder as they observe behaviour. This produces qualitative data. Such data can be coded or categorised (see above) and help to add detail to quantitative data. The diary method is another technique where observers can take notes of behaviour. This can be self-reported behaviour. The diary method has the advantage of providing genuine information in the participants' own surroundings. However, participants often find it difficult to complete on a long-term basis.

Qualitative data and questionnaire surveys

Qualitative data is mainly collected from open-ended questions where participants are invited to give an answer using their own words. Such data is less likely to be biased by the interviewer's pre-conceived ideas. Analysis of this data can involve content analysis, categorisation or the use of quotations as described above.

Qualitative data and interviews

Interviews have been described above. Interviews are likely to be transcribed and can then be analysed using many of the qualitative techniques described above. Unstructured interviews are most suitable for qualitative analysis. The interpretation of interview data is open to subjective interpretation. However, this lack of objectivity may be overcome by the detail that such a method allows.

Qualitative data analysis: evaluation

Qualitative data analysis tends to be subjective, although there are methods for checking both reliability (through replication) and validity (through the use of other methods). In any case, many qualitative researchers argue that subjectivity and the personal opinion of a participant are extremely valuable and would actually strengthen any research study. Qualitative data analysis can, however, be extremely time consuming.

Measures of central tendency and dispersion

MEASURES OF CENTRAL TENDENCY

These are used to summarise large amounts of data into a typical value or average. They are ways of estimating the mid-point of scores. There are three averages:

The mean: where all the scores are added up and divided by the number of scores.

✓ It is a very sensitive measure.

✓ It includes all the information from the raw scores and is one of the most powerful methods.

✓ It is most appropriate with interval or ratio data. This is data measured using units of equal interval. They reflect a real difference and involve 'public' units of measurement e.g. height, time, distance, weight. For example, the times of runners in the London Marathon.

✗ It is less useful if some of the scores are skewed. That is, if there are very large or small scores ('outliers') in the distribution of scores (the median should be used instead).

✗ Often, the mean score is not one of the original scores. It may involve decimal points.

The median: This is the central score in a list of rank-ordered scores. With an odd number of scores, the median is the middle number. With an even number of scores, the median is the mid-point between the two middle scores.

✓ It is not affected by extreme scores (outliers).

✓ It is most appropriate with ordinal data. This is data that can be ranked or ordered e.g. 1st, 2nd, 3rd. Intervals between the rankings are likely to be unequal. For example, where the runners finished in the London Marathon.

The mean height of these two teams is the same but it gives a misleading impression as to how well-matched they are

✘ It is not as sensitive as the mean, because the raw scores are not used in the calculation.

e.g 1 1 2 3 4 5 6 7 8   the median is 4

2 3 4 6 8 9 12 13   the median is 7

The mode: The most common or 'popular' number in a set of scores.

✔ It is not affected by extreme scores.

✔ It sometimes makes more sense. The average number of children in a British family is better described as 2 (the mode) rather than 2.4 children (the mean).

✔ It is most appropriate with nominal data. This is frequency or category data. The simplest form of data. It merely involves counting the frequency of occurrence in each category. For example, how many runners completed the London Marathon, how many runners didn't.

✘ There can be more than one mode in a set of data
e.g. 2 3 6 7 7 7 9 13 15 16 16 16 20 (modes are 7 and 16).

✘ It tells us nothing about the other scores.

MEASURES OF DISPERSION

These are measures of the variability or spread of scores. They include:

The range: this is calculated by taking away the lowest value from the highest value in a set of scores. *(Note: Some psychologists also add 1 to the range if the measurement is in whole numbers.)*

✔ It is easy and quick to work out.

✔ It includes extreme values, but does not incorporate individual values.

✘ It can be distorted by extreme 'freak' values and does not show whether data are clustered or evenly spread around the mean.
e.g. 2 3 4 5 5 6 7 8 9 21 and 2 5 8 9 10 12 13 15 16 18 21
The range of these two sets of data is the same, despite the data being very different.

Semi-interquartile range: shows the middle 50% of a set of scores. When the scores are in rank order, the first 'quartile' (Q1) is the first 25% of scores. The third quartile (Q3) includes the first 75% of scores. The inter-quartile range is half the distance between Q1 and Q3. To obtain this, you subtract Q1 from Q3 and divide by two.

e.g.   1   2   4   6   7   8   9   12   14   16   19

Q1 ◄— this is the inter-quartile range —► Q3

Q3−Q1 = 14−4 = 10. 10 divided by 2 = 5 = semi-interquartile range.

✔ It is easy to calculate.

✘ It is not affected by extreme scores.

✘ It is inaccurate if there are large intervals between the scores.

Standard deviation: is a measure of the spread or variability of a set of scores from the mean. The larger the standard deviation, the larger the spread of scores.

✔ It is a more sensitive dispersion measure than the range since all scores are used in its calculation.

- What is meant by the terms 'conformity', 'ecological validity' and 'informed consent'? (2 + 2 + 2 marks)

2. Concepts or contributory factors: This might include differences or similarities between concepts or a description of factors (i.e. ways, assumptions, limitations, implications) that might contribute to a particular concept. For example:

- Outline **two** differences between STM and LTM. (3 + 3 marks)

- Outline **two** factors that can modify the effects of stressors. (3 + 3 marks)

3. Theories or explanations: This might involve outlining or describing a particular theory, explanation or approach.

- Outline Bowlby's maternal deprivation hypothesis. (6 marks)

- Describe one psychological approach to stress management. (6 marks)

4. Essential (APFCC) Studies: This will involve asking a question concerning the APFCC (Aims, Procedure, Findings, Conclusions and Criticisms) of any of the Essential Studies. Examiners won't name a particular research study. They might ask for up to two criticisms of a particular study. For example:

- Describe the aims and findings of **one** research study into obedience to authority. (3 + 3 marks)

- Outline the findings of **one** study into anorexia nervosa and give **two** criticisms of this study. (3 + 3 marks)

Sometimes students find it difficult to write enough for 3 marks to an APFCC question. In this case, you must try to *expand* your answer. One way of doing this would be to include brief details of, say, the Procedure if they asked about the Aim and you don't feel you have enough material to gain the 3 marks. However, you *must* relate your material to the question.

For example: Question: Outline the aim of *one* study into the capacity of STM (3 marks). Answer: Jacobs' (1887) aim was to investigate the capacity of STM using the immediate digit span technique which involved reading aloud lists of either letters or numbers. He gradually increased the length of the lists until recall was only successful 50% of the time. Using this innovative technique, he achieved his aim of measuring how much can be stored in STM.

5. Research: This involves knowing about research (theories **and** studies) related to all areas of the Specification. Examiners might ask you to outline findings or conclusions of the research into a particular area. Knowing the Essential Studies in detail should also help here. For example:

- Outline findings of research into the role of 'control' in stress. (6 marks)

- Outline conclusions from research that has investigated the accuracy of eyewitness testimony. (6 marks)

AO1 Exam Terms

Term	Meaning
Define	You must explain what is meant by a particular term such as one used to identify a particular concept.
Describe	You must present evidence of your knowledge of the stipulated topic areas.
Explain	You must convey understanding of the stipulated topic area and make the explanation coherent and intelligible.
Outline	You must offer a summary (brief) description of the stipulated topic area.

Part (c) Exam Questions

Each Part (c) question is worth 18 marks and should take 18 minutes to answer. There are 6 marks for AO1 and 12 marks for AO2. The Part (c) questions can involve a combination of AO1 and AO2 terms.

AO1 and AO2 Exam Terms

Terms	Meaning
Consider **'To what extent...'**	You must demonstrate knowledge and understanding of the stipulated topic area and an awareness of the strengths and limitations of the material presented.

For example:

- Give a brief account of (AO1) **one** alternative to the multi-store model of memory and consider its strengths **and** limitations. (AO2) (18 marks)

- Consider (AO1 and AO2) whether the findings from social influence research can justify the methods used to obtain such findings. (18 marks)

- To what extent (AO1 and AO2) does psychological research support the view that eyewitness testimony is unreliable? (18 marks)

- Outline (AO1) some criticisms of the biological model of abnormality and consider (AO2) whether these are fair. (18 marks)

AO2 Exam Term (this would be combined with an AO1 term such as 'Outline')

Term	Meaning
Evaluate	You must make an informed judgement regarding the value of the stipulated topic area, based on systematic analysis and examination.

For example:

- Outline (AO1) and evaluate (AO2) **one or more** psychological explanation(s) of attachment. (18 marks)

- Briefly describe (AO1) and evaluate (AO2) physiological approaches to stress management. (18 marks)

MARKING ALLOCATIONS

The AQA Specification A exam uses a positive mark scheme which means that any irrelevant answers are ignored and only the relevant ones are marked. This occurs even if the irrelevant material comes first. The only exception to this is in the Research Methods questions where the first answer only is accepted. This means that there is no reason to cross out any (incorrect) answer *except* in Research Methods.

The marking allocations tend to be similar for each question with the same mark allocations. In summary, these are:

AO1

6 mark questions	3 mark questions	Mark allocation
5–6 marks	3 marks	The description is accurate and detailed.
3–4 marks	2 marks	The description is generally accurate but less detailed.
1–2 marks	1 mark	The description is lacking in detail and may be muddled and/or flawed.
0 mark	0 mark	The description is inappropriate, incorrect and/or irrelevant.

(Note: There can also be 2 + 2 + 2 mark allocations (see 2 or 3 mark allocation below))

Exam Hint: When answering a 3-mark question, think of the following:

- **Name**: what you are going to describe using terms from the Essential Glossary
- **Explain**: exactly what the question asks for
- **Research**: try to give a research or everyday example to illustrate your answer.

AO2

12 mark questions	Mark allocation
11–12 marks	There is informed commentary, thorough analysis of the relevant psychological material and it has been used in a highly effective way.
9–10 marks	There is informed commentary, reasonably thorough analysis of the relevant psychological material and it has been used in an effective way.
7–8 marks	There is reasonable commentary, slightly limited analysis of the relevant psychological material but it has been used in an effective way.
5–6 marks	There is reasonable commentary, limited analysis of the relevant psychological material but it has been used in a reasonably effective way.
3–4 marks	There is superficial commentary, rudimentary analysis of the relevant psychological material and there has been minimal interpretation of this.
1–2 marks	There is just discernible commentary, analysis is weak and muddled and the material presented may be irrelevant.
0 marks	The commentary and any analysis is wholly irrelevant to the question.

Most commonly with Research Methods there are 2 mark or 3 mark allocations as follows:

2 or 3 mark questions	Marking allocation
2–3 marks	Accurate and informed description or explanation
1 mark	Brief or muddled answer
0 marks	Incorrect or inappropriate answer

For more detailed help, refer to the document available from AQA entitled Psychology Specification A: Specimen Units and Mark schemes (www.aqa.org.uk)

HINTS ON WRITING EVALUATION (AO2 SKILL)

There are some general points that apply to much research. In order to develop your AO2 skills of analysis and evaluation you could consider the following:

1. Demand characteristics: People change their behaviour to adapt to the situation (Orne, 1962). Also 'screw you' effect (see page 141).

2. Ethics: Does the research follow ethical guidelines? Which does it break? Could it be repeated in a more ethical way? (see page 140)

3. Date of study Is it very old – out of date? Was it conducted pre-ethical guidelines (BPS produced in 1975). Is the theory/study outdated?

4. Ethnocentrism: Does it look at people from a restricted cultural viewpoint? Why does this matter? Is the theory/study biased?

5. Sample: Many studies use a restricted sample. Many use white, middle class Psychology undergraduates. Are they representative? Sear (1986) found 75% of studies from 1980–85 used US undergraduates as participants. Can such results be generalised to other groups? Students are said to differ from the wider population in the following ways:

- Self concept not fully formed
- Less stable peer relationships
- More egocentric
- Less stable views & attitudes
- Stronger need for peer approval

6. What's the point? Miller (1969) argued that psychology should promote human welfare. Does the study do this? If not, why bother with it? Does the theory/study help to open up or extend debate? Has the research helped psychologists look at a topic in a different light?

7. Place where study took place: Psychological research mainly involves laboratory studies which take place in an academic environment and over-emphasise cognitive aspects of behaviour at the expense of emotional ones. Typically, they also remove the participant from the support of their peers. An experiment is 'a social situation' and as such is open to all kinds of social effects.

8. Ecological validity: Is the study applicable to real-life experiences and can it be generalised to the wider population? (e.g. sampling above)

9. Coherence: What is the quality of the research argument? Is the study coherent (does it make cognitive sense)? Does the research have 'face validity'?

10. Status: What is the reputation of the researcher? e.g. **Freud, Pavlov, Skinner, Piaget, Asch and Milgram**. Their work has stimulated other research world-wide. Some of their ideas have been formulated into a paradigm (an approach followed by many psychologists). Have their ideas stood the test of time? Has the theory/study defined or helped to clarify the meaning of any concepts in psychology? Does the theory/study add to our understanding in this area of psychology? Is the theory/study likely to be of any use to psychologists in the future?

11. Methodological problems? Consider the methodology employed in the research. What are the advantages and disadvantages associated with them? Is the study reliable? Is the study valid? (see page 139)

12. Empirical evidence: Is the theory/study well supported by empirical evidence? Is there a lot of conflicting research? Are there other possible explanations and areas of analysis which the theory/study overlooks?

13. Operationalisation: Does the theory/study employ concepts and definitions that can be criticised?

Some sentences which will encourage AO2 commentary:

- . . . 's study can be evaluated in a number of ways. These include . . .

- To evaluate . . . 's study it is important to consider . . .

- Further support for this argument/study can be taken from the work of . . . who found evidence to suggest that . . .

- . . . 's study is useful but . . .

- A contrasting view is that of . . . , who found that . . .

- . . . 's study does not take into account . . .

- The problem with . . . 's research, however, is that it is unreliable/ethnocentrically biased because . . .

- . . . 's research methodology can be questioned, particularly his/her use of . . .

- A conflicting view is expressed by . . . because . . .

- . . . 's study is useful/effective because . . .

- Therefore the study is not applicable because . . .

- . . . 's study lacks . . . . This is a problem because . . .

- Contrary to . . . 's research, . . . suggests that . . .

(adapted from Psychology Review Vol 4 No. 3 pp 8–10)

Examiners always stress the need to elaborate your AO2 commentary. This means to give details about the evaluative point that is being made. *Why* is it a problem? For example: Why is a small sample size a problem? Why is low ecological validity a problem? and so on.

EXAM TIPS

1. Make a **revision timetable** and **try** to stick to it.

2. Employ psychology: The optimum learning time is about 20 minutes. Reward yourself at the end of your revision sessions.

3. Active revision: Read, condense notes, highlight essential points. Use different revision techniques. Variety beats boredom. Does your teacher use the same teaching technique for each and every lesson? Of course not!

4. Revise with friends: Discuss revision strategies and topics with your friends. Share your difficulties, friends might be able to solve some of your problems. This will also help their revision.

5. As a bare minimum you should ensure you've learnt the **Glossary, Essential Studies (APFCC)** and **SAs** in this book.

6. Start with the easiest topics: This will give you confidence and help you move through the material more quickly.

7. Know the Specification content. Questions can **only** be set from the Specification. **If it's not on the Specification, it won't be in the exam.**

8. Know the format of the exam paper. Remember the allocation of AO1 and AO2 marks. (AO3 marks only apply to Research Methods.)

9. Choose your questions carefully based on the 18 mark Part (c) question. It's worth the most marks (60%) and is therefore the most important. Read the questions carefully.

10. Answer the question: Don't waffle. It's quality, not quantity that counts. Make sure all of your answers are relevant.

11. Time allocation: Allocate your time appropriately in the exam. Don't be tempted to spend more time on your favourite answers. The first few marks are the easiest to obtain. Always answer the correct number of exam questions.

12. 'Mark a minute' format: Spend the same number of minutes on a question as there are marks available. There are 30 marks available for each 30-minute question. Spend 3 minutes on a 3-minute question and so on.

13. Practise exam questions: 'Practice makes perfect.' With the exception of research methods questions, there are a limited number of questions that can be asked. The more past paper questions you practice, the better your examination technique will be. If you're fortunate, you may even have practised a question that comes up in the exam.

Finally, remember, examiners mark to the standard of a *'notional 17-year-old'* – they don't expect perfect answers.

The very best of luck.

Sample Answers (SAs)

Introduction:

All the 'sample answers' below are derived from the Exam tips Boxes. If you feel you could answer all the 18 mark questions below then you'll be brilliantly prepared for the AS exam. Don't forget you'll have a choice of questions in the exam, so, with luck, two of them should come up in some form or another.

You can think of the answer as writing three paragraphs, each about 100–130 words long. The first one could comprise the description (AO1) and is worth 6 marks. The final two paragraphs could comprise the commentary (analysis and evaluation (AO2)) and are worth 12 marks. You can, of course, mix the description and commentary throughout the three paragraphs – just remember the mark allocations for AO1 (6) and AO2 (12).

Some examiners recommend you concentrate on writing just the AO2 commentary (analysis and evaluation) in your answer since the AO1 (description) will inevitably appear when you have to briefly describe the studies you choose to analyse and evaluate. Note that we've included most of the Part c questions you could be asked, but we haven't tried to cover every possibility. All the Part c questions which follow are worth 18 marks.

COGNITIVE PSYCHOLOGY: HUMAN MEMORY

1. Give a brief account of the different characteristics of short-term and long-term memory and evaluate research that demonstrates these differences.

2. Outline and evaluate the multi-store model (MSM) of memory.

3. Give a brief account of **one** alternative to the multi-store model (MSM) of memory and consider its strengths and limitations.

4. Give a brief account of **one** alternative to the multi-store model (MSM) of memory and consider its strengths and limitations.

5. Consider psychological research into explanations of forgetting in short-term memory.

6. Consider psychological research into explanations of forgetting in long-term memory.

7. To what extent is there psychological evidence to support the idea of repression in forgetting?

8. Briefly describe and evaluate research into the way emotional factors influence forgetting.

9. *'There are so many factors that influence memory that we cannot be sure that any memories are not merely biased reconstructions.'* To what extent does psychological research support this view of reconstructive memory?

10. To what extent has psychological research shown eyewitness testimony to be unreliable?

DEVELOPMENTAL PSYCHOLOGY: ATTACHMENTS

1. Consider psychological research into individual differences in attachment.

2. Give a brief account of **one** psychological explanation of attachment and consider its strengths **and** limitations.

3. Give a brief account of and evaluate Bowlby's maternal deprivation hypothesis.

4. To what extent does psychological research show that deprivation is harmful to children's development?

5. Consider psychological research into the effects of privation on children's development.

6. *'While going out to work may benefit mothers of young children, the children themselves may suffer compared with those whose mothers stay at home.'* To what extent does psychological research support this view of the effects of day care on children's social development?

PHYSIOLOGICAL PSYCHOLOGY: STRESS

1. To what extent does stress play a role in cardiovascular disorders?

2. Consider research into the effects of stress on the immune system.

3. Consider psychological research into the role of life events as a source of stress.

4. Consider psychological research into the effects of workplace stressors.

5. To what extent have the effects of stress been shown to be modified by personality?

6. Give a brief account of psychological methods of stress management and consider their strengths **and** limitations.

INDIVIDUAL DIFFERENCES: ABNORMALITY

1. Briefly describe definitions of abnormality and assess to what extent they have taken into account cultural differences.

2. Outline and evaluate the different attempts to define abnormality.

3. Briefly describe and evaluate the biological (medical) approach to abnormality.

4. Give a brief account of the psychodynamic approach to abnormality and assess its strengths **and** limitations.

5. Give a brief account of the behavioural model of abnormality and consider its strengths **and** limitations.

6. Outline and avaluate the cognitive approach to abnormality.

7. *'Anorexia nervosa is a biological rather than a psychological disorder.'* Assess to what extent research supports the view that anorexia nervosa (AN) is caused by biological factors.

8. Outline and evaluate psychological approaches as explanations of AN.

SOCIAL PSYCHOLOGY: SOCIAL INFLUENCE

1. Consider psychological research into majority influence (conformity).

2. Give a brief account of psychological explanations of conformity and consider their strengths **and** limitations.

3. Give a brief account of psychological explanations of obedience and consider their strengths **and** limitations.

4. To what extent can use of deception in social influence research studies be justified?

5. To what extent can ethical guidelines ensure that the major ethical issues involved in research with human participants are properly dealt with?

It's worth answering these Part c questions yourself using the textbook material and *then* comparing your answer with the SAs that follow. Ensure your answers:

● Are about the same number of words (could you write them in 18 mins?).

● Are divided up into the same AO1 (6 marks – one-third of essay) and AO2 format (12 marks – two-thirds of essay).

● Match the marking allocations for AO1 and AO2 outlined on page 156.

SAMPLE ANSWERS (SAs)

COGNITIVE PSYCHOLOGY: HUMAN MEMORY

Give a brief account of the different characteristics of short-term and long-term memory and evaluate research that demonstrates these differences. (18 marks)

First paragraph: Description: AO1: worth 6 marks

The main differences between STM and LTM relate to encoding, capacity and duration. STM tends to favour 'acoustic' coding whereas long-term memory tends to favour 'semantic' coding (Baddeley, 1966). STM has a limited capacity of 7 +/- 2 words (Jacobs, 1887) whereas LTM is regarded as having an infinite capacity. STM duration is very short (<18 seconds – Peterson & Peterson, 1959) whereas LTM can last a lifetime (Bahrick, 1975). Another key difference is that rehearsal is vital for STM whereas it is not essential for maintenance in LTM. People also tend to be aware of information in their STM whereas this is not necessarily the case with LTM.

Note: It's not possible to describe all the studies supporting STM/LTM differences in the time available. Evidence to support these differences can come in later paragraphs.

Second and third paragraphs: AO2: 12 marks

Many of the studies that demonstrate STM/LTM differences are robust, reliable and easily replicable. Evaluation of the research will cover encoding and duration differences.

Baddeley demonstrated that acoustically similar words are recalled less well than acoustically dissimilar words in a STM task and that semantically similar words are recalled less well in a LTM task. However, the STM difference was quite small (64% to 71%) suggesting semantic coding does occur in STM (as does some visual). Also, we can recall holiday places, smells, tastes and faces extremely well from LTM suggesting that LTM can, and does, use more than merely semantic coding.

The Peterson and Peterson STM duration study used nonsense trigrams that students had to remember for differing time periods whilst completing a distractor task. Criticisms of this study are that nonsense syllables lack ecological validity in that they do not represent everyday memories. Furthermore the sample of students may not be representative of the wider population and thirdly, the distractor task introduced another cognitive processing task that, although preventing rehearsal, might also have led to some interference. However, it has to be accepted that a 'number counting' distractor task would be least likely to interfere with a 'letter' recall task. The Bahrick (1975) study testing 440 participants on their recall of high school friends demonstrated the duration of LTM. This study used everyday, real-life memories of a large and diverse age sample and as a result the findings of very long-term memories (VLTM) were ecologically valid and important. However, the study inevitably lacked some important controls such as whether participants had 'refreshed' their memories in the intervening period since school by reminiscing with friends or by viewing their old yearbook. To be fair, Bahrick did try to examine this influence.

Note: Two different characteristics of STM and LTM along with analysis and evaluation of the relevant research have been covered.

Outline and evaluate the multi-store model of memory. (18 marks)

First paragraph: Description: AO1: worth 6 marks

Atkinson and Shiffrin (1968) believed there were three components of memory (sensory memory, STM and LTM). Sensory memory only processes about 1/20th of the information received through the senses – it is the 'gatekeeper of information'. The information selected is passed onto the STM that has a limited capacity (+/– 2 magic 7) and duration (30 seconds). Through rehearsal, information is transferred from STM to LTM. The longer information is rehearsed in STM the more likely it is that information will be transferred from STM to LTM for more permanent storage. Information in STM not rehearsed will be quickly forgotten.

A diagram of the multi-store model would be appropriate but the description is essential.

Second and third paragraphs: AO2: 12 marks

Experiments support the multi-store model by demonstrating differences between STM and LTM with respect to encoding, duration and capacity. They demonstrate that STM favours acoustic encoding (semantic in LTM) and has a far smaller capacity and duration than LTM (Baddeley, 1966). These findings are robust and replicable both within a laboratory and in a more real-life setting. The serial position curve study (Murdock, 1962) strongly supports the notion of two separate stores with the primacy effect demonstrating LTM (through acoustic rehearsal) and the recency effect demonstrating STM. Work in the clinical field also gives weight to the STM/LTM distinction. Studies such as KF (Shallice & Warrington, 1970) whose LTM was fine but STM was poor support this idea of dual stores. However, the MSM does not explain how KF's LTM can remain normal with STM so poor since *all* information is supposed to be processed through STM. Since case studies deal with 'one-off' situations this evidence must be treated with caution.

However, the MSM is criticised for being over-simplified, passive and a linear ('one-way') model. It is argued that it is not rehearsal itself that is important but what we do with the information (Bekerian and Baddeley, 1980). For example, the model does not easily explain flashbulb memories. Researchers have suggested that the LTM (episodic, semantic and procedural) and STM (working memory model) are split into several different, not unitary, stores. Studies have shown that LTM is actively involved in all aspects of memory and also demonstrate the two-way flow of information between the STM and LTM and hence challenge the idea that STM only contains new information (Morris *et al*, 1985).

Note: We've written one paragraph supporting the model and one criticising it. You could choose to write two paragraphs either supporting OR rejecting the model.

SAMPLE ANSWERS (SAs)

Give a brief account of ONE alternative to the multi-store model (MSM) of memory and consider its strengths and limitations. (18 marks)

First paragraph: Description: AO1: worth 6 marks

Baddeley & Hitch (1974) proposed that the STM should be replaced by a system that allows several pieces of information to be processed and interrelated concurrently (hence 'working memory' title). They argued that STM was far more complex than just a 'stopping off' station for information to transfer to LTM. The components are: the central executive, in overall charge, which is an attentional system of limited capacity allocating resources to the other 'slave' systems. These are the articulatory loop (a verbal rehearsal system or inner voice), the visuo-spatial sketch pad (a visual rehearsal system or inner eye) and, later, the primary acoustic store or phonological store (auditory system or inner ear).

Note: A diagram of the working memory model would be appropriate but the description is essential.

Second and third paragraphs: AO2: 12 marks

There are a number of positive points that can support the working memory model. Psychologists generally accept that STM is better viewed as comprising a number of different processing systems and is more realistic in explaining how memory works in everyday life. Each of the components is supported by experimental evidence, for example, dual task studies (Baddeley, 1973). The model is supported by physiological evidence from PET scans where four different brain areas have been shown to be active during different STM processing tasks. These areas correspond to the model's components. Such studies involve 'normal' patients and evidence can be more easily generalised than those using case studies. Nevertheless, brain-damaged patients who suffer selective deficits to their STM also support the model (e.g. KF's motorcycle accident mainly affected only verbal information – Warrington & Shallice, 1970).

Weaknesses of the model include the fact that we know least about the most important aspect of the model, namely, the central executive store. Since its precise function is unknown it has been argued that this is as inappropriate as one single STM store. Also the capacity of the central executive has never been measured. A further criticism is that the model does not explain changes in processing ability that occur as the result of practice or time. Much of the evidence to support the model has been confined to the laboratory and it may therefore lack what it claims to do, that is, explain memory in real-life settings. Even Baddeley stated: 'We have a long way to go before we can be sure of the details of the model'.

Note: We've chosen the Working Memory model here as an alternative to the MSM and written one paragraph supporting the model and one criticising it. You could choose to write two paragraphs either supporting OR rejecting the model.

Give a brief account of ONE alternative to the multi-store model (MSM) of memory and consider its strengths and limitations. (18 marks)

First paragraph: Description: AO1: worth 6 marks

Craik & Lockhart '72 Levels of Processing (LOP) approach stated that memory should not be viewed as a 'structural' model but rather a process – it's not where information goes that's important but what we do with it. They see memory as the by-product of the processing of information: the durability of the memory is a function of the depth of processing. They believe that stimuli are processed through a series of levels that become progressively more complex. The simplest level is 'visual' (e.g. analysing material by the shape of the word), 'acoustic' (e.g. analysing material according to its sound) and 'semantic' (e.g. analysing material by its meaning). The level used depends on both the nature of the stimulus and the processing time available.

Second and third paragraphs: AO2: 12 marks

The LOP approach changed the direction of memory research from searching for simple models to looking for complex processes. Experimental work supports the superiority of semantic processing. Craik and Tulving's (1975) experiment demonstrated that words that are semantically encoded by participants are significantly better recalled than acoustically or visually processed ones. These results have also been supported by experiments by Hyde and Jenkins (1973). The LOP approach also makes 'cognitive sense'. Imagine trying to learn all your AS material by sound or visual analysis, you have to understand the meaning of the material to process it deeply and hence recall it later.

The LOP approach is too simplistic and descriptive rather than explanatory. It presents a circular argument in that there is no independent way of measuring depth. The model predicts deep processing will lead to better retention and, in turn, better retention is taken as evidence for deeper processing. Another criticism is that depth of processing may not be the only factor influencing retention. Tyler et al (1979) showed that difficult anagrams were later recalled better than simple anagrams. The LOP approach would suggest they should be recalled equally well since they were processed at the same semantic level. However, this criticism may have been answered to some extent since later research extended 'depth' to include 'organisation', 'distinctiveness', 'elaboration' and 'effort'.

Note: We've chosen the Levels of Processing model here as the alternative to the MSM. Although we've tried to stick to the three paragraphs format, description (AO1), 'for' and 'against' paragraphs (AO2), inevitably, sometimes AO1 and AO2 come into each of the different paragraphs. This doesn't matter. Just ensure that one-third of the material you present is descriptive (AO1 = 6 marks) and two-thirds analysis and evaluation (AO2 = 12 marks).

SAMPLE ANSWERS (SAs)

Consider psychological research into explanations of forgetting in short-term memory. (18 marks)

First paragraph: Description: AO1: worth 6 marks

The trace decay theory suggests that stimuli create nerve cell activity in the brain but it may not be strong enough to create a structural neural change. Thus, a memory trace or engram would be encoded in STM but would not have made a permanent trace in the LTM. Metabolic processes degrade the trace (unless it is maintained by repetition and rehearsal), which means the memory rapidly fades from STM. Whilst trace decay focuses on time, displacement theory focuses on capacity. STM has a capacity of 7 +/−2 and therefore in order to hold more information, old information has to be displaced or 'pushed out'. This old information is thus forgotten.

Second and third paragraphs: AO2: 12 marks

Displacement theory is supported by Waugh and Norman's serial probe task where 16 digits are presented at a rate of either one or four per second. One of the digits (the probe) is repeated and participants must report the digit that followed this probe. When the probe is given near the end of the list, recall is good; but when it was near the beginning, recall was poor. This supports displacement theory since it is assumed that later ones displace the earlier digits. However, this finding can also support decay theory since the earlier the probe is in the list the more time it has to decay. To further support decay theory, they used the different presentation rate conditions and found that the faster the list was presented, the better the recall. Although Shallice (1967) later confirmed these findings, it was found that elapsed time (decay) was less influential than number of subsequent items (displacement). One criticism is that decay and displacement cannot be easily separated.

Peterson and Peterson's STM duration study supports the decay theory since they demonstrated that information was largely lost from STM after an 18 seconds delay. However, the rehearsal prevention task (counting backwards) may have interfered or displaced the original material, thus questioning support for trace decay. Reitman (1971) cleverly overcame this problem by using a 'tonal attention' intervening task. She obtained similar results supporting decay theory without the associated problems of interference or displacement. All of these studies are laboratory based and most often involve rather meaningless lists to learn. The value of such results to everyday memory can be questioned.

Consider psychological research into explanations of forgetting in long-term memory. (18 marks)

First paragraph: Description: AO1: worth 6 marks

Interference occurs because memories interfere with and disrupt one another. In retroactive interference, new memories can disrupt old memories. Proactive interference is when old memories disrupt new memories. Retrieval failure is another explanation of LTM. It suggests that failure to recall memories occur because there are insufficient cues or clues to help locate the memory. This explanation suggests that the memory is not accessible at a particular point in time. The 'tip of the tongue' phenomenon, state and context dependent studies demonstrate retrieval failure forgetting.

Second and third paragraphs: AO2: 12 marks (some AO1)

Many experiments using meaningless word lists and nonsense syllables and the paired associate word technique have demonstrated interference in the laboratory (Keppel & Underwood, 1962). However, these procedures (and thus the findings) do not seem to apply to everyday life. Interference theory seems to explain laboratory studies that involve learning compressed in time but not learning that occurs in 'real life' with more meaningful material (Solso, 1995). It would seem from interference experiments that the more material we try to remember, the more likely there is to be interference. However, experts in a particular field with great pre-existing knowledge (and thus the greater likelihood of interference effects) tend to suffer from less interference when they try to learn new relevant information than a 'novice'.

There are numerous studies that support the idea of retrieval failure forgetting. Godden & Baddeley (1975) found evidence for context-dependent retrieval with their study of divers recalling and learning information underwater or on dry land. However, Fernandez and Glenberg, despite trying to replicate context-dependent studies, have never found reliable evidence for such claims. Goodwin (with alcohol) and Darley (with marijuana) have also found state-dependent effects, although the ethical stance of such studies has been questioned. Ucros (1989) with a meta-analysis of the effect of mood on retrieval found rather weak support for it. Support cited for retrieval failure theory of forgetting comes from both within and outside the laboratory. Indeed, returning to one's old school, tasting or smelling something one has not experienced for years often appears to trigger 'long lost' memories and this led Eysenck to conclude that *'it seems probable that this (retrieval failure) is the main reason for forgetting in LTM'*.

Note: The question asks for explanations so you have to include at least TWO: trace decay and displacement. A more difficult question could ask you how much research into forgetting has revealed about the nature of STM and LTM. You'd have to deal with STM/LTM differences (see earlier) and then evaluate studies that demonstrate these such as Waugh & Norman (1965), Murdock (1965) and Babrick et al (1975).

SAMPLE ANSWERS (SAs)

To what extent is there psychological evidence to support the idea of repression in forgetting? (18 marks)

First paragraph: Description: AO1: worth 6 marks

Freud claimed that some forgetting is motivated and the mechanism for this is repression. Freud believed that we forget things that are a source of anxiety and/or guilt. These memories are not lost (i.e. they are available) but they are no longer in the unconscious mind (i.e. they are inaccessible). Freud used the example of 'freudian slips' to explain this. This refers to a situation when one word is 'accidently' replaced with another. Freud claimed that this was due to an unresolved conflict and that 'innocent forgetting' simply did not exist.

Second and third paragraphs: AO2: 12 marks (some AO1)

Much of Freud's claims were based on clinical case studies. Also in support of Freud's theory, Parkin claimed that repression could be related to psychogenic amnesia caused by severe emotional shock (as opposed to physical trauma or disease). Parkin claimed that repression was beneficial to sufferers of post traumatic stress disorder (PTSD) and presented clinical studies to demonstrate this. It has also been suggested that 'recovered memories' of sexual abuse from childhood are evidence of repression. However, this is a highly controversial area with serious moral and ethical implications and there has been conflicting evidence to support these claims.

One of the major criticisms of repression is that there is very little scientific, quantitative data to support it. However, some argue that this is because it is difficult and often unethical to study the effects of emotional stress. Despite this, Kline argues that you can adequately demonstrate repression in the laboratory. He told participants that they had failed a test and asked them to recall questions from the test at a later date. He found relatively poor recall scores for those given the negative feedback of failing the test compared to those participants given their correct scores. However, Eysenck disputed these results by pointing out that similar poor recall scores were present in participants given 'success feedback'. Eysenck believed that poor recall was due to the high state of arousal in that particular participant, not the negative feedback. However, other laboratory research has reported evidence of repression (Levinger & Clark, 1961).

Overall, Freud's theory was largely derived from rather subjective case studies and findings cannot be generalised because they concern individuals. Also there is far more scientific and reliable evidence to support other theories of forgetting such as retrieval-cue failure and interference.

Note: You don't have to provide a balanced argument – you can take one side or the other.

Briefly describe and evaluate research into the way emotional factors influence forgetting. (18 marks)

First paragraph: Description: AO1: worth 6 marks

Emotional factors do appear to influence forgetting; some seem to minimise forgetting and others seem to increase it. State dependent studies that investigate physiological factors present at encoding and recall have shown that good moods can reduce forgetting. McCormick and Mayer supported this with regard to happy memories. According to Freud, anxiety-provoking memories are deliberately forgotten or repressed and thus increase forgetting. An extremely detailed and vivid memory of an event or incident is called a 'flashbulb' (FB) memory and these are more likely if the event is personally and emotionally significant. FB memories thus reduce forgetting.

Second and third paragraphs: AO2: 12 marks (some AO1)

Freud reported case studies that he believed demonstrated motivated forgetting. However, such case studies lack objectivity and findings cannot be generalised to a wider population. Studies of patients with psychogenic amnesia support the idea of severe emotional trauma causing forgetting (Parkin, 1993) as do studies that report 'recovered' memories of child abuse (Williams, 1994). Due to ethical considerations, experimental evidence of repression is difficult. But, Levinger & Clark (1961) showed that emotionally charged words were more difficult to recall that neutral ones. However, the poorer recall of the emotional words could have been because they were more difficult to visualise than the neutral words!

Conway et al (2003) support the existence of FB memory since 75% of Americans had near perfect recall of the September 11th 2001 tragedy. However, they've only tested FB memories up to one year later. Brown & Kulik's (1977) 'racial relevance' findings also support the idea that emotionally-arousing events cause unforgettable memories. However, other studies question the accuracy of FB memories. Wright (1993) found people reporting inaccurate memories for the Hillsborough tragedy but it can always be claimed that events not remembered do not fit the criteria required for a FB memory (e.g. unexpected, emotionally and personally significant). It has also been claimed that FB memories are not forgotten because they are repeated over and over again. Repeated rehearsal of any memory aids recall and emotional factors do not play a significant part in FB memories.

It would seem that emotional factors can *help* remembering and in some cases they can *increase* forgetting.

Note: A difficult question since so much information could be included. Note that some AO1 appears in the last two paragraphs and some AO2 occurs in the first paragraph. This doesn't matter – it's perhaps a little artificial for us to separate them out. We've done this to try to aid clarity. You can mix description and analysis & evaluation throughout the paragraphs. Just remember the proportion of marks available for AO1(6) and AO2 (12).

SAMPLE ANSWERS (SAs)

'There are so many factors that influence memory that we cannot be sure that any memories are not merely biased reconstructions.' To what extent does psychological research support this view of reconstructive memory? (18 marks)

First paragraph: Description: AO1: worth 6 marks

Bartlett (1932) was one of the first psychologists to question the accuracy of memory and to suggest that all memories are reconstructed based on prior knowledge and experiences (schemas). He claimed that remembering is an active process which involves *'effort after meaning'*, that is, making the past more coherent to fit in with existing knowledge. Schemas are an important factor in memory reconstruction since they allow people to interpret their world and events in a simplified and stereotyped way. This can also lead to inaccurate memory reconstructions.

Second and third paragraphs: AO2: 12 marks (also some AO1 included)

Bartlett's (1932) classic study into the 'War of the Ghosts' supports the reconstructive nature of memory by showing that reproductions of an unfamiliar story are altered in significant ways. For example, the reproductions are shortened and made more coherent (intrusions, omissions and normalisation) from the cultural viewpoint of the participant. However, the methodology employed by Bartlett was questionable. The analysis of the story reproductions was subjective and the stories used were culturally unfamiliar and, as such, do not represent everyday memories. Allport & Postman (1947) also support the reconstructive nature of memory with their study demonstrating the effect of racial stereotyping. Both of these studies are exceptionally old and the Allport and Postman, in particular, may not be so valid today.

EWT is a particular aspect of memory where research predominantly supports the view that memory is reconstructive. Loftus has conducted numerous studies which illustrate this. However, again there are criticisms of her work in that most of it involved laboratory experiments using film clips of incidents rather than real-life events. A contrasting view is that of Yuille & Cutshall (1989) who, using a real-life shooting incident, showed that memories are not so easily reconstructed, even when using misleading questions. Further support from Wynn & Logie (1998) using real-life events suggests that memories are very accurate and not subject to reconstruction and the accuracy of flashbulb memories is not easily explained using the reconstructive idea of memory.

Note: You could choose to answer this question using EWT research exclusively. There is certainly enough information in EWT to successfully do this. However, this answer predominantly deals with Bartlett, schemas and related research.

To what extent has psychological research shown eyewitness testimony to be unreliable? (18 marks)

First paragraph: Description: AO1: worth 6 marks

There are numerous studies that question the accuracy of EWT. Loftus has shown consistently with numerous experimental studies that EWT can be influenced by people's willingness to make their memories fit their schemas. Loftus and Palmer (1974) showed the effect of changing a single verb on witness statements of the speed of a crashing car. Using the verb 'smashed into' led to a faster speed estimate (41 mph) than use of the verb 'contacted' (32 mph). Loftus (1975) also provides evidence that the style of questioning used with eyewitnesses can actually distort memories. Eyewitnesses asked about a car passing a barn on a country road were later more likely to report having seen a barn when, in fact, the barn did not exist.

Second and third paragraphs: AO2: 12 marks (also some AO1 included)

Criticisms of many of these studies are that they are low in ecological validity in that they do not take place in real-life situations and that the emotional effects associated with seeing such incidents may affect memory recall and that this is unlikely to be replicated in the laboratory setting. In addition, most of the studies used students as participants so there are questions as to the generalisation of the findings. Other factors such as race, clothing and social influence have been shown to affect the accuracy of EWT.

However, Baddeley questions whether EWT research is so clear-cut. He argues that research does not prove destruction of the memory trace but merely interference with its retrieval. This suggests that reconstructive questioning of witnesses is all-important. Yuille & Cutshall (1986) using witnesses to a real-life serious crime (in contrast to Loftus' methodology) found memories to be accurate, detailed and not easily distorted: in essence, EWT can be very reliable. Foster *et al* (1994) also found memories for real-life crimes to be more accurate than simulations. In summary, it is suggested EWT can be inaccurate if misleading information concerns insignificant details and if witnesses have little reason to distrust it.

SAMPLE ANSWERS (SAs)

DEVELOPMENTAL PSYCHOLOGY: ATTACHMENTS

Consider psychological research into individual differences in attachments. (18 marks)

First paragaraph: Description: AO1: worth 6 marks

Ainsworth *et al* (1971, 1978) devised the Strange Situation, a method for studying attachments in one-year-olds. This consists of eight episodes, involving the baby, its mother, and a female stranger. They were most interested in the baby's reunion behaviours. Ainsworth *et al* identified three types of attachment. 70 per cent were classified as securely attached (Type B). They became upset when the mother left the room, and wanted her to comfort them as soon as she returned. 15 per cent were classified as anxious-avoidant (Type A). These babies were indifferent towards their mother, and barely reacted when she returned. 15 per cent were anxious-resistant (Type C). They became quite distressed when the mother left, but when she returned they showed ambivalence towards her. Many other studies have been conducted using the Strange Situation, including cross-cultural studies.

Second and third paragraphs: AO2: worth 12 marks

Ainsworth *et al*'s study is the most important in all of attachment research. But the sample was small. However, several more recent studies, using larger samples, have supported their original claim that the mother's sensitivity determines whether the baby is securely or insecurely attached (van Iizendoorn & Schuengel, 1999). Cross-cultural studies using the Strange Situation have shown important differences, both within and between cultures. For example, Van Iizendoorn & Kroonenberg (1988) reviewed the research. They found that although Type B is the most common type, Type A is relatively more common in Western European countries, and Type C in Israel and Japan. This suggests that the Strange Situation may not be equally valid as a way of measuring attachment in different countries.

Attachment types are often regarded as fixed characteristics of the child. But if the family's circumstances change (such as the mother's stress levels), the child's attachment type can change. This couldn't happen if attachment style were a fixed characteristic. Also, a child's attachment to its mother may be different from attachment to its father. It could be securely attached to one but not to the other. This shows that attachments are a feature of unique relationships, rather than characteristics of the child. The Strange Situation has also been criticised as highly artificial (it lacks ecological validity). And surely it's unethical for psychologists to deliberately expose babies to stress, even if this sometimes happens in real life.

Give a brief account of *one* psychological explanation of attachment and consider its strengths *and* limitations. (18 marks)

First paragraph: Description: AO1: worth 6 marks

According to Bowlby (1969, 1973), newborn human babies are completely helpless. So, they're genetically programmed to behave towards their mothers (or mother-figures) in ways that ensure their survival. These species-specific behaviours include cuddling, looking, smiling, and crying. Babies use them to shape and control their caregivers' behaviour. Mothers are also genetically programmed to respond to the baby's attachment behaviours. There's a critical period for attachment formation (Bowlby, 1951). Mothering is useless for most children after 12 months, and for all children after two-and-a-half to three years. Generally, attachment behaviours are more evident when the child is distressed, unwell, afraid, or in unfamiliar surroundings. Babies also display monotropy, a strong innate tendency to become attached to one particular adult female. This attachment to the mother-figure is unique.

Second and third paragraphs: AO2: worth 12 marks

Bowlby's theory was opposed to 'cupboard theories' of attachment such as learning theory. He rejected learning theory's claim that attachments are based on the baby's need for food by drawing on Lorenz's (1935) study of imprinting in goslings, and Harlow's (1959) study of contact comfort in rhesus monkeys. Their research showed the importance of instinct, but we can't necessarily apply these findings to humans. However, Schaffer & Emerson's (1964) longitudinal study of Scottish babies also contradicted the learning theory explanation. They showed that babies were often attached to people who weren't involved in their physical care, and often the main carer wasn't the baby's main attachment figure. But these attachment figures included fathers, and this seems to contradict Bowlby's monotropy theory.

Also, babies and young children display a wide range of attachment behaviours towards various attachment figures other than their mothers. That is, mothers aren't special or unique as implied by monotropy. Schaffer and Emerson also showed that it's quite common for young children to form multiple attachments (it's the 'rule'). Although Bowlby accepted that this can happen, he thought it was the exception rather than the rule. Bowlby also believed that fathers aren't of any direct emotional importance to the baby. Their main role is to provide emotional and financial support to the mother. But Schaffer and Emerson's findings suggest that fathers are attachment figures in their own right.

Give a brief account of and evaluate Bowlby's maternal deprivation hypothesis. (18 marks)

First paragraph: Description: AO1: worth 6 marks

Bowlby's maternal deprivation hypothesis (MDH) is based on two of the central elements from his attachment theory. First, there's a critical period for the development of attachments. For most children, if they haven't formed an attachment during their first year, it will be too late to form one later on. For all children, this becomes impossible after two-and-a-half to three years. Second, monotropy refers to the innate tendency to become attached to one particular female adult (not necessarily the biological mother). The attachment to her is the first to develop, and is the child's strongest attachment. This makes it unique. Specifically, the MDH claims that if the mother-baby attachment were broken in the first years of life, the child's emotional and intellectual development would be seriously and permanently harmed.

Second and third paragraphs: AO2: worth 12 marks

The MDH was based largely on studies of children raised in orphanages and other institutions (such as Goldfarb, 1943; Spitz, 1945, 1946; and Spitz & Wolf, 1946). According to these researchers, and Bowlby, in all these institutions the common factor was lack of maternal care. This was the crucial harmful influence on the children growing up in them. This is what Bowlby later called maternal deprivation. But these studies had some serious methodological weaknesses. For example, in Goldfarb's study the children who were raised in institutions and those who were raised by foster parents weren't randomly assigned to these two 'conditions' (as would happen in a true experiment). It's possible that the latter were more 'desirable' in various ways, which is why they were fostered in the first place. This makes it difficult to make direct comparisons between the two groups.

Also, the institutionally-reared children lived in almost complete social isolation for their first year. All the institutions involved were extremely unstimulating environments, and this lack of stimulation (social and intellectual) could have been responsible for the children's poor development, in addition to, or even rather than, the lack of maternal care (maternal 'deprivation'). Also, as Rutter (1981) points out, maternal 'deprivation' refers to loss of a mother-figure. Strictly speaking, the children raised in institutions suffered maternal 'privation', because they lacked the opportunity to form an attachment with anyone in the first place. Deprivation and privation refer to very different types of early experience, with very different types of effect. Studies of institutionally-raised children provide evidence for the effects of privation (not just maternal), rather than deprivation.

To what extent does psychological research show that deprivation is harmful to children's development? (18 marks)

First paragraph: Description: AO1: worth 6 marks

Deprivation refers to the loss, through separation, of an attachment figure. Short-term deprivation usually lasts days or weeks, such as when a child goes into a residential nursery, or stays with foster parents, while its mother goes into hospital. Or the child might go into hospital itself. Long-term deprivation includes the death of a parent, and separation through parental divorce. Another example is day care. According to Bowlby (1969, 1973), children become distressed when separated from their mothers, which was illustrated by Robertson & Robertson's (1969) study of John. He displayed the three components of distress, namely protest, despair, and detachment. According to Schaffer (1996), most children are adversely affected by parental divorce, but most are resilient enough to adapt eventually (Hetherington & Stanley-Hagan, 1999). One important effect of long-term deprivation is separation anxiety.

Second and third paragraphs: AO2: worth 12 marks

John became increasingly distressed as his stay in the residential nursery went on. But the Robertsons and Bowlby disagreed as to the exact cause of his distress. For the Robertsons, John suffered bond disruption. In his mother's absence, there was no one to take her place. For Bowlby, it was loss of his mother that was crucial (that is, John suffered maternal deprivation). But Robertson & Robertson (1989) argue that they provided clear evidence that a young child's separation from his mother triggers a sequence of psychological reactions likely to have long-term effects. The children they fostered in subsequent studies showed much less distress than John, and good quality substitute care should always involve a 'substitute mother'. Nevertheless, they concluded that separation is always dangerous and should be avoided if possible.

Apart from the quality of the substitute care, the degree of distress is affected by several factors. For example, separation will probably be most distressing between the ages of 12–18 months (Maccoby, 1980), for boys (although there are wide differences between boys and between girls), if there have been any behaviour problems (such as aggression) before separation, and if the child hasn't been separated from the mother before. Similarly, the nature, severity, and duration of the effects of divorce are influenced by several factors. These include continuity of contact with the non-custodial parent, the financial status/lifestyle of the custodial parent, and whether the custodial parent remarries and the nature of the resulting step-family. So, it may not be separation (short- or long-term) itself that's harmful, but factors associated with it.

'While going out to work may benefit mothers of young children, the young children themselves may suffer compared with those whose mothers stay at home.' To what extent does psychological research support this view of the effects of day care on children's social development? (18 marks)

First paragraph: Description: AO1: worth 6 marks

Day care includes all types of non-maternal care of children who normally live with their parent(s). Examples include creches, day nurseries, childminders, and nannies. One view of the harmful effects of day care on children's social development is that such children are more likely to develop insecure attachments to their mothers. According to Bowlby, children whose mothers go out to work suffer maternal deprivation. Belsky & Rovine (1988) reported evidence that compared with 'home-reared' babies, those who'd been in day care for at least four months before their first birthday, and for more than 20 hours per week, were more likely to develop insecure attachments. Several other studies have shown that children who were in day care as babies are as self-confident and emotionally well-adjusted as those who weren't (Clarke-Stewart, 1989).

Second and third paragraphs: AO2: worth 12 marks

Bowlby's attachment theory, and his maternal deprivation hypothesis, have both influenced the still widely held view that children should be cared for by their own mothers. Any criticisms of Bowlby's theories weaken the argument that day care is non-normative. But most modern British and American mothers with school-age children go out to work. So, shared childcare is actually the norm, and has always been shared (Scarr, 1998). Belsky & Rovine's findings were based on the Strange Situation. But this is an inappropriate technique to use with children in day care. It assumes that repeated separations from the mother are stressful for the child. But day care children are used to such separations. What looks like indifference to the mother (implying insecure attachment) may just be independence and self-reliance (Clarke-Stewart, 1989).

Day care doesn't necessarily weaken attachments to the mother. Provided the day care is stable and of a reasonable quality, children don't suffer any ill effects. They might actually benefit from it (Schaffer, 1996). Where the quality of the day care is poor, children are likely to be rated lower on social and emotional development. However, the quality of day care chosen by parents is correlated with their personal characteristics or circumstances. For example, children from families with single working mothers or low income are more likely to experience low quality care. So, we can't be sure whether it's the quality of day care or parental circumstances which influence children's development. This confusion between the two variables has led to an overestimation of the effects of day care (Scarr, 1988).

Consider psychological research into the effects of privation on children's development. (18 marks)

First paragraph: Description: AO1: worth 6 marks

Privation refers to the failure to develop an attachment to any individual. This is often associated with children growing up in institutions. The effects are mainly long-term, and a major example is affectionless psychopathy, the inability to care and have deep feelings for other people. The early studies of children raised in institutions (such as Goldfarb, 1943) on which Bowlby based his maternal deprivation hypothesis, actually show the effects of privation. Hodges & Tizard's (1989) longitudinal study of children raised in institutions for at least their first two years provides evidence both for and against the view that the effects of early privation are reversible. Case studies of children who've endured extreme early privation (such as the Czech twins studied by Koluchova, 1972, 1991) are also relevant.

Second and third paragraphs: AO2: worth 12 marks

Bowlby et al's (1956) study of TB sanatorium children was originally discussed in relation to deprivation. The children who'd spent time in a sanitorium before the age of four weren't any more likely to show affectionless psychopathy than a control group. But they did show more signs of emotional disturbance. Bowlby admitted that factors other than separation were responsible for this disturbance, including illness and death in their families. Some of the sanitorium children may have suffered privation. Hodges and Tizard's data for the 16-year-olds who'd spent their early years in institutions suggests that there may be a critical period for developing attachments with peers later in life (so supporting Bowlby). But they also showed that early privation may not prevent the formation of attachments to adoptive parents later on (so contradicting Bowlby).

However, longitudinal studies like that of Hodges and Tizard suffer from the problem of participant drop-out. It's unclear how representative the 16-year-olds were of the original sample. It's also unclear what determined whether the institutional children were adopted or returned to their biological families. This is important, because only the adopted children successfully developed attachments with their parents. However, at each point in the study the children were compared both with themselves (at earlier ages) and with a matched control group. Koluchova's study of the Czech twins supports the findings of other studies involving children who suffer extreme privation and then are 'rescued'. That is, it's possible to reverse the effects of prolonged early privation, which doesn't predestine them to a life of severe handicap (Clarke & Clarke, 2000).

PHYSIOLOGICAL PSYCHOLOGY: STRESS

To what extent does stress play a role in cardiovascular disorders? (18 marks)

First paragraph: Description: AO1: worth 6 marks

Selye (1956) defined stress as the non-specific response of the body to any demand made upon it. This response reflects the General Adaptation Syndrome (GAS), the body's defence against stress. The body responds in the same way to any stressor, whether it's environmental (such as extreme temperature, or electric shock) or arises from within the body itself. The GAS comprises three stages, alarm reaction, resistance, and exhaustion. By this last stage, the body's resources are becoming depleted, and psychophysiological disorders develop. These include cardiovascular disorders such as high blood pressure/BP (hypertension), coronary artery disease (CAD), and coronary heart disease (CHD). Friedman & Rosenman (1974) found evidence for the role of individual differences in men's ways of dealing with stressful situations. They concluded that men who displayed Type A behaviour (TAB) were far more likely to develop CHD than other men.

Second and third paragraphs: AO2: worth 12 marks

Selye's concept of stress as a non-specific bodily response was based upon his observations of hospital patients. But research into the GAS involved mainly rats' responses to stressors. So, it hasn't been tested directly with human beings. Nevertheless, it helps to account for the physiology of stress. For example, the alarm reaction involves the fight-or-flight response (FOFR), which is a well-established reaction to stressful situations. This is also crucial to the evolutionary explanation of how stress makes us ill. Most modern-day stressors have a much greater psychological element than those faced by our ancestors. Stress is more likely to be chronic, which involves repeated episodes of increased heart rate and BP, causing plaque formation within the cardiovascular system. Selye has been criticised for largely ignoring the psychological aspects of stress.

Friedman and Rosenman's American study of TAB showed how psychological factors (personality) can produce physiological effects (CHD). It was a long-term study involving a very large sample. All the participants were free of heart disease at the start, and the researchers were able to separate out the effects of risk factors (such as smoking) from the effects of personality. But the measures used to assess Type A and Type B behaviour have been criticized. Also, their results can't be generalised to women, since their sample was all-male. Their basic findings have been replicated in other countries. But most Type A men don't develop CHD, and many Type Bs do. Also, their evidence is only correlational. There's no evidence to support their claim that personality actually causes CHD.

Consider research into the effects of stress on the immune system. (18 marks)

First paragraph: Description: AO1: worth 6 marks

The immune system is a collection of billions of cells which travel through the bloodstream. They move in and out of tissues and organs, defending the body against foreign bodies (antigens), such as bacteria, viruses, and cancerous cells. The main types of immune cells are white blood cells (leucocytes). When we're stressed, the immune system's ability to fight off antigens is reduced. This is why we're more susceptible to infections. The immunosuppressive effects of stress were demonstrated by Kiecolt-Glaser et al's (1984) study of medical students facing important exams, and in Schliefer et al's (1983) study of men whose wives had died from breast cancer. Riley's (1981) study of tumour development in mice implanted with cancer cells also demonstrates the immunosuppressive effects of stress.

Second and third paragraphs: AO2: worth 12 marks

There are always important ethical issues raised by experiments with non-humans which involve subjecting them to painful or life-threatening procedures. In Riley's experiment, not only were the high-stress condition rats deliberately subjected to stress, but they developed large tumours before being killed. There are also scientific issues. In particular, what can studies of mice placed on rotating turntables tell us about the immunosuppressive effects of stress in humans? However, studies using human participants are broadly consistent with Riley's results. In Kiecolt-Glaser et al's study, blood samples from the medical students were analysed for the amount of leucocyte activity; specifically, how much natural killer cell activity. These help fight off viruses and tumours.

Kiecolt-Glaser et al's study was a natural experiment. The exams would have happened anyway, and all the participants volunteered for the study. So, there are no ethical problems raised by the study, unlike Riley's. Also, the medical students were compared with themselves when the two blood samples were taken (prior to and on the first day of the exams). This controls for important participant variables, such as personality. But we can't be sure that it was exam stress alone which caused the change in immune function. Nevertheless, different stressors, including exams, death of spouse, caring for relatives with Alzheimers' disease (Kiecolt-Glaser et al, 1995) have all been shown to be involved in reduced immune function.

SAMPLE ANSWERS (SAs)

Consider psychological research into the role of life events as a source of stress. (18 marks)

First paragraph: Description: AO1: worth 6 marks

Life events include changes which happen to most people, such as leaving school, and marriage, and much less common ones, such as imprisonment, and being fired at work. Holmes & Rahe (1967) constructed an instrument for measuring stress, which they defined as the amount of change a person has to deal with during a particular period of time. Their Social Readjustment Rating Scale (SRRS) comprises 43 life events, each given a life change unit (LCU) score. They found that the higher someone's overall LCU score (how many life events they'd experienced during the previous year), the more likely they were to show symptoms of both physical and psychological illness. They claimed that stress actually makes us ill.

Second and third paragraphs: AO2: worth 12 marks

Holmes and Rahe's SRRS was the first attempt to measure stress objectively and to examine its relationship to illness. It assumes that any change is stressful. But the list of life events are largely negative, especially those with the highest LCU scores (such as death of spouse). So, the SRRS may be confusing 'change' with 'undesirability'. Some of the life events could refer to positive or negative change, and there's no reference to the problems of old age, or natural or man-made disasters. Also, it seems that only those life events classified as uncontrollable are correlated with later illness. By definition, most of the 43 life events aren't everyday occurrences. This is in contrast with Kanner et al's (1981) hassles scale, which includes traffic jams, bad weather, and financial worries.

Kanner et al found that daily hassles were correlated with undesirable psychological symptoms. Also, hassles were a more powerful predictor of both physical and psychological symptoms than the SRRS's life events. Delongis et al (1982) confirmed these findings, but they also reported a correlation between life events and physical symptoms for the 2–3 years prior to the study. Instead of life events causing illness, it could be that some life events are early signs of an illness that's already developing (Penny, 1966). Studies like Rahe et al's (1970) study of navy personnel are merely correlational, so we cannot be sure what's cause and what's effect. Also, participants are often asked to recall both their illnesses and the stressful life events that occurred during the preceding year. Retrospective studies like this often produce unreliable data.

Consider psychological research into the effects of workplace stressors. (18 marks)

First paragraph: Description: AO1: worth 6 marks

Some occupations are more stressful than others. Four of the most stressful are nursing, social work, teaching, and the emergency services. Nurses have to deal constantly with patients' pain, anxiety, and death, give emotional support to relatives, and are often in the front line when major incidents occur. Business executives constantly have to make important decisions. Brady's (1958) executive monkey experiment was an attempt to test the relationship between high stress levels, and increased hormone production and the development of ulcers. He was mainly interested in the effects of stress in business executives. Whenever the executive monkey failed to press the lever to prevent electric shock, the yoked control would also receive shock. But only the executives developed severe ulcers and eventually died.

Second and third paragraphs: AO2: worth 12 marks

Brady concluded that it was stress, not the shocks, that caused the ulcers. This seems to contradict other research (involving humans) which shows that control helps to reduce (not increase) stress. But his monkeys weren't randomly assigned to the executive/yoked control conditions. They were allocated according to how quickly they learned to avoid shock. This makes his conclusions less valid. In Weiss's (1972) replication of Brady's experiment, the shock was preceded by a warning signal. Under these conditions, the executive rats were less likely to develop ulcers than the controls. This suggests that what's stressful is having to be constantly vigilant (as Brady's monkeys had to be). Indeed, human executives and air-traffic controllers have the highest incidence of stomach ulcers of any US occupational groups. The latter especially have to be constantly vigilant.

Apart from being unethical, Brady's and Weiss's experiments can only suggest why stress is harmful for humans. But other evidence suggests that people low down on the occupational ladder, who lack control, are more susceptible to stress-related illness (for example, Marmot et al, 1997). This and other studies suggest that having too little stress can damage your health, both physical and mental. Other sources of workplace stress include work overload (too much to do, or doing a job that's beyond one's capabilities) and underload (not having enough to do, or not being stretched/stimulated enough). Stress may also arise from role ambiguity and conflict, job insecurity and redundancy, lack of career structure, and poor interpersonal relationships and lack of support.

SAMPLE ANSWERS (SAs)

To what extent have the effects of stressors been shown to be modified by personality? (18 marks)

First paragraph: Description: AO1: worth 6 marks

Friedman & Rosenman's (1974) study of Type A behaviour (TAB) was intended to provide evidence for the role of non-physiological factors, in the form of personality, in coronary heart disease (CHD). They showed how psychological factors, in the form of personality, can have physiological effects (CHD). TAB describes a typical way of reacting to life in general, and work-related situations in particular, such that Type A men have a greater chance of developing CHD compared with other types. More recent research has suggested that specific Type A characteristics, in particular hostility, may be a better predictor of CHD than TAB as a whole. Type C personalities, who tend to suppress their anger, are cancer-prone (Temoshok, 1987). Women diagnosed with breast cancer showed significantly more emotional suppression than those with non-life-threatening breast disease (Greer & Morris, 1975).

Second and third paragraphs: AO2: worth 12 marks

Friedman and Rosenman's study has been criticised on many counts. For example, the sample was all male, so the results don't necessarily apply to women, and the two measures of TAB produced different scores for some men, so they might have been measuring different things. Also, hostility specifically seems to be a better predictor of CHD than TAB as a whole. However, their basic findings have been replicated outside the US, and their results suggest that the harmful effects of stressors can be mediated through psychological factors. It's how people perceive and react to stressors that's (potentially) dangerous to health.

Greer *et al* (1979) investigated how women with breast cancer use coping mechanisms. Women who either used denial or showed a 'fighting spirit' were significantly more likely to be free of cancer five years later than those who either showed 'stoic acceptance' or 'gave up'. A follow-up at 15 years later confirmed the improved prognosis (Greer *et al*, 1990). These findings lend scientific support to the advice to 'think positive', and it might be possible to teach people such strategies (Hegarty, 2000). But personality or coping mechanisms can only have an indirect effect on cancer through their effect on the immune system. Also, personality interacts with gender. For example, women are less likely than men to display TAB, which may reflect the male gender role. This, in turn, implies the role of culture. Women are also less hostile than men.

Give a brief account of psychological methods of stress management and consider their strengths *and* limitations. (18 marks)

First paragraph: Description: AO1: worth 6 marks

Formally, stress management (SM) refers to a range of techniques, both psychological and physiological, used deliberately by professionals, singly or in combination, to help people reduce their stress levels. Psychological examples include stress inoculation training/SIT (Meichenbaum, 1976), and increasing hardiness (Kobasa, 1979, 1982). SIT attempts to reduce stress through changing cognitions. The individual's self-defeating internal dialogue is first identified, then s/he is helped to make positive, coping statements, and finally is guided through increasingly threatening situations. Hardiness can be increased in three ways. Focusing involves helping people to identify the physical signs of stress; reconstructing past stressful situations helps to make a more realistic assessment of different stressors; and compensation through self-improvement is about taking on challenges that we can meet in the face of unavoidable stressors.

Second and third paragraphs: AO2: worth 12 marks

SIT, like other forms of cognitive restructuring, is a practical application of cognitive psychology. It's based on a widely held belief that our emotional responses and behaviour are largely determined by the way we think. So, if you can change the thoughts which normally produce stress reactions, you can reduce people's stress levels. Meichenbaum believes that people sometimes find things stressful because they think about them in catastrophising ways. This is an extreme example of the view that it's how people interpret events or situations that makes them stressful. Meichenbaum (1997) believes that SIT's 'power-of-positive-thinking' approach can successfully change people's behaviour. Some behaviourist psychologists believe that focusing on internal thoughts is unscientific, but it's proved successful, especially in reducing exam nerves and the anxiety associated with severe pain.

Increasing hardiness is a practical application of Kobasa's theory of personality. Hardy people have high internal locus of control (Rotter, 1966). Research shows that events seen as uncontrollable are the most stressful. So, helping people to gain control should help reduce their stress levels. In turn, locus of control is related to learned helplessness (Seligman, 1975; Miller & Norman, 1979). Psychological methods don't suffer from some of the disadvantages of physiological methods, such as the side-effects of anxiolytic drugs, or the need for biofeedback's specialised equipment. But perhaps SIT or increasing hardiness are effective not because of the specific techniques involved, or the underlying theory, but simply the attention and support given by the therapist. By contrast, physiological methods are more likely to work because of the specific physiological changes they induce. But even here, psychological factors still play a part.

INDIVIDUAL DIFFERENCES: ABNORMALITY

Briefly describe definitions of abnormality and assess to what extent they have taken into account cultural differences. (18 marks)

First paragraph: Description: AO1: worth 6 marks

The 'statistical infrequency' definition of abnormality refers to behaviour that is statistically or numerically infrequent in a given population. Specific characteristics can be measured and plotted on a 'normal' distribution. Anybody who deviates from the average is classified as 'abnormal'. The 'deviation from social norms' definition regards abnormality as any behaviour that deviates from accepted norms or rules within society. It would include any behaviour that *is beyond the bounds of social acceptability*. The 'failure to function adequately' definition is applied to people who cannot live a 'normal' life. They do not experience 'normal' emotions and/or display everyday behaviours. The 'deviation from ideal mental health' definition involves a comparison between a person's thoughts and behaviours with a list of 'normal', desirable or ideal characteristics. The further people are from these ideals the more abnormal they are.

Note: The question asks for definitions (plural) and therefore you could choose to write about only two definitions if you wish. Examiners will recognise the 'trade-off' between depth and breadth in your choice.

Second and third paragraphs: AO2: worth 12 marks

Since there are no universal measures of behaviour the 'statistical infrequency' definition fails to take account of cultural differences. Standards of behaviour can only be set within specific populations or cultures. Screaming aloud as a response to unhappiness would be statistically infrequent in Western cultures and thus be regarded as abnormal. However, Lee (1961) found this be a common response for Zulu women. It is also clear that cultures differ in their reporting of mental illness. Rack (1982) found that depression is rarely reported in Asian cultures. Thus, statistical measures of mental illness in different countries may reflect reporting levels rather than actual prevalence. The statistical infrequency definition would appear to only apply *within* cultures and not *across* cultures. However, even this has been questioned. With many different groups of people within society it may be more accurate to apply this definition within sub-cultures only in an attempt to avoid sweeping generalisations.

Similar criticisms can be made of the 'deviation from social norms' definition. Since norms vary across cultures there can be no universal agreement on what constitutes normal or abnormal behaviour. Evidence to support this criticism comes from the diagnosis rates of ethnic minorities in Britain. The rate of black African-Caribbean immigrants diagnosed with schizophrenia is far greater than whites (Cochrane, 1977). Since this finding is not replicated in other countries, it is unlikely to reflect true morbidity rates. Therefore, it is suggested that British psychiatrists diagnose behaviour on the basis of social norms prevalent in the 'white' population. There is a cultural bias in diagnosis. However, many psychiatrists claim that so-called 'disadvantaged' ethnic groups are exposed to more stressful life experiences (e.g. racism) and this may account for the differences. This explanation can also be applied to the 'failure to function adequately' and 'deviation from ideal mental health' definitions.

It's difficult to produce a culture-free definition of abnormality. What is regarded as abnormal behaviour differs between cultures. This suggests that the concept of abnormality is a social construction.

Note: Due to time limitations, this answer concentrates primarily on the first two definitions. However, points are made relevant to the last two definitions. Analysis is difficult but material is presented which questions many of the points outlined.

Outline and evaluate the different attempts to define abnormality. (18 marks)

First paragraph: Description: AO1: worth 6 marks

The first paragraph here can be exactly the same as the one on the left.

Second and third paragraphs: AO2: worth 12 marks

The 'statistical infrequency' definition fails to distinguish between desirable and undesirable behaviour. Statistically speaking, many extremely gifted individuals could be classified as 'abnormal' using this definition. The use of the term 'abnormal' in such cases is inappropriate. It has also been shown that as many as 50% of Americans suffer from a mental disorder during their lifetime and thus such behaviours are not really that 'statistically infrequent'. The knowledge that men are less likely to report mental problems than females also suggests that the prevalence rate for mental disorders reflects reporting levels rather than true incidence of any disorder. The 'deviation from social norm' definition reflects the 'norms' of a particular culture. Such norms change across and within cultures over time. The definition fails to account for the fact that it can be beneficial to break social norms as in the case of the suffragettes. 'Conforming neurotics' are individuals who conform so strictly to social norms that they become neurotic about following them. Paradoxically, their adherence to social norms makes them abnormal!

The main problems with the 'failure to function adequately' definition of abnormality is that there are individuals who carry on functioning within society perfectly well and yet must be suffering from a mental disorder. Such individuals would include Harold Shipman who managed to continue working as a GP despite being a serial killer. To a certain extent, all the definitions can be considered as arbitrary and subjective definitions with many problems attached. There is no single 'perfect' definition. There is little objective evidence to support one definition over another. The concept of 'abnormality' can be viewed as a social construction within a particular culture.

Note: You do not have to cover all the definitions, although you should include at least TWO. You could also include the cross-cultural problems that psychologists have encountered with their attempts to define abnormality. These have not been covered here in much detail to avoid replication with the previous answer.

SAMPLE ANSWERS (SAs)

Briefly describe and evaluate the biological (medical) approach to abnormality. (18 marks)

First paragraph: Description: AO1: worth 6 marks

The Biological (Medical) Model assumes that abnormality has a physiological cause related to the physical structure or functioning of the brain. Genetic factors are believed to play a part in the development of mental disorders that appear to 'run in the family'. Biochemical explanations propose that many disorders can be explained by neurotransmitter imbalances. Infections are also implicated in many mental disorders. It's also assumed that, like physical illnesses, mental illnesses can be diagnosed accurately by examining patient symptoms. It follows that treatments based on this model involve physical, invasive techniques involving drugs, electro-convulsive therapy and psychosurgery.

Second and third paragraphs: AO2: worth 12 marks

Objective, scientific evidence to support the biological model includes brain scans of people who have been found to suffer from mental dysfunction due to physical brain damage such as a tumour. Kendler *et al* (1985) found supporting evidence for a genetic component to mental disorder. They found that relatives of schizophrenics were 18 times more likely to develop the illness than matched controls. Neurotransmitter imbalances (excess dopamine) have also been detected in the brains of schizophrenics. Barr *et al* (1990) found evidence that mothers who developed flu whilst pregnant were more likely to subsequently develop schizophrenia. This suggests a possible correlational link between the infection and the disorder. The successful use of physical treatments including drugs and the objective clinically controlled tests of their effectiveness also provide evidence to support the biological approach.

One of the main problems with such physiological evidence is that it could be the *effect* of mental disorder rather than the *cause*. Is an excess of dopamine the *result of* schizophrenia or the *cause* of it? Studies on animals suggest it is more likely to be the latter. However, it remains uncertain whether animals are actually experiencing a particular disorder in a similar way to humans and whether such findings can be generalised. The reliability of psychiatric diagnosis using the biological approach has been questioned by Rosenhan (1973). He showed that psychiatrists could not reliably distinguish between the 'sane and insane'. Although the use of deception in this study has been criticised, the study highlights the lack of objective tests used within the biological approach. Psychiatrists have to rely on patient self-report of their symptoms and these could well be unreliable. The biological approach has also been criticised for being reductionist and ignoring patient thoughts, feelings and experiences. It's suggested that other environmental factors must contribute to the development of mental disorders and these are largely ignored by the biological approach.

Note: There is a wealth of information that could be included here. Evaluation of the medical approach could also include a consideration of whether it is a humane approach, whether it labels people and results in the stigmatising of vulnerable individuals.

Give a brief account of the psychodynamic approach to abnormality and assess its strengths *and* limitations. (18 marks)

First paragraph: Description: AO1: worth 6 marks

The psychodynamic approach suggests that mental illness is caused by psychological forces. These forces remain 'unconscious' and explain why people do not know the reasons for their behaviour. According to Freud, there are three parts to the personality: the id (a person's basic instinctual drives), the ego (their 'reality manager') and the superego (their conscience). There is a perpetual conflict between the ego and superego and it is balanced by the ego. When this balance is not achieved, abnormal behaviour occurs. Conflict is particularly marked during childhood when the personality is still developing and thus childhood experiences play a vital part in adult development. Distressing events in childhood can be repressed (placed in the unconscious) only to re-emerge in adulthood. Freudian psychoanalysis is a 'talking cure' and concentrates on making the 'unconscious conscious'. It's assumed that re-experiencing past conflicts helps people to deal with them in the present.

Second and third paragraphs: AO2: worth 12 marks

Freud was the first to recognise the importance of psychological factors on the development of mental disorders. This, along with his emphasis on the influence of childhood, is widely accepted today. In addition, the idea of the unconscious having some affect on conscious behaviour attracts much support. The therapy seeks to treat the whole person and is therefore not reductionist. Psychodynamic therapeutic practice is extensive and widespread. The psychodynamic approach has been influential and long lasting. Its influence extends beyond the narrow constrains of psychology into film, literature and art. It is suggested that an unimportant theory would have been dismissed many years previously.

The main criticism of the psychodynamic approach is that it cannot be scientifically tested. Evidence 'recovered' from the unconscious can support the approach and any evidence that is not forthcoming can be claimed to still be in the unconscious! The predominant use of case studies ensures that such findings cannot be easily generalised. Indeed, the majority of Freud's patients were middle class, Viennese women – not a particularly representative sample. Evidence to support the approach is often reported by the therapists themselves and thus could be open to interpretative bias. It is generally accepted that Freud exaggerated the effectiveness of his psychodynamic therapy for his own patients. Eysenck (1952) in a comprehensive review of 7000 cases claimed that the therapy does more harm than good.

Although influential, evidence to support the psychodynamic approach remains weak and questionable.

Note: You do not have to consider evidence that both supports and rejects the approach. You could choose to evaluate the approach from one viewpoint. Although a fairly balanced answer is provided above, it is perhaps easier to find evidence to reject the approach.

Cross-cultural variations in attachment: The *patterns* of attachment type (secure, anxious-avoidant, anxious-resistant) that exist both between and within cultures.

Day care: All varieties of non-maternal care of children who normally live with their parents or close relatives. Examples include crèches, day nurseries, childminders ('out-of-home' facilities), (non-resident) nannies, and grandparents ('in-the-home' arrangements). It *excludes* foster care, and institutional (residential) care.

Deprivation: The loss (through separation) of an attachment figure (usually the mother-figure). This can be *short-term* (for example, when the child goes into care while the mother is in hospital) or *long-term* (as in divorce or the death of a parent). The most common (short-term) effect of deprivation is distress.

Insecure attachment: A relationship with another person in which the attachment figure is either treated with *indifference* and much like a stranger (anxious-avoidant: Type A); or shown *ambivalence* following a period of separation (anxious-resistant: Type C). In neither case does the attachment figure provide a sense of security and safety.

Institutionalisation: The fact of growing up in an institution (such as an orphanage or residential nursery) or the effects of such an upbringing. Institutionalisation is associated with privation.

Privation: In relation to attachment, the absence of an attachment figure or the lack of opportunity to form an attachment. More generally, the lack of particular kinds of stimulation. Privation is usually associated with children raised in institutions and/or under conditions of extreme hardship. The most common (long-term) effect is developmental retardation (such as affectionless psychopathy).

Secure attachment (Type B): A (usually) long-term relationship with another person, who provides a sense of security and comfort at times of stress, and separation from whom causes distress and sorrow.

Separation: Disruption to the relationship with an attachment figure. This can be short-term/temporary (as when a child's mother goes into hospital) or long-term/permanent (as in parental divorce or death).

Social development: Changes in the child's social relationships, in particular, its ability to become attached to a mother-figure. In relation to day care, it is claimed that children experiencing day care are more likely to develop *insecure attachments*.

11.1 PHYSIOLOGICAL PSYCHOLOGY

Cardiovascular disorders: Disorders/diseases of the heart and the circulatory system. Examples include high blood pressure/BP (hypertension), coronary artery disease (CAD), and coronary heart disease (CHD).

Control in the perception of stress: Only those life events classified as 'uncontrollable' seem to be correlated with later illness. One of the 'three Cs of hardiness' (Kobasa) corresponds to a high internal locus of control (Rotter), that is, taking responsibility for your actions, and viewing yourself as being in charge of what happens to you. Locus of control is related to learned helplessness (Seligman), the belief that nothing you do will make any difference to your situation.

General Adaptation Syndrome (GAS): According to Selye, the body's defence against any stressor, either environmental or arising from within the body itself. It consists of the alarm reaction (*shock* and *countershock phases*), resistance, and exhaustion.

Immune system: A collection of (billions of) cells, produced mainly in the spleen, lymph nodes, thymus, and bone marrow, which travel through the bloodstream, defending the body against antigens (such as bacteria, viruses, and cancerous cells). The major type of immune cells are white blood cells (leucocytes).

Life changes: Events that require us to adapt. In Holmes and Rahe's Social Readjustment Rating Scale (SRRS), the degree of stress (that is, change) associated with particular life events is measured in Life Change Units (LCUs). Death of spouse, divorce, and marital separation are rated as being the most stressful. Change in sleeping habits, Christmas, and minor violations of the law are rated as being the least stressful.

Physiological approaches to stress management: Formal attempts to reduce the effects of stress, such as the use of psychotherapeutic drugs (in particular, *anxiolytic* – anxiety-reducing – drugs), and biofeedback (which helps patients control their BP, heart rate, muscle tension, and other *autonomic functions*).

Psychological approaches to stress management: Both formal and informal attempts to reduce the effects of stress. *Formal* attempts include stress inoculation training (SIT), a form of cognitive restructuring, and increasing hardiness. *Informal* attempts refer mainly to coping strategies/mechanisms, such as problem-focused and emotion-focused helping (Lazarus and Folkman).

Sources of stress: The different kinds of stressors which can induce a stress response. These include environmental 'insults' (such as electric shock, and excessive heat or cold), life changes (such as death of spouse), and workplace stressors (such as work overload, and role conflict).

Stress: (a) An environmental event or situation (a stressor) which induces a stress-response in us; (b) our response to a stressor, in particular the physiological/bodily responses (such as the General Adaptation Syndrome/GAS); (c) interaction between an individual and their environment, in particular the belief that they don't possess the resources needed to deal with the demands of a situation. But people differ in what makes them feel stressed, how much stress they feel, and how they try to deal with it.

Stress management: (a) A range of techniques used, deliberately, by professionals to help people reduce their stress levels. These can be psychological (as in cognitive restructuring and increasing hardiness) or physiological (as in the use of psychotherapeutic drugs and biofeedback). This is *formal* stress management. (b) *Informal* stress management involves what we do spontaneously in our attempts to reduce stress, such as when we use coping strategies/mechanisms.

Stressors: An environmental event or situation which we feel unable to deal with, and which induces a stress response.

Workplace stressors: Stressors which are either common to many occupations (such as work overload/underload, role ambiguity/conflict, job insecurity/redundancy), or which are related to the nature of the particular occupation (such as nurses having to deal constantly with suffering and death, and air traffic controllers having to be vigilant for long periods).

11.2 INDIVIDUAL DIFFERENCES

Abnormality: Since abnormality can take many different forms, there is no single feature that encompasses the term. Generally, abnormality can be defined as *deviating from the norm or average* but it is difficult to determine this norm or average. Attempts to define abnormality include: statistical infrequency, deviation from social norms, failure to function adequately and deviation from ideal mental health.

Anorexia nervosa: *(literally means 'nervous loss of appetite')* Primarily a female eating disorder characterised by a refusal to maintain normal body weight (<85% normal weight). Accompanied by an intense fear of being over-weight, a distortion of body image and a general, evident physical decline with the cessation of menstruation (amenorrhoea), dry, cracking skin and constipation. In some cases AN can be fatal. Depression and low self-esteem is also common.

Behavioural model of abnormality: This approach isn't associated with mental disorders but with maladaptive behaviour. It assumes that all behaviour is learnt through the process of classical and operant conditioning and thus can be unlearnt using the same principles. Treatment involves behaviour therapy and behaviour modification. This approach is scientifically tested and proven to be effective for less serious disorders.

Biological (medical) model of abnormality: An approach which assumes that abnormal behaviour has an underlying physical cause. Diagnosis involves the identification of symptoms. Studies into genetic inheritance, biochemistry and infection support this approach. Treatment involves invasive techniques such as drugs, ECT and psychosurgery. There is considerable scientific evidence to support this approach, although it is argued that it treats the symptoms rather than the root cause of any illness.

Bulimia nervosa: *(literally means 'ox hunger')* Primarily a female eating disorder characterised by periods of binge eating frequently followed by purging (expulsion of food). Accompanied by an intense fear of being fat, the physical effects are not obvious but include the deterioration of tooth enamel and digestive tract damage. BN is rarely fatal.

Clinical characteristics: This refers to the symptoms displayed by individuals which help in the diagnosis of patients. The list of symptoms is gained through observation, examination and self-report.

Cognitive model of abnormality: Assumes that abnormal behaviour is caused by an individual's disturbed thoughts. It assumes that thoughts affect behaviour. Individuals make 'cognitive errors' such as magnifying failures and minimising successes. Therapy involves cognitive restructuring. Irrational and negative thoughts need to be replaced by rational and positive ones. This approach is both modern and popular.

Cultural relativism: The assertion that behaviour must be judged within the context in which it originates. Each culture has its own values and practices, and psychologists should not make value judgments about cultural differences.

'Deviation from ideal mental health': This definition concentrates on the 'normal' characteristics people should possess for ideal mental health. This list includes positive self-esteem, autonomy and resistance to stress. If people do not possess these characteristics they are said to be abnormal. Limitations of this include the subjective nature of the over-demanding criteria. Indeed, based on the criteria proposed by Jahoda (1958) most people might be classified as abnormal!

'Deviation from social norms': Abnormality is seen as any behaviour that violates the social norms within a society. Social norms are unwritten rules for acceptable behaviour (i.e. how one ought to behave). This definition has limitations in that it can be subjective and norms change over time and vary across cultures.

Eating disorders: A term that applies to psychological and physical illnesses that are associated with harmful eating patterns or behaviour. The most well-known of these are anorexia nervosa and bulimia nervosa.

'Failure to function adequately': This definition involves a list of behaviours that prevent a person from coping with their day-to-day life. This list includes personal distress, unpredictability and maladaptive behaviour. The more of these indicators a person has, the more abnormal they are seen to be. One limitation is that some people who would be classified as abnormal (e.g. Harold Shipman) appear to function adequately in society.

Psychodynamic model of abnormality: Assumes that mental disorders are psychological in origin. Childhood experiences and the conflict in the personality (id, ego and super-ego) play an important part in the development of mental disorders. Traumatic events are placed in the unconscious through repression. The goal of psychodynamic therapy is to make the 'unconscious conscious'. This is achieved through insight and is a 'talking cure'. The psychodynamic model remains controversial and is difficult to evaluate scientifically.

Psychological models of abnormality: This is an 'umbrella' term to refer to any approach which explains abnormal behaviour with the exception of the biological (medical) model. It includes the psychodynamic, behavioural and cognitive models.

Statistical infrequency: This definition of abnormality defines any behaviour that is statistically rare as abnormal. It has the advantage of being objective but fails to distinguish between statistically rare desirable and undesirable behaviour. It is also difficult to measure all behaviours and to determine the 'cut-off' point for normality. When is behaviour sufficiently rare as to be defined as 'abnormal'?

12.1 SOCIAL INFLUENCE

Conformity (majority influence): Yielding to group pressure. It is the influence that a group has over an individual (hence, 'majority influence'). The group consists of the individual's peers (that is, they are all of equal status).

Deception: Misleading research participants about the true purpose of a research study. This can be done through telling them that the study is concerned with one thing (such as the effects of punishment on learning), when it's really about something else (such as obedience, as in Milgram's experiments). Participants can also be deceived if certain information is *withheld*. Deception, therefore, prevents participants from giving their informed consent.

Ecological validity: Being able to generalise the findings of a study beyond the particular laboratory setting in which they were collected. This includes more naturalistic ('real-life') situations. Also called mundane realism.

Ethical guidelines: Formal, written documents which provide a framework within which psychologists should carry out their research. For example, the *Ethical Principles* published by the British Psychological Society (BPS) help determine what's an acceptable psychological investigation.

Ethical issues: Considerations that relate to the welfare and well-being of participants in psychological research. Major issues, which have been highlighted by research into social influence, include deception, informed consent, protection of participants from psychological harm, and withdrawal from the investigation.

Experimental validity: The belief of participants in an experiment that the experimental situation is real. For example, the teacher-participants in Milgram's obedience studies believed that they were actually administering electric shocks to the learner (Mr Wallace), and that he, like them, was a volunteer. Also called experimental realism.

Informed consent: Agreeing to participate in psychological research (giving your consent) in the full knowledge of the true purpose of the research. If participants have been deceived to any degree then they haven't given informed consent.

Minority influence: The ability of the numerical minority to change the views of the majority. As in majority influence, all the individuals involved are of equal status.

Obedience to authority: Complying with the demands or instructions of an authority figure. By definition, this figure has greater power in the particular situation or setting in which they make their demands.

Protection of participants from psychological harm: One of the ethical issues highlighted by social influence research in particular. The harm may be physical and/or psychological. Ethical guidelines are designed to help define what is acceptable research. Researchers must consider the consequences of their research *for the participants*, whose psychological well-being, health, values, and dignity mustn't be threatened in any way.

Social influence: The various ways in which other people affect what we do and think. In conformity, other people's influence is indirect and often we're unaware of it. The people concerned are of equal status to us (our peers), and they affect us by example. This also applies to minority influence. But in obedience, someone with greater power or authority than us tries to directly influence our behaviour by giving us orders or instructions.

12.2 RESEARCH METHODS

There aren't any questions that ask you to define Research Methods terms. You'll have to understand the meaning of the terms in relation to the particular research described in the Stimulus Material. However, the following terms are mentioned in the Specification.

(Note: Unlike the other Sections, the terms are set out in Specification order and not alphabetical order. We think that grouping them like this makes more sense.)

Quantitative research methods: Techniques that lend themselves to the collection of numerical and statistical data. Experimental methods would be examples of this.

Qualitative methods: Techniques that lend themselves to the collection of non-numerical data (e.g. the written or spoken word). Interviews and naturalistic observations would be examples of this.

Experiments: A situation where the independent variable is deliberately manipulated to find the effects on the dependent variable, whilst controlling extraneous variables.

- **Laboratory experiments**: An experiment that occurs in a carefully controlled environment, usually a laboratory.

- **Field experiments**: An experiment that takes place in the real world as opposed to a laboratory. The IV is still manipulated by the experimenters.

- **Natural experiments**: An experiment that takes place in the real world and where the IV occurs naturally. There is no manipulation of the IV.

Investigations using correlational analysis: A method of data analysis which allows the strength of the relationship between two (or more) co-variables to be measured.

Naturalistic observations: A study where an observer objectively records the behaviour of participants in their natural environment.

Questionnaire surveys: Written methods of data collection. They can involve open or closed questions. Surveys tend to involve a large sample of participants.

Interviews: A verbal method of data collection that involves the researcher asking questions in a face-to-face way. They can vary from very structured (formal) to unstructured (informal).

Aims: An outline of the general purpose of the research study. A statement of *why* the research study is taking place.

Hypotheses: These are predictions made about the possible outcomes of a study that is yet to be conducted. A statement of *what* is expected to happen.

- **Experimental/alternative hypothesis**: The prediction made before the study takes place that an IV will have an effect on the DV. There are two types: directional (one-tailed) and non-directional (two-tailed).

- **Directional (one-tailed) hypothesis (H1)**: This hypothesis states the direction of any difference that is expected. In correlations, the hypothesis is predicted as being either positive or negative.

- **Non-directional (two-tailed) hypothesis (H1)**: The prediction that there will be a significant difference between the results of the two conditions (or a correlation between the variables). It does not predict the direction that difference (or correlation) will take.

- **Null hypothesis (Ho)**: This hypothesis states that there will be no difference between the results of the two conditions, the results are simply due to chance. The hypothesis of 'no difference' or 'no correlation'.

Experimental design: A procedure used in experiments that allows for the control of participant variables. Without this control, the experimental results would be jeopardised. There are three types: independent groups design, repeated measures design and matched pairs design.

- **Independent groups design**: Different participants are randomly allocated to the different experimental conditions.

- **Repeated measures design**: The same participants are tested in all the experimental conditions. They 'repeat' all the conditions.

- **Matched participants (or pairs) design**: The same as independent groups design except that similar participants are randomly allocated to the different experimental conditions. They are previously 'matched' on whatever criteria are judged to be important for the study. This might include age and sex.

Independent variable (IV): The variable that is directly manipulated by the experimenter to see the effect it has on the dependent variable (DV)

Dependent variable (DV): The variable that is measured by the experimenter. So-called because changes in this variable are *dependent* on the IV.

Extraneous variables: Anything, other than the IV, which might have an effect on the DV. Extraneous variables should be controlled.

Confounding variables: Extraneous variables that aren't controlled can adversely affect or 'confound' results. They're called 'confounding' variables.

Operationalisation: The appropriate way to define or measure the variable in question. For example, can you operationalise 'good' driving in terms of the number of accidents you've had?

Pilot studies: Small scale 'practice' investigations that allow the researcher to check all aspects of their research. Appropriate improvements can then be made to the 'real' study.

Reliability: Means consistency. Research should be consistent over time and across different researchers. In other words, the research should be repeatable, replicable and the same (or similar) results should be obtained. If this occurs, the research is reliable.

Validity: Means accuracy. Is the research measuring what it is supposed to be measuring?

- **Internal validity**: Refers to whether the research is accurate *within* the confines of the experimental setting. The research must not be affected by investigator effects or demand characteristics. If results can be directly attributed to the manipulation of the IV, then the research is internally valid.

- **External (ecological) validity**: Refers to whether the research results are accurate and can thus be generalised *beyond* the confines of the experimental setting.

Participants: The people who take place in the research study. They form the sample.

Random sampling: A technique where every member of the population has an equal chance of being selected. The simplest way to do this is to draw names out of a hat.

Demand characteristics: Refers to the situation where participants try to guess the purpose of the study and amend their behaviour accordingly. They act according to what they feel are the 'demands' of the study or experiment.

Investigator effects: This refers to the process whereby a researcher inadvertently influences the results of the study. This could be due to physical characteristics of the researcher affecting respondents' answers or behaviour.

Measures of central tendency: These are data values that represent the typical mid-point value of a set of scores. They're 'averages' and the most commonly used measures are the mean, median and mode.

- **Mean**: The arithmetic average obtained by adding up all the scores and dividing by the number of scores. Most appropriate with interval/ratio data.

- **Median**: The middle value when scores are placed in rank order. Most appropriate with ordinal data.

- **Mode**: The value that occurs most frequently. Most appropriate with nominal data.

Measures of dispersion: These are measures of the variability or spread of scores. They include the range and standard deviation.

- **Range**: The difference between the highest and lowest scores.

- **Inter-quartile range**: The spread of scores for the middle 50% of the scores.

- **Standard deviation**: A measure of the distribution of scores around the mean. A large SD suggests a wide scatter of scores, a small SD suggests that scores are close to the mean.

Positive correlation: Where one variable increases the other variable increases (e.g. ice cream sales increase as temperature increases). It is expressed from 0 (no correlation) to +1 (perfect positive correlation).

Negative correlation: Where one variable increases the other variable decreases (e.g. raincoat sales decrease as temperature increases). It is expressed from 0 (no correlation) to -1 (perfect negative correlation).

Histograms: A type of graph used for frequency data. The area of each column is proportional to the number of cases it represents. The X axis must involve continuous data and is divided into appropriate intervals.

Bar charts: A type of graph used to visually present discrete (non-continuous) or nominal data.

Frequency polygons: Similar to a histogram except that two or more frequency distributions can be plotted on the same graph in order to aid comparison.

Scattergraphs: A type of graph used to plot correlations. Allows any clear relationship between two variables to be seen at a glance. So-called because the scores are 'scattered' across the graph.

References

Abrams, D., Wetherell, M., Cochrane, S., Hogg, M.A. & Turner, J.C. (1990) Knowing what to think by knowing who you are: Self-categorization and the nature of norm formation. *British Journal of Social Psychology, 29,* 97–119.

Ainsworth, M.D.S. (1967) *Infancy in Uganda: Infant Care and the Growth of Love.* Baltimore, MD: Johns Hopkins University Press.

Ainsworth, M.D.S., Bell, S.M.V. & Stayton, D.J. (1971) Individual differences in strange-situation behaviour of one-year olds. In H.R. Schaffer (Ed.) *The Origins of Human Social Relations.* New York: Academic Press.

Ainsworth, M.D.S., Blehar, M.C., Waters, E. & Wall, S. (1978) *Patterns of Attachment: A Psychological Study of the Strange Situation.* Hillsdale, N.J: Lawrence Erlbaum Associates Inc.

Alberge, D. (1999) Dancers take lessons in eating. *The Times,* 18 August.

Allport, G.W. & Postman, L. (1947) *The Psychology of Rumour.* New York: Holt, Rinehart & Winston.

American National Association of Anorexia Nervosa and Associated Disorders: www.anad.org.

Anokhin, P. K. (1973) The forming of natural and artificial intelligence. *Impact of Science on Society,* Vol. XXIII, 3.

Asch, S.E. (1951) Effect of group pressure upon the modification and distortion of judgements. In H. Guetzkow (Ed.) *Groups, Leadership and Men.* Pittsburgh, PA: Carnegie Press.

Atkinson, R.C. & Shiffrin, R.M. (1968) Human memory: a proposed system and its control processes. In K.W. Spence & J.T. Spence (Eds) *The Psychology of Learning and Motivation,* Vol.2. London: Academic Press.

Atkinson, R.C. & Shiffrin, R.M. (1971) The control of short-term memory. *Scientific American,* 224, 82–90.

Baddeley, A.D., Grant, S., Wight, E. & Thomson, N., (1973) Imagery and Visual Working in P.M.A. Rabbitt & S. Darnit (Eds) *Attention & Performance V,* London: Academic Press.

Baddeley, A.D. & Hitch, G. (1974) Working memory. In G.H. Bower (Ed.) *Recent Advances in Learning and Motivation,* Vol.8. New York: Academic Press.

Baddeley, A.D. (1966) The influence of acoustic and semantic similarity on long-term memory for word sequences. *Quarterly Journal of Experimental Psychology, 18,* 302–309.

Baddeley, A.D. (2001) Is working memory still working? *American Psychologist, 56,* 861–864.

Baddeley, A.D., Thomson, N. & Buchanan, M. (1975) Word length and the structure of short-term memory. *Journal of Verbal Learning and Verbal Behavior, 14,* 575–589.

Bahrick, H.P., Bahrick, P.O. & Wittinger, R.P. (1975) Fifty years of memory for names and faces: A cross-sectional approach. *Journal of Experimental Psychology: General, 104,* 54–75.

Barr, C.E., Mednick, S.A. & Munk-Jorgenson, P. (1990) Exposure to influenza epidemics during gestation and adult schizophrenia: A forty-year study. *Archives of General Psychiatry, 47,* 869–874.

Bartlett, F.C. (1932) *Remembering.* Cambridge: Cambridge University Press.

Baumrind, D. (1964) Some thoughts on the ethics of research: After reading Milgram's behavioural study of obedience. *American Psychologist, 19,* 421–423.

Baydar, N. & Brooks-Gunn, J. (1991) Effects of maternal employment and child-care arrangements on pre-schoolers' cognitive and behavioural outcomes. *Developmental Psychology, 27,* 932–945.

Beck, A.T. (1967) *Depression: Causes and Treatment.* Philadelphia: University of Philadelphia Press.

Bekerian, D.A. & Baddeley, A. D. (1980) Saturation advertising and the repetition effect. *Learning and Verbal Behaviour, 19,* 17–25.

Belsky, J. & Rovine, M.J. (1988) Non-maternal care in the first year of life and the infant–parent attachment. *Child Development, 59,* 157–167.

Berry, J.W., Poortinga, Y.H. Segall, M.H. & Dasen, P.R. (1992) *Cross-cultural psychology: Research and applications.* Cambridge: Cambridge University Press.

Bickman, L. (1974) Clothes make the person. *Psychology Today, 8(4),* 48–51.

Bowlby, J. (1951) *Maternal Care and Mental Health.* Geneva: World Health Organisation.

Bowlby, J. (1969) *Attachment and Loss.* Volume 1: *Attachment.* Harmondsworth: Penguin.

Bowlby, J. (1973) *Attachment and Loss.* Volume 2: *Separation.* Harmondsworth: Penguin.

Bowlby, J., Ainsworth, M., Boston, M. & Rosenbluth, D. (1956) The effects of mother–child separation: A follow-up study. *British Journal of Medical Psychology, 29,* 211.

Bradley, L.A. (1995) Chronic benign pain. In D. Wedding (Ed.) *Behaviour and Medicine* (2nd edition). St. Louis, MO: Mosby-Year Book.

Brady, J.V. (1958) Ulcers in executive monkeys. *Scientific American, 199,* 95–100.

Briere J. & Conte, J. (1991) Self reported amnesia for abuse in adults molested as children. *Journal of Traumatic Stress.* 6, 21–31.

British Psychological Society (1993) Ethical principles for conducting research with human participants (revised). *The Psychologist, 3(6)* 269–272.

Brown, R. & Kulik, J. (1977) Flashbulb memories. *Cognition, 5,* 73–99.

Brown, R. & McNeill, D. (1966) The 'tip-of-the-tongue' phenomenon. *Journal of Verbal Learning and Verbal Behaviour, 5,* 325–337.

Brown, R.J. (1988) Intergroup relations. In M. Hewstone, W. Stroebe & G.M. Stephenson (Eds.) *Introduction to Social Psychology* (2nd edition). Oxford: Blackwell.

Bulik C.M., Wadt T.D., & Kendler K.S. (2001) Characteristics of Monozygotic twins discordant for bulimia nervosa. *International Journal of Eating Disorders, 29,* 1–10.

Burt C. (1955) The Evidence for the concept of intelligence. *British Journal of Psychology, 25,* 158–177.

Bushnell, J.A., Wells, J.E., McKenzie, J.M., Hornblow, A.R. Oakley, Browne, M.A. & Joyce, P.R. (1994) Bulimia co-morbidity in the general population and in the clinic. *Psychological Medicine, 20,* 605–611.

Cannon, W.B. (1927) The James-Lange theory of emotions: A critical examination and an alternative theory. *American Journal of Psychology, 39,* 106–124.

Chisolm, K., Carter, M.C., Amers, E.W. & Morison, S.J. (1995) Attachment security and indiscriminately friendly behaviour in children adopted from Romanian orphanages. *Development & Psychopathology, 7,* 283–294.

Clarke, A. & Clarke, A. (2000) *Early Experience and the Life Path.* London: Jessica Kingsley.

Clarke-Stewart, K.A. (1989) Infant day care: Maligned or malignant? *American Psychologist, 44,* 266–273.

Clarke-Stewart, K.A. (1991) A home is not a school. *Journal of Social Issues, 47,* 105–123.

Cobb, A. (1993) *Safe and effective? MIND's views on psychiatric drugs, ECT and psychosurgery.* London: MIND Publications.

Cochrane R. (1977) Mental illness in immigrants in the UK. *Social Psychiatry, 12,* 23–35.

Cohen, C.E. (1981) Person categories and social perception: Testing some boundaries of the processing effects of prior knowledge. *Journal of Personality and Social Psychology, 40,* 441–452.

Cohen, F. & Lazarus, R. (1979) Coping with the stresses of illness. In G.C. Stone, F. Cohen & N.E. Ader (Eds.) *Health Psychology: A Handbook.* San Francisco, CA: Jossey-Bass.

Cohen, G., Eysenck, M. & Le Voi, M. (1996) *Memory: A Cognitive Approach.* London. Open University Press.

Cohen, S., Tyrrell, D.A.J. & Smith, A.P. (1991) Psychological stress and susceptibility to the common cold. *New England Journal of Medicine, 325,* 606–612.

Conrad, R. (1964) Acoustic confusion in immediate memory. *British Journal of Psychology, 55,* 75–84.

Conway, A. R., Skitka, L.J., Hemmerich, J. & Kershaw, T. (2003) Flashbulb memory of Sept 11th 2001 (Personal Correspondence. Paper submitted to Psychological Science).

Conway, M.A., Anderson, S.J., Larsen, S.F., Donnelly, C.M., McDaniel, M.A., McClelland, A.G.R. & Rawles, R.E. (1994) The formation of flashbulb memories. *Memory and Cognition, 22,* 326–343.

Coolican, H. (1999) *Research Methods and Statistics in Psychology* (3rd Ed) London: Hodder & Stoughton.

Cooper, C. & Faragher, B. (1993) Psychological stress and breast cancer: the interrelationship between stress events, coping strategies and personality. *Psychological Medicine, 23,* 653–662.

Cooper, R.S., Rotimi, C.N. & Ward, R. (1999) The puzzle of hypertension in African-Americans. *Scientific American, 253,* 36–43.

Craik, F.I.M. & Lockhart, R (1972) Levels of processing. *Journal of Verbal Learning and Verbal Behaviour, 11,* 671–684.

Craik, F.I.M. & Tulving, E. (1975) Depth of processing and retention of words in episodic memory. *Journal of Verbal Learning and Verbal Behaviour, 12,* 599–607.

Craik, F.I.M. & Watkins, M.J. (1973) The role of rehearsal in short-term memory. *Journal of Verbal Learning and Verbal Behaviour, 12,* 599–607.

Crutchfield, R. S. (1954) A new technique for measuring individual differences in conformity to group judgement. *Proceedings of the Invitational Conference on Testing Problems,* 69–74.

Darley, C.F., Tinklenberg, J.R., Roth, W.T., Hollister, L.E. & Atkinson, R.C. (1973) Influence of marijuana on storage and retrieval processes in memory. *Memory and Cognition, 1,* 196–200.

Davison, G.C. & Neale, J.M. (2001) *Abnormal Psychology* (8th ed.). New York: John Wiley & Sons Inc.

DeLongis, A., Coyne, J.C., Dakof, G., Folkman, S. & Lazarus, R.S. (1982) The impact of daily hassles, uplifts and major life events to health status. *Health Psychology, 1*, 119–136.

Deutsch, M. & Gerard, H.B. (1955) A study of normative and informational social influence upon individual judgements. *Journal of Abnormal & Social Psychology, 51*, 629–636.

Eagles, J.M., Andrew, J.E., Johnston, M.I., Easton, E.A. & Millar, H.R. (2001) Season of birth in females with anorexia nervosa in Northern Scotland. *International Journal of Eating Disorders, 30* (2); 167–175.

Ellis, N.C and Hennelley R.A. (1980) A bilingual word-length effect: implications for intelligence testing and the relative ease of mental calculation in Welsh and English. *British Journal of Psychology, 71*, 43–52.

Eysenck, H. (1952) The effects of psychotherapy: an evaluation. *Journal of Consulting Psychology, 16*, 319–324.

Eysenck, H.J. & Wilson, G.D. (1973) (Eds.) *The Experimental Study of Freudian Theories*. London: Methuen.

Eysenck, M. (1998) Memory. In M. Eysenck (Ed.) *Psychology: An integrated approach*. Harlow: Longman.

Eysenck, M.W. (1986) Working memory. In G. Cohen, M.W. Eysenck & M.A. Le Voi (Eds.) *Memory: A Cognitive Approach*. Milton Keynes: Open University Press.

Fearn, N. (1999) Anorexia via TV. *The Independent*, 27 May.

Fernandez, A. & Glenberg, A.M. (1985) Changing environmental context does not reliably affect memory. *Memory and Cognition, 13*, 333–345.

Fichter, M.M. & Pirke, K.M. (1995) Starvation models and eating disorders. In G. Szmulker, C. Dare & J. Treasure (Eds.) *Handbook of eating disorders: Theory, treatment and research*. Chichester: Wiley.

Field, A.E., Camargo, C.A., Taylor, C.B., Berkey, C.S. & Colditz, G.A. Alison E. Field, ScD; Carlos (1999) Relation of peer and media influences to the development of purging behaviors among preadolescent and adolescent girls. *Archives of Pediatrics and Adolescent Medicine, 153*, 1184–1189.

Fink, M. (2002) *Electroshock – Healing Mental Illness*. Oxford: Oxford University Press.

Flanagan, C. Psychology Review, Vol. 9, No.1. Exam Corner (pp. 6–8).

Foster, R.A., Libkuman, T.M., Schooler, J.W. & Loftus, E.F. (1994). Consequentiality and eyewitness person identification. *Applied Cognitive Psychology, 8*, 107–121.

Frankenhauser, M. (1983) The sympathetic–adrenal and pituitary–adrenal response to challenge: Comparison between the sexes. In T.M. Dembroski, T.H. Schmidt & G. Blumchen (Eds.) *Behavioural Bases of Coronary Heart Disease*. Basle: S. Karger.

Freud, S. (1901) *Psychopathology of Everyday Life*. Translation by A. A. Brill (1914). London: Fisher Unwin.

Freud, S. (1910) The origin and development of psychoanalysis. *American Journal of Psychology, 21*, 181–218.

Freud, S. (1915) *Repression*. In Freud's Collected Papers, Vol. IV. London: Hogarth.

Friedman, M. & Rosenman, R.H. (1974) *Type A Behaviour and Your Heart*. New York: Harper Row.

Garner, D.M., Garfinkel, P.E., Schwartz, D. & Thompson, M. (1980) Cultural expectations of thinness in women. *Psychological Reports, 47*, 483–491.

Glanzer, M. & Cunitz, A.R. (1966) Two storage mechanisms in free recall. *Journal of Verbal Learning and Verbal Behavior, 5*, 351–360.

Godden, D. & Baddeley, A.D. (1975) Context-dependent memory in two natural environments: On land and under water. *British Journal of Psychology, 66*, 325–331.

Goldfarb, W. (1943) The effects of early institutional care on adult personality. *Journal of Experimental Education, 12*, 106–129.

Goodwin, D.W., Powell, B., Bremer, D. Hoine, H. & Stern, J. (1969) Alcohol and recall: State dependent effects in man. *Science, 163*, 1358.

Greer, A., Morris, T. & Pettingdale, K.W. (1979) Psychological response to breast cancer: Effect on outcome. *The Lancet, 13*. 785–787.

Greer, S. & Morris, T. (1975) Psychological attributes of women who develop breast cancer: A controlled study. *Journal of Psychosomatic Research, 19*, 147–153.

Groesz, L.M., Levine, M.P. & Murnen, S.K. (2001) The effect of experimental presentation of thin media images on body dissatisfaction: a meta-analytic review. *International Journal of Eating Disorders, 31* (1), 1–16.

Harlow, H.F. (1959) Love in infant monkeys. *Scientific American, 200*, 68–74.

Hennighausen, K., Enkelmann, D. Wewezer, C. & Remschmidt, H. (1998) Body image distortion in Anorexia Nervosa – is there really a perceptual deficit? *European Child and Adolescent Psychology, 8(3)*, 200–7.

Hetherington, E.M. & Stanley-Hagan, M. (1999) The adjustment of children with divorced parents: A risk and resiliency perspective. *Journal of Child Psychology & Psychiatry, 40(1)*, 129–140.

Hodges, J. & Tizard, B. (1989) Social and family relationships of ex-institutional adolescents. *Journal of Child Psychology & Psychiatry, 30*, 77–97.

Hofling, K.C., Brotzman, E., Dalrymple, S., Graves, N. & Pierce, C.M. (1966) An experimental study in the nurse–physician relationship. *Journal of Nervous & Mental Disorders, 143*, 171–180.

Holland, A.J., Sicotte, N. & Treasure, J. (1988) Anorexia nervosa: Evidence for a genetic basis. *Journal of Psychosomatic Research, 32*, 561–572.

Holmes, T.H. & Rahe, R.H. (1967) The social readjustment rating scale. *Journal of Psychosomatic Research, 11*, 213–218.

Hyde, T.S. & Jenkins, J.J. (1973) Recall for words as a function of semantic, graphic and syntactic orienting tasks. *Journal of Verbal Learning and Verbal Behaviour, 12*, 471–480.

Jacobs, J. (1887) Experiments on 'prehension'. *Mind, 12*, 75–79.

Jahoda, M. (1958) *Current Concepts of Positive Mental Health*. New York: Basic Books.

Johnson, J.H. & Sarason, I.G. (1978) Life stress, depression and anxiety: Internal/external control as a moderator variable. *Journal of Psychosomatic Research, 22*, 205–208.

Judd, J. (1997) Working mothers need not feel guilty. *Independent on Sunday*, 27 November, 5.

Kagan, J., Kearsley, R. & Zelago, P. (1978) *Infancy: Its Place in Human Development*. Cambridge, MA: Harvard University Press.

Kanner, A.D., Coyne, J.C., Schaefer, C. & Lazarus, R.S. (1981) Comparison of two modes of stress measurement: Daily hassles and uplifts versus major life events. *Journal of Behavioural Measurement, 4*, 1–39.

Kendler, K.S. Masterson, C.C. & Davis, K.L. (1985) Psychiatric illness in first degree relatives of patients with paranoid psychosis, schizophrenia, and medical controls. *British Journal of Psychiatry, 147*, 524–531.

Kendler, K.S., Maclean, C., Neale, M., Kessler, R., Heath, A. & Eaves, L. (1991) The genetic epidemiology of bulimia nervosa. *American Journal of Psychiatry, 148*, 1627–1637.

Kenrick, D.L. and McFarlane, S.W. (1986) Ambient temperature and horn honking: a field study of the heat/aggression relationship. *Environment and Behaviour, 18,* 179–191.

Keppel, G. & Underwood, B.J. (1962) Pro-active inhibition in short-term retention of single items. *Journal of Verbal Learning and Verbal Behaviour, 1,* 75–121.

Keys, A., Brozek, J., Henschel, A., Michelsen, O. & Taylor, H.L. (1950) *The Biology of Human Starvation.* Minneapolis, MN: University of Minneapolis Press.

Kiecolt-Glaser, J.K., Garner, W., Speicher, C.E., Penn, G.M., Holliday, J. & Glaser, R. (1984) Psychosocial modifiers of immunocompetence in medical students. *Psychosomatic Medicine, 46,* 7–14.

Kiecolt-Glaser, J.K., Marucha, P.T., Malarkey, W.B., Mercado, A.M. & Glaser, R. (1995) Slowing of wound healing by psychological stress. *The Lancet, 346,* 1194–1196.

Kline, P. (1972) *Fact and fantasy in Freudian theory.* London: Methuen.

Kline, P. (1989) Objective tests of Freud's theories. In A.M. Coleman & J.G. Beaumont (Eds.), *Psychology Survey No.7.* Leicester: British Psychological Society.

Kobasa, S. (1979) Stressful life events, personality and health: An inquiry into hardiness. *Journal of Personality & Social Psychology, 37,* 1–11.

Kobasa, S. (1986) How much stress can you survive? In M.G. Walraven & H.E. Fitzgerald (Eds.) *Annual Editions: Human Development, 86/87.* New York: Dushkin.

Koluchova, J. (1972) Severe deprivation in twins: A case study. *Journal of Child Psychology & Psychiatry, 13,* 107–114.

Koluchova, J. (1991) Severely deprived twins after 22 years observation. *Studia Psychologica, 33,* 23–28.

Kremer, J. (1998) Work. In K. Trew & J. Kremer (Eds) *Gender and Psychology.* London: Arnold.

Laing, R.D. (1959) *The Divided Self – An Existential Study in Sanity & Madness.* Pelican Books.

Lambe, E.K., Katzman, D.K., Mikulis, D.J., Kennedy, S.H. & Zipursky, R.B. (1997). Cerebral grey matter volume deficits after weight recovery from anorexia nervosa. *Archives of General psychiatry, 54,* 537–542.

Lazarus, R.S. & Folkman, S. (1984) *Stress, Appraisal, and Coping.* New York: Springer.

Lee, S.G. (1969) Spirit Possession among the Zulu. In J. Beattie and J. Middleton. (Eds) *Spirit Mediumship and Society in Africa.* New York: Africana.

Levinger, G. & Clark, J. (1961) Emotional factors in the forgetting of word associations. *Journal of Abnormal and Social Psychology, 62,* 99–105.

Loftus, E.F. (1975) Leading questions and the eyewitness report. *Cognitive Psychology, 1,* 560–572.

Loftus, E.F., & Palmer, J.C. (1974) Reconstruction of automobile destruction: An example of the interaction between language and memory. *Journal of Verbal Learning and Verbal Behavior, 13,* 585–589.

Loftus, E.F., Miller, D.G. & Burns, H.J. (1978) Semantic integration of verbal information into visual memory, *Journal of Experimental Psychology, 4(1),* 19–31.

Lorenz, K.Z. (1935) The companion in the bird's world. *Auk, 54,* 245–273.

Maccoby, E.E. (1980) *Social Development-Psychological Growth and the Parent–Child Relationship.* New York: Harcourt Brace Jovanovich.

Maier, S.F. & Seligman, M.E.P. (1976) Learned helplessness: Theory and evidence. *Journal of Experimental Psychology: General, 105,* 3–46.

Marmot, M., Bosma, H., Hemingway, H., Brunner, E. & Stansfield, S. (1997)

Contribution of job control and other risk factors to social variation in health disease incidence. *The Lancet, 350,* 235–239.

Maslow, A. (1968) *Towards a psychology of being (2nd Ed).* New York: Van Nostrand Reinhold.

Maslow, A.H. (1943) A theory of human motivation. *Psychological Review, 50,* 370–396.

McClelland, L. & Crisp, A. (2001) Anorexia nervosa and social class. *International Journal of Eating Disorders,* 29 (2), 150–156.

McCloskey, M. & Zaragoza, M.S. (1985) Misleading post-event information and memory for eents: Arguments and evidence against memory impairment hypotheses. *Journal of Experimental Psychology: General, 114,* 1–16.

McCloskey, M., Wible, C.G. & Cohen, N.J. (1988) Is there a special flash-bulb memory mechanism? *Journal of Experimental Psychology: General, 117,* 171–181.

Meichenbaum, D. (1976) Towards a cognitive therapy of self-control. In G. Schwartz & D. Shapiro (Eds.) *Consciousness and Self-Regulation: Advances in Research.* New York: Plenum Publishing Co.

Meichenbaum, D. (1997) The evolution of a cognitive-behaviour therapist. In J.K. Zeig (Ed.) *The Evolution of Psychotherapy: The Third Conference.* New York: Brunner/Mazel.

Milgram, S. (1963) Behavioural study of obedience. *Journal of Abnormal & Social Psychology, 67,* 391–398.

Milgram, S. (1974) *Obedience to Auithority.* New York: Harper & Row.

Miller, G. (1969) Psychology as a means of promoting human welfare. *American Psychologist, 24,* 1063–1075.

Miller, G.A. (1956) The magical number seven, plus or minus two: some limits on our capacity for processing information. *Psychological Review, 63,* 81–97.

Miller, I. & Norman, W. (1979) Learned helplessness in humans: A review and attribution theory model. *Psychological Bulletin, 86,* 93–118.

Mind 2002: http://www.mind.org.uk/information/factsheets/P/psychosurgery/Psychosurgery.asp#Introduction

Morris, P.E., Tweedy, M. & Gruneberg, M.M. (1985) Interest, knowledge and the memorising of soccer scores. *British Journal of Psychology, 76,* 415–425.

Moscovici, S. & Faucheux, C. (1972) Social influence, conforming bias and the study of active minorities. In L. Berkowitz (Ed.) *Advances in Experimental Social Psychology,* Volume 6. New York: Academic Press.

Moscovici, S., Lage, E. & Naffrechoux, M. (1969) Influence of a consistent majority on the responses of a majority in a colour perception task. *Sociometry, 32,* 365–380.

Murdock, B.B. (1962) The serial position effect in free recall. *Journal of Experimental Psychology, 64,* 482–488.

Nemeth, C., Swedund, M. & Kanki, G. (1974) Patterning of the minority's reponses and their influence on the majority. *European Journal of Social Psychology, 4,* 53–64.

Nobles, W.W. (1976) Extended self: Rethinking the so-called Negro self-concept. *Journal of Black Psychology, 2,* 99–105.

Orne, M.T. & Holland, C.C. (1968) On the ecological validity of laboratory deceptions. *International Journal of Psychiatry, 6,* 282–293.

Orne, M.T. (1962) On the social psychology of the psychological experiment: with particular reference to demand characteristics and their implications. *American Psychologist, 17,* 776–783.

Parkin, A.J. (1993) *Memory: Phenomena, Experiment and Theory.* Oxford: Blackwell.

Paulescu, E., Frith, C.D. & Frackoviak, R.S.J. (1993) The neural correlates of the verbal component of working memory. *Nature, 362,* 342–345.

Penny, G. (1996) Health Psychology. In H. Coolican *Applied Psychology.* London: Hodder & Stoughton.

Peterson, L.R. & Peterson, M.J. (1959) Short-term retention of individual verbal items. *Journal of Experimental Psychology, 58,* 193–198.

Pippard, J. (1992) Audit of electroconvulsive therapy in two National Health Service Regions. *British Journal of Psychology,* 160, 621–637.

Rack, P. (1982) *Race, culture and mental disorder.* London: Tavistock.

Rahe, R.H., Mahan, J. & Arthur, R. (1970) Prediction of near-future health-change from subjects' preceding life changes. *Journal of Psychosomatic Research, 14,* 401–406.

Reitman, J.S. (1971) Mechanisms of short-term memory. *Cognitive Psychology, 2,* 185–195.

Richards, M.P.M. (1995) The International Year of the Family – family research. *The Psychologist, 8,* 17–20.

Riley, V. (1981) Psychoneuroendocrine influence on immuno-competence and neoplasia. *Science, 212,* 1100–1109.

Robertson, J. & Robertson, J. (1967–73) Film Series, *Young Children in Brief Separation:* No. 3 (1969). John, 17 months, 9 days in a residential nursery. London: Tavistock.

Robertson, J. & Robertson, J. (1989) *Separation and the Very Young.* London: Free Association Books.

Romans, S.E., Gendall, K.A., Martin, J.L. and Mullen, P.E. (2001) Child sexual abuse and later disordered eating: A New Zealand epidemiological study. *International Journal of Eating Disorders,* 29 (4), 380–392.

Rosenhan, D.L. & Seligman, M.E. (1989) *Abnormal Psychology.* New York: Norton.

Rosenhan, D.L. (1973) On Being Sane in Insane Places. *Science 179,* 250–257

Rotter, J.B. (1966) Generalised expectancies for internal versus external control of reinforcement. *Psychological Monographs, 30*(1), 1–26.

Rutter, M. (1981) *Maternal Deprivation Reassessed* (2nd edition). Harmondsworth: Penguin.

Savin, H.B. (1973) Professors and psychological researchers: conflicting values in conflicting roles. *Cognition, 2*(1), 147–149.

Scarr, S. & Thompson, W. (1994) Effects of maternal employment and nonmaternal infant care on development at two and four years. *Early Development & Parenting, 3*(2), 113–123.

Scarr, S. (1998) American child care today. *American Psychologist, 53*(2), 95–108.

Schaffer, H.R. (1971) *The Growth of Sociability.* Harmondsworth: Penguin.

Schaffer, H.R. (1996) *Social Development.* Oxford: Blackwell.

Schaffer, H.R. & Emerson, P.E. (1964) The development of social attachments in infancy. *Monographs of the Society for Research in Child Development, 29* (Whole No. 3).

Schaffer, R. (1998) Deprivation and its effects on children. *Psychology Review, 5*(2), 2–5.

Schliefer, S.J., Keller, S.E., Camerino, M., Thornton, J.C. & Stein, M. (1983) Suppression of lymphocyte stimulation following bereavement. *Journal of the American Medical Association, 250,* 374–377.

Sear, D.O. (1986) College sophomores in the laboratory: influences of a narrow database on psychology's view of human nature. *Journal of Personality and Social Psychology, 51,* 515–530.

Sebrechts, M.M., Marsh, R.L. & Seaman, J.G. (1989) Secondary memory and very rapid forgetting. *Memory and Cognition, 17,* 693–700.

Seligman, M.E.P. (1975) *Helplessness: On Depression, Development and Death.* San Francisco: W.H. Freeman.

Selye, H. (1956) *The Stress of Life.* New York: McGraw-Hill.

Shallice, T. & Warrington, E.K. (1970) Independent functioning of verbal memory stores: A neurophysiological study. *Quarterly Journal of Experimental Psychology, 22,* 261–269.

Shallice, T. (1967) Paper presented at NATO symposium on short-term memory. Cambridge, England. Cited in A.D. Baddeley (1976*) The Psychology of Memory.* New York. Harper & Row.

Shepard, R.N. (1967) Recognition memory for words, sentences and pictures. *Journal of Verbal Learning and Verbal Behaviour, 6,* 156–63.

Sheridan, C.L. & King, R.G. (1972) Obedience to authority with an authentic victim. *Proceedings of the 80th Annual Convention, American Psychological Association, 7* (1) 165–166.

Sherif, M. (1935) A study of social factors in perception. *Archives of Psychology, 27,* Whole No. 187.

Simon, H.A. (1974) How big is a chunk? *Science, 183,* 482–488.

Slamecka, N.J. (1966) Differentiation versus unlearning of verbal associations. *Journal of Experimental Psychology, 71,* 822–828.

Solso, R.L. (1995) *Cognitive Psychology* (4th Ed.) Boston: Allyn & Bacon.

Spitz, R.A. & Wolf, K.M. (1946) Anaclitic depression. *Psychoanalytic Study of the Child, 2,* 313–342.

Spitz, R.A. (1945) Hospitalism: An enquiry into the genesis of psychiatric conditions in early childhood. *Psychoanalytic Study of the Child,1,* 53–74.

Spitz, R.A. (1946) Hospitalism: A follow-up report on investigation described in Vol. 1, 1945. *Psychoanalytic Study of the Child, 2,* 113–117..

Starbuck, M. (1998) A practical guide to evaluation. *Psychology Review, 4,* 3, 8–10.

Szasz, T.S. (1962) The myth of mental illness. *American Psychologist, 15,* 113–118.

Temoshok, L. (1987) Personality, coping style, emotions and cancer: Towards an integrative model. *Cancer Surveys, 6 ,* 545–567 (Supplement).

Tyler, S.W., Hertel, P.T., McCallum, M.C. and Ellis. H. (1979) Cognitive effect and memory. *Journal of Experimental Psychology*: Human Learning and Memory, 5 (6), 607–617.

Tyrka, A.R., Waldron, I., Graber, J. and Brooks-Gunn, J. (2002) Prospective predictors of the onset of anorexic and bulimic syndromes. *International Journal of Eating Disorders, 32,* 282–90.

Ucros, C.G. (1989) Mood state-dependent memory: A meta-analysis. *Cognition and Emotion, 3,* 139–167.

Van Ijzendoorn, M.H. & Kroonenberg, P.M. (1988) Cross-cultural patterns of attachment: a meta-analysis of the strange situation. *Child Development, 59,* 147–156.

Wade, T., Martin, N.G. & Tiggemann, M. (1998). Genetic and environmental risk factors for weight and shape concerns characteristic of bulimia nervosa. *Psychological Medicine, 28,* 761–72.

Watson, J.B. & Raynor, R. (1920) Conditioned emotional responses. *Journal of Experimental Psychology, 3,* 1–14.

Waugh, N.C. & Norman, D.A. (1965) Primary memory. *Psychological Review, 72,* 89–104.

Wayforth, D. & Dunbar, R.I.M. (1995) Conditional mate choice strategies in humans – evidence from lonely hearts advertisements. *Behaviour, 132,* 755–779.

Weiss, J.M. (1972) Psychological factors in stress and disease. *Scientific American, 226,* 104–113.

Williams, L.M. (1994). Recall of childhood Trauma: A prospective study of women's memories of childhood abuse. *Journal of Consulting and Clinical Psychology, 62,* 1167–76.

Woods, J. (1990) The Good Freud Guide. Guardian, 25th August.

Wright, D.B. (1993) Recall of the Hillsborough disaster over time: Systematic biases of 'flashbulb' memories. *Applied Cognitive Psychology, 7,* 129–138.

Wynn, V.E. & Logie, R.H. (1998) The veracity of long-term memories – did Bartlett get it right? *Applied Cognitive Psychology, 12,* 1–20.

Yuille, J.C. & Cutshall, J.L. (1986) A case study of eyewitness testimony of a crime. *Journal of Applied Psychology, 71,* 291–301.

Zimbardo, P.G., Banks, W.C., Craig, H. & Jaffe, D. (1973) A Pirandellian prison: The mind is a formidable jailor. *New York Times Magazine,* 8 April, 38–60.

Index